D0324648

signed.
AB & 10^{00}
m1

$ale
NN
final
$2^{50}
RP

KIPAWA RIVER
CHRONICLES

Adventures In The North Woods

KIPAWA RIVER
CHRONICLES

Adventures In The North Woods

SCOTT SORENSEN

Copyright © 1999 by Scott Sorensen. All rights reserved.
No part of this book may be used or reproduced in any manner
whatsoever without written permission except in the case of
brief quotations embodied in critical articles and reviews.
Inquiries should be addressed to: Scott Sorensen
Mountman@burgoyne.com
or
Box 69, Fabre, Quebec J0Z 1Z0

Photography credits: Unless otherwise noted,
photographs are from the personal collection of Scott Sorensen.
Cover art and book layout by
Diamond Design and Cerulean Publishing.
Printed in USA
Paper edition published 1999, ISBN 0-9672983-0-X

Table of Contents

For Pat, and our little ladies five.

*If one advances confidently in the direction of his dreams
and endeavors to live the life he has imagined,
he will meet with a success unexpected in common hours.*
—Henry Thoreau

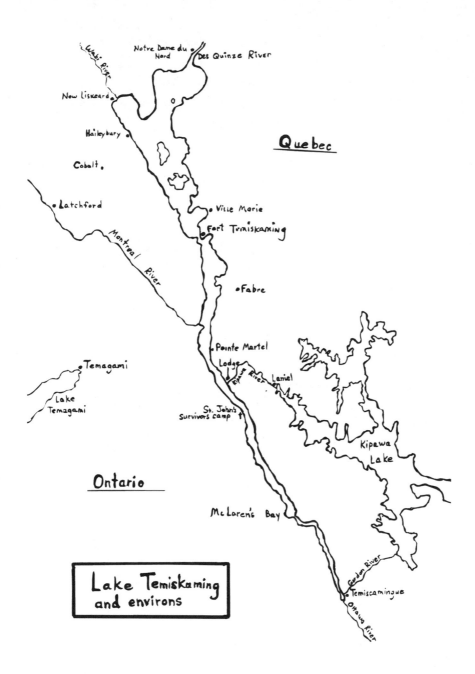

Wabi River

Notre Dame du Nord

Des Quinze River

New Liskeard

Quebec

Haileybury

Cobalt

Latchford

Montreal River

Ville Marie

Fort Temiskaming

Fabre

Temagami

Pointe Martel
Lodge

Kipawa River

Laniel

Lake
Temagami

St. John's
Survivors camp

Kipawa
Lake

Ontario

McLaren's Bay

Gordon River

Temiscamingue

Ottawa River

Lake Temiskaming
and environs

Acknowledgments

With gratitude to Pat, loyal companion and willing accomplice in a thousand and one adventures.

Together, Pat and I thank Lorraine and Larry Wiwchar for years of encouragement, advice, inspiration, and much labor in preparing the manuscript.

We also express deep appreciation to Audette and Ron Huywan, who have been there from the beginning and helped us "pick up the pieces."

To Rhea Topping for valuable assistance in obtaining photographs of her father, grandmother, uncle, Sonja Henie, and Lana Turner.

And to our friend Don Bair, whose enterprising spirit and belief in a young river guide opened the door when opportunity knocked.

We are forever grateful to wonderful parents, Nonie and Maynard Sorensen and Helen and Bill Halls, whose generosity and influence touches our lives daily.

Finally, we give thanks to the "Friends of the Kipawa River." May they prevail in their struggle to save this natural wonder.

Charlie Hastings in front of Hollywood Rapid.

Chapter 1

DIVERTING THE KIPAWA RIVER

*Eventually, all things merge into one,
and a river runs through it.*
—Norman Maclean

"You're not going to believe it, but somebody wants to divert the Kipawa River!" cried Charlie Hastings, whose 240-pound frame completely blocked my cabin door.

"What are you talking about Charlie?" I asked raising myself up off the couch. It was 10:30 P.M. and I had just sat down to read a book when Charlie burst through the door.

"Come see for yourself," he motioned as he turned and started back up the trail towards the River Cabin. "Two guys from the town of Temiscamingue just showed up on motor bikes with some terrible news," he yelled over his shoulder, then disappeared like a ghost into the night. For a moment, I just stood in shocked amazement. His words had hit me like a tidal wave. Charlie and I had kayaked the rapids of the Kipawa River together for twelve years. He could be a practical joker at times, but on the night of June 5, 1998, there was an edge of raw anger in his voice. I knew he wasn't joking.

"You'd better put some shoes on and get moving," said my wife, Pat, as she climbed out of bed and turned up the kerosene lamp. "Charlie seems pretty upset."

I pulled on a pair of sweats, then dashed up the trail toward the River Cabin, which stands like a sentinel above Hollywood Rapid. A group of my paddling friends from Toronto were inside the cabin, up for a weekend of kayaking. Halfway up the trail I realized I had forgotten to grab a flashlight. But that didn't matter. The moon was almost full, and I had walked this trail a thousand times in the past twenty-four

1

years. Every dip, rock, and tree root were as familiar to me as my own backyard. In fact, it is my backyard. And the Kipawa River runs right through it.

The roar of Hollywood Rapid was pounding in my ears, just fifty feet away. When I suddenly stepped from the shadow of a towering white pine, the scene that lay before me caused my heart to leap into my throat. Moonlight was dancing on the rapids as wisps of foam and jets of spray spouted up from the river where whitewater crashed and boiled between the rocks below. "No one would divert this river," I thought to myself as I stepped over a large boulder. "That would be like burning the Mona Lisa."

Inside the cabin, Charlie was talking to Peter Arthur and about a dozen other members of the Ontario Voyageur Kayak & Canoe Club (OVKC). "What's going on?" I interrupted, stepping inside the door. Peter turned and introduced me to a couple of young men wearing dark leather jackets and leggings. Bikers, I thought to myself. What in the world are they doing out in the bush on a night like this?

One of them, a tall, powerfully built man in his mid-twenties, turned to me and said, "My name is Daniel Marinier. When I saw your friends driving through Temiscamingue today with kayaks tied to their vehicles I knew they were headed to the Kipawa. As soon as I got off work, I called my friend Richard, and we hopped on our bikes to pay you a visit. Are you aware that Hydro Quebec has proposed to build a dam twelve miles south of here near Lost Creek?"

"I haven't heard anything about it," I replied a bit skeptically as I pulled up a chair.

"I'm surprised," he continued. "Their plans will affect you more than anyone else. On the other hand, I've only known about the project for three weeks and I'm the Aquatics Director at the Temiscamingue Recreation Center where the meetings are being held. Hydro Quebec has succeeded in keeping this whole thing pretty quiet. Richard and I have been paddling the upper half of the Kipawa for the past year, and we intend to fight this proposal to the very end. Hydro Quebec plans to dig a canal from Kipawa Lake, then flood the area behind their proposed dam and send the water down a pipe to a generating station in Lost Creek where it flows into Lake Temiskaming. It is water that would normally flow right here in front of your cabin. They're diverting the Kipawa River!"

For a moment, there was a heavy, sickening silence in the room. His words hung in the air like a foul stench, as if someone had dragged in a bloated, dead goat and thrown it on top of the table. Charlie

Hastings was grinding his fist into the palm of his left hand as he spoke. "Hydro companies are like beavers. When they hear the sound of flowing water or see a rapid coursing through a gorge, they get nervous and try to dam it up or run it through a pipe to make electricity."

"You're absolutely right," Peter Arthur agreed. "I will never forget the time I sat in a meeting with a couple of hydro engineers watching a video of some waterfalls near Quebec City. One of them turned to the other and said, "What a waste! All that water pouring over a ledge, and for what? It's money down the drain.""

"Yeah, but we're not talking about Quebec City or Montreal," I interjected, rising from my chair. "We're talking about the Kipawa River, jewel of the north, my own backyard!"

"Save your breath, Mr. Sorensen," said the biker, Richard Moreau. "Hydro Quebec doesn't care where the river runs, so long as they can dam it or divert it and sell the power to Montreal or New York City. You should see what they did at James Bay in the backyard of the Cree Indians. Don't think for a minute they won't do it here. And they're in a hurry. The first public meeting was held two weeks ago in Laniel. A second meeting will be at Notre Dame du Nord ten days from now, and a third meeting is scheduled for June 22 at the Recreation Center in the town of Temiscamingue. They want to wrap up all their environmental studies and public hearings by December and start construction next year."

"But they can't possibly assess all the impacts in just seven months," I replied. "Why the big push?"

"It has something to do with the year 2000 and the North American Free Trade Agreement," said Daniel Marinier. "Apparently restrictions on the sale of electricity, natural gas, and other forms of energy will be lifted in 2000. Hydro Quebec has its eye on every source of running water left in the province that is not already tapped. Even if they decide to drop this proposal, there is a group of private investors from Montreal with another project in mind that would also divert water from the Kipawa to the Gordon River."

At that point, Daniel handed me a stack of papers and said, "See how many signatures you can get from fishermen, kayakers, tourists, or even sightseers coming here to view the waterfalls at Grande Chutes. Anyone who wants to protect the natural beauty of the Kipawa River and keep water flowing down its channel needs to sign this petition."

Mike McCubbin, a paddler from northern Ontario, asked to see a copy of the petition. "I will make sure that kayakers from all over Canada are made aware of this proposal, via the Internet, as soon as I get back to town. This whole thing is madness. We are talking about a project that will destroy the most beautiful river in northwestern Quebec. Not to mention the loss of the best whitewater within three hundred miles of here."

I took the petitions and thanked Daniel and Richard for the effort they had made to inform us of Hydro Quebec's plans. As I left the cabin and started back down the trail, I paused again to watch the moonlight dancing with the shadows on the rapids. The Kipawa River, which had run its natural course for ten thousand years, was about to fall victim to technology and the folly of men. A deep, overwhelming sadness swept over me as I reflected on the twenty-four years I had lived on its shores.

River Cabin overlooking Hollywood Rapid, Kipawa River.

Chapter 2

LOST IN THE WILDS

I went to the woods because I wished to live deliberately,
to front only the essential facts of life,
and see if I could not learn what it had to teach,
and not when I came to die,
discover that I had not lived.
—Henry David Thoreau

The discovery that I had not yet really lived came to me like a flash when I first saw the rapids of the Kipawa River. I have kept watch on those rapids where they tumble into the waters of Lake Temiskaming for a generation since. Although no one has officially appointed me the sentinel on the Kipawa, I have felt it a privilege to stand watch lest the power, grace, and beauty of this magnificent river go unnoticed by man. Much as Thoreau never expected financial compensation for being the self-appointed inspector of snowstorms in the woods around Walden Pond, I have never felt cheated in my capacity as the watchman of the Kipawa River. On the contrary, I would be a poorer man had I never seen the beauty, heard the roar, or felt the power of this wild river. It has taken a grip on me which grows tighter every spring when I leave my home in Utah and return to this huddle of log buildings in northern Quebec.

I am not the first to have fallen under its spell. For a hundred years the camp on the Kipawa River has lured lumberjacks, fishermen, movie stars, and millionaires; and for centuries prior to that, it received Algonquin and Ojibwa Indians, French Canadian voyageurs, and Catholic priests in search of a flock.

I first came to live on Lake Temiskaming in 1975 as caretaker of the lodge on the Kipawa River. The owner of the lodge, Don Bair, a friend of mine from Indianapolis, had fallen under the Kipawa River's spell several years before when he landed a twenty-pound lake trout from the mouth of its raging waters. At that time the lodge was up for sale, and Don was anxious to secure the property for a private retreat where he could send friends, employees, and business associates for a few days of rest, relaxation, and fishing. Don, of course, intended to spend a good deal of time at those various pursuits as well.

When he offered me the position of manager–caretaker, I

proposed that my close friend and hunting partner, Jim Karpowitz, accompany me as my assistant. Don agreed. Jim and I left Salt Lake City in the spring of 1975. We were twenty-three years old and adventure bound in a Volkswagen bug loaded to the gills with fishing gear and hunting rifles. We had high hopes of losing ourselves in the wilds of northern Canada.

Don Bair, owner of the lodge 1975 - 1982.

Upon arriving in Fabre, Quebec, we immediately set out for the lodge on foot down a seven-mile logging trail that the locals called "a two-hour walk through the woods." Under normal conditions, we would have traveled to the camp by boat from the Fabre Public Docks twelve miles north on Lake Temiskaming, but the date was May 2, and due to a late spring there remained a two-foot layer of mushy ice on the lake.

We started down the trail that morning with the sun shining, birds singing, and visions of arriving at the camp in the afternoon to spend a quiet evening grilling lake trout on the coals of a roaring fire. Nine hours and fifteen miles later, the two of us were struggling up a muddy hillside under darkening skies that had poured down rain, sleet, and snow since noon. We were thoroughly soaked and discouraged. The trail we had started on had branched off in various directions, meandering through swamps and gulleys, then vanishing altogether on a cliff overlooking Lake Temiskaming. It was there we had expected to find the lodge alongside the rapids of the Kipawa River. But to our chagrin, we found an ice-covered lake, shrouded in fog, and little hope of spending the night in a warm cabin by a roaring fire.

As we stood on the hill staring into the gloom, Jim turned to me and said, "I can hear water rushing somewhere out in the distance." I listened intently for a moment, then detected a faint noise like waves breaking onto a beach. But fog has a way of altering and even obliterating sounds.

"Could be our imagination just playing tricks on us, Jim," I replied. "On the other hand, what can we lose by hiking along the shoreline for a while?" For three hours we crawled under deadfall, climbed over rocky ledges, and listened to the sound of rushing water that alternately faded then grew louder in the distance. At 9:00 PM, we ended our trek on top of a hill in total darkness and deep frustration. We finally had to admit we were lost, but by this time we felt too cold, tired, and hungry to really care.

Jim and I had been raised in the shadows of the Wasatch Mountains, and for many years, we had trained ourselves in the skills necessary to survive in the outdoors. We took a certain pride in our ability to start a fire using anything from bow drills to flint and steel, not to mention matches in a waterproof container. But that night, as we searched desperately for a few scraps of dry wood, I learned to appreciate the difference between the semi-arid mountains of the West and the rain-drenched forests of the East. Everything was soaked. After one hour and two dozen matches, we kindled a small blaze with punk from the center of a rotten log. For dinner we shared the soggy remains of a box of oatmeal cookies, then lay down on some pine boughs to spend a long, almost sleepless night. We determined to retrace our steps

Jim and Scott trapping beaver in the Wasatch Mountains, 1975.

back to the road in the morning, for even the sound of running water that had lured us on for so many hours had now faded entirely. We took turns feeding the fire with bits of punk and wet branches that smoked more than burned. It was hardly the roaring blaze I had envisioned while walking down the trail that morning, but even the smallest fire brings comfort and warmth when you are lost in the bush. As I watched the tiny flames flicker and dance in their attempt to ward off darkness and cold, I thought how natural it was that primitive man worshiped the god of fire. I have nearly done the same on nights such as that.

While Jim and I talked and contemplated the sorry situation in which we found ourselves, our conversation drifted to stories of trappers and mountain men whose legend and lore had captivated us when we were growing up in the Rocky Mountains. Some of their epic struggles with nature made our plight seem rather trivial. I recalled the saga of Jedediah Smith, who was attacked by a grizzly bear. The bear succeeded in getting most of Smith's head into its mouth. When his companions finally drove it off, they found Jedediah in bad straits. The bear had raked long strands of scalp from Smith's head, leaving deep, ragged gashes through which traces of white skull bone were visible. The trappers soon discovered that he was also missing an eyebrow and the better part of an ear. While they were discussing various courses of action, which included burying him, Jedediah sat up and told his friend James Clyman to fetch a needle and sew him back together.

I could see Jim wince ever so slightly as I described in vivid detail how Clyman began to patch and sew the scalp back into place. The old mountain man was thoroughly perplexed, however, by the missing ear. When one of the trappers found the ear lying in some brush, Jed Smith suggested that Clyman attempt to stitch it back on. Clyman was not optimistic but proceeded with his friend's request. Months later, after the wounds had healed, a fellow trapper observed that the ear seemed a bit crooked and out of place. Jedediah grinned and told him that Clyman had purposely sewed it on a little further back than normal so he could better hear if a bear was sneaking up behind him.

"Haw, haw," Jim roared in mock exaggeration of the deep, throaty laughter we had heard booming through the entryway of a local bar in the town of Laniel the night before. Jim always laughed at my stories, even though he'd heard most of them at least a dozen times before. We had a silent but mutual agreement to laugh at each other's mountain man tales no matter how old they were or how often we retold them. It comes with the territory when there are just two of you in a thousand miles of wilderness. Anyway, we were partners, and partners should always laugh at each other's stories. If they don't, they might end up strangling one another after a few months in the bush.

Jim laid another damp stick on the fire and then, not to be outdone, recounted the story of Hugh Glass. Glass was an old mountaineer who was also mauled by a grizzly, then left to die by his comrades, who felt helpless to do anything for him. They managed to kill the bear, but only after it had torn huge gaping wounds on Hugh's back, broken his leg, and left him unconscious. To make matters worse, the small trapping brigade was trying to avoid an angry swarm of Arikara Indians over whose territory they had trespassed for several days. So they laid poor Hugh on the hide of the bear that had mauled him, then abandoned him to his fate.

Several days later, when he should have been dead, Glass regained consciousness. He tried to sit up but was racked with pain as an unseen force pulled him back to the ground. The hair from the heavy bearskin had become stuck and scabbed to the wounds on his back. I felt myself cringe as Jim described how "Old Hugh" slowly rolled over onto his stomach, then, with the bearskin still attached, dragged himself down to a small stream where he soaked for several hours. Eventually the hide loosened, while minnows nibbled and fed on the maggots that had infested his wounds.

After Hugh got free of the bearskin, he crawled from the stream to a thicket of chokecherry and alder brush. There he found a stout, forked limb into which he jammed the heel of his broken leg. By bracing himself and pulling backwards away from the limb, he was able to straighten and set the fractured bone. Next he splinted the leg with a couple of branches and some buckskin lacing. Now all that remained was to hobble and crawl a couple of hundred miles back to Fort Henry on the Yellowstone River. It took him two months, but he made it.

"Waugh!" Jim snorted as he poked the coals of our fire. "That ol' coon had the har of the bar. I reckon if Hugh Glass could do all that with a broken leg, we ought to be able to hike back to the highway tomorrow."

I nodded in agreement, then rolled over so my back could feel the fire's warmth. The hot coals sputtered and hissed as drops of freezing rain continued filtering down through the pine boughs above. I drifted in and out of sleep thinking about grizzled old Hugh, abandoned in the wilderness, dragging himself around with a bear hide stuck to his back. Compared to us, he seemed pretty tough and heroic. We seemed more like a couple of lost boys. Boys who didn't have enough sense to follow a map or get out of the rain.

9

At the first light of dawn, I awoke to the chirping of chickadees in the branches overhead. There were four of them, black-capped little puffballs of down preening their feathers, oblivious to the misty cold that had penetrated me to the bone. Our fire was dead and I was shivering, but something soft and warm was moving in my hand. I raised my head from the ground, and there, curled up in my palm, was a tiny field mouse who had taken refuge from the storm. When I moved, it hopped to the ground and ran into our empty oatmeal cookie box. After stirring around in the box for awhile, it reappeared with bulging cheeks and crumbs stuck to its whiskers. Then, sensing that the palm of my hand was no longer a safe haven, the mouse made its way over to Jim, who was fast asleep on the ground. For a moment, the tiny animal surveyed the sleeping giant, then disappeared into an opening where Jim's beard and coat collar met. It seemed to me that we had truly become one with nature. With his head in the mud, rain falling on his face, pine needles strewn throughout his hair, one foot in the ashes of our fire, and a mouse crawling around in his beard, Jim was snoring like an old man in a rest home. Suddenly he bolted upright and began pawing at his beard. "Something was climbing around in my shirt," he grumbled. I told him he had been dreaming and it was time to get up and start the long walk back to our vehicle.

As we gathered up our gear, the fog over the lake began to lift, and once again I heard the sound of rushing water. I do not know how to explain my next move except to say that once a person has spent an entire day and half a night chasing noises in the fog he becomes obsessed and finds it hard to quit when the noise seems to be right around the bend. "Let's follow that sound for another thirty minutes," I suggested. "If we haven't found the lodge by then, we'll turn back to the road."

Our route took us down from the hill, then along a rocky beach for three hundred yards to the base of another steep, but not particularly large, hill. As we made our way to the top, small patches of sunlight began to peek through the fog. All at once we found ourselves staring like lost and lonely pilgrims at the rapids of the Kipawa River. We had spent that long, cold, miserable night just fifteen minutes from the warmth and comfort of the lodge.

⚜ Dam Update

Saturday, June 13, 1998
Kipawa River Lodge (Topping's Camp) 10:00 A.M.

Several boats are anchored in the mouth of the river. I visit each one and explain Hydro Quebec's proposal and the purpose of our petition to keep the river flowing at current levels. They all sign it. Most are cottage owners on Lake Temiskaming but have not been informed of the project. One of them has a camp at McMartin's Point, less than a mile from the proposed dam. They are all competing in Sean Gustafson's annual fishing derby at McClaren's Bay eighteen miles south of the lodge. The derby runs today between sunrise and 5:00 P.M.

At 7:30 P.M., I notice Sean's boat anchored in the mouth of the river. Sean is a fisherman in the purest sense of the word. He and his wife, Marie, have come for the evening run on walleye. Marie is in the back of the boat strumming her guitar and singing. She has the most beautiful voice on either side of Lake Temiskaming. I paddle the canoe out and explain Hydro Quebec's proposal to them. They look bewildered. Nobody at McClaren's Bay is aware of the plan. They sign the petition and vow further investigation.

"So what size of fish won the derby?" I ask.

Sean's grin is huge. "A 5 lb. 9 oz. walleye from right here at the mouth of the Kipawa River."

Jim's first catch, a 5 lb. northern pike.

Chapter 3

A HOWLING NORTH WIND

And suddenly there came a sound from heaven
as of a rushing, mighty wind.
—Acts 2:2

Jim and I spent the next two days sleeping, stoking the fire, and foraging for food. Our backpacks contained two boxes of macaroni and cheese, a dozen hot dogs, three chocolate bars, and eight strips of jerky. We had hiked into the camp, assuming the previous occupants would have left something in the way of provender. However, a thorough search of the three guest cabins turned up nothing. Each of the cabins was a spacious, beautifully crafted, three-and four-bedroom log structure with stone fireplaces and handmade furniture, but no food. After combing the Main Lodge for nearly an hour, Jim discovered a trapdoor beneath a rug in the living room. We pried it open with a hunting knife, and there below in the corner of a dark, dingy cellar, we struck the mother lode—one case of canned asparagus. The cellar was about five feet deep with a rickety set of stairs and walls lined with river stone. It was cold, damp, and strewn with cobwebs. I climbed inside and passed the case of asparagus up to Jim. He took one look at the cans and condemned them. "These are no good. The tops are bulged out. If we eat this stuff, we'll die!"

I was less critical. "If we don't eat this stuff, we might starve to death. Maybe the cans are deformed from freezing last winter."

Using the knife, I gouged a jagged hole in the top of a can and poured some stringy, foul-smelling, greenish-gray liquid into a pan. It looked deadly.

"Go ahead," Jim taunted, "cook yourself up a bowl of botulism. I'm going fishing."

Jim had tied a fishing pole to his pack frame and brought along two silver lures with red eyes. "These are popeyes. Best pike lure ever invented," he bragged as he attached one to the steel leader at the end of his line. "My old Scoutmaster, Clements Horlocker, turned me onto these ten years ago on a trip to northern Saskatchewan."

I eyed him suspiciously. In the ten years I had known Jim he had never mentioned a Scoutmaster with the unlikely name of Clements Horlocker or anything about a fishing trip to northern Saskatchewan. I decided to test him.

"Yeah, it reminds me of the time my den mother, Beulah Bullwhacker, took a bunch of us Cub Scouts to the Gulf of Alaska on a polar bear hunt back in '63. Beulah wouldn't let us use guns though. We had to cut a big hole in the ice, then sprinkle frozen peas around the hole for bait. Then when . . . "

"I know the rest," Jim growled indignantly. "When the bear came up to take a pea, you kicked him in the ice hole. Ha, Ha, real funny, but in fact I did have a Scoutmaster named Clements Horlocker who took me fishing in Saskatchewan, and that is just one small fragment of my vast and illustrious past of which you are both ignorant and uninformed." Then he marched off in a huff toward the mouth of the river with his fishing pole in hand.

It was obvious Jim didn't want any company for awhile. Even though we had rationed our food for two days, we were now reduced to four strips of jerky and a chocolate bar. Hunger, or at least the prospect of hunger, was beginning to put a strain on our relationship as partners in the operation of a hopefully soon-to-be-successful fishing lodge.

I wandered over to the boathouse, a large thirty-by-sixty-foot log building that housed two fourteen-foot aluminum boats, one fifteen-foot fiberglass boat, and a sixteen-foot wooden skiff. The boats had no motors. They were useless anyway until the ice departed from the lake, at which time we would bring the big tri-hull in from town. The tri-hull was our workhorse—a heavy, wide, twenty-foot-long fiberglass boat with an Evinrude 150 mounted on its transom. It was stored in a garage behind the filling station in Fabre along with several small outboards, a couple of chain saws, and a portable generator. Providing ourselves with food, transportation, and other conveniences would be a simple matter once the ice was gone.

When I turned to leave the boathouse, a large object alongside the far wall caught my attention. It was a cedar-strip canoe lying upside down, nearly hidden from view by the other boats. Stepping cautiously in between the boats and the other equipment, I walked to the opposite end of the building and unlatched two large, gate-like doors that faced directly out on Lake Temiskaming. As they swung open on creaky hinges, the boathouse was flooded with sunlight. The canoe turned out to be a seventeen-foot Peterborough with a squared-off stern. It was painted bright red and when I tipped it over, a pair of wooden paddles tumbled out from beneath the thwarts, clattering loudly on the floor. Now, here was a vessel I could use.

The lake was free from ice directly in front of the lodge for about two hundred yards due to the powerful current pouring in at the mouth of the river. And south around the point beyond the river inlet, there appeared to be more open water than ice for at least a mile. That was the direction I intended to explore.

The distance from the boathouse door to the lake was less than forty feet, but the weight of the canoe surprised me. I had to drag it bow-first to the water's edge. After placing a paddle and a life jacket near the center thwart, I set one foot inside and pushed off with the other.

When it comes to water travel, for me nothing compares to the quiet glide of a wooden canoe on a calm lake. The Peterborough was a wide and sturdy vessel. In fact, it was so stable that I could stand up between the center thwart and the stern and paddle it like a Venetian gondola. At least that was the position I assumed as I glided out past the point where Jim was happily casting his shiny popeye into the mouth of the river. I hailed him with a musical refrain in Italian, using my deepest, most operatic voice. Jim pretended to ignore me. He turned the other way and kept right on fishing. Nonetheless, I caught him peeking over his shoulder. No one I've ever met enjoys canoeing more than Jim, especially when it's done with style and flair. On the other hand, no one I've ever met dislikes opera more than Jim, especially when it's done poorly.

After rounding the point, I assumed a kneeling position near the stern and settled into a smooth rhythmic paddling. The morning was sunny and brisk, with a swatch of billowy white clouds floating high above the Ontario shore. A cool breeze was drifting off the ice a few hundred yards to the west, creating tiny ripples on the water in front of my bow. As I paddled south, the roar of the rapids slowly diminished. After a mile the sound was indiscernible, hardly more than a whisper floating in the air. Once the noise had faded altogether, the silence was so complete I felt a strange emptiness. I came to the realization that living so close to the rapids was like having music playing in the background twenty-four hours a day. If I listened closely, I could hear the various notes and even the changing octaves. It was a music so subtle and sublime I began to take it for granted when day after day it continued to play its soft harmony as we went about our activities. Only in its absence, when I left the camp for several hours or days, did I realize how soothing and lovely the sound of rushing water was. Years later, while sitting in a concert hall listening to Handel's Water Music, I felt my spirit transcend the auditorium and alight in the stern of a cedar-strip canoe at the mouth of the Kipawa River, where it rocked to the rhythm of that glorious sound.

A mile and a half south of the lodge I came upon the tallest, most precipitous cliffs I had yet to see on the lake. They rose to heights of three and four hundred feet, towering above my canoe like a great stone curtain. Mentally, I made a note to tell Jim about them and return with some harnesses, ropes, and carabineers for a day of climbing and rappelling.

The sun was nearly overhead as I drifted along the base of the cliffs. Its radiant warmth penetrated the folds of my wool shirt, making me drowsy and listless. Lying back against the stern, using my life jacket for a pillow, I yawned long and deep and gave into the gentle force that was pulling my eyelids shut.

I do not know how long I dozed with the hot, luxuriant sun beating down on the canoe, but suddenly the tranquility was shattered by a shrill, ear-piercing scream that sent chills coursing down my spine. I bolted upright in a state of alarm and turned my head around 180 degrees to look behind the canoe. I braced myself, expecting some sort of onslaught or attack.

At first glance, I saw nothing out of the ordinary. My eyes began scouring the shoreline just fifty yards away. Perhaps it was Jim, pulling some prank. Maybe he was still angry about being teased about old Horlocker and had followed me down the lake to get revenge. It seemed unlikely though. Either he would have had to swim the mouth of the river in thirty-two-degree water and then hike the rugged shoreline for two miles, or else have dragged out one of the aluminum boats and rowed up behind me.

All at once an odd-looking creature broke the surface of the water between my canoe and the shore. It appeared to be a duck with a large dark head, mysterious red eyes, and a long rapier-like beak which would have been the envy of any woodpecker. Its back was almost as dark as its head but was crisscrossed with elegant white lines, creating a checkerboard pattern. Like most ducks, it had a lightly shaded breast and small, insignificant tail feathers. It moved effortlessly about the surface of the lake, dipping and bobbing its head below the waterline as if searching for food.

So engrossed was I watching the unusual bird that I nearly forgot the startling sound of a moment before. Suddenly the bird cocked its head toward the heavens, opened its beak, and wailed out the most wild, unearthly cry I could imagine coming from any creature, much less a duck. That solved the mystery of the noise that had startled me moments earlier. Still, I had no clue what strange, ill-mannered fowl sat before me, looking pleased and proud to have interrupted my nap. I had hunted waterfowl with my father around the marshes of the Great Salt Lake from the time I was six-years-old and could readily identify mallards, pintails, widgeons, scaups, gadwals, redheads, shovellers, and a half-dozen other species, but now I was baffled. I had never seen a duck that even remotely resembled the alien fowl that continued dunking its head and shrieking at me like a red-eyed maniac. As I turned the canoe and began paddling back toward the lodge, the mysterious bird was joined by its mate. The two of them harangued me with a chorus of shrieks and cries that continued for several minutes until quelled by the roar of the rapids as I neared the camp.

When I approached the mouth of the river, Jim was still standing on the same large rock persistently casting his line into the current. He seemed despondent.

"So, no luck with old Horlocker's popeye?" I chided him.

"Au contraire, mon frere. I had a ten-pound lake trout up alongside the bank, but he shook the hook loose right at my feet. I tried to horse him onto shore without using a net."

Now it was I who felt despondent. I had been imagining trout filets roasted over hot coals as an alternative to a stick of jerky and a bloated can of asparagus.

"Cheer up!" Jim laughed as he reached into the water at his feet and held up a nylon stringer with a thirty-inch fish swinging wildly from one end. "The trout got away, but I landed a five-pound pike. Stoke up the fire while I gut this fish. We're having pike for dinner tonight!"

That evening we dined on northern pike baked over coals in aluminum foil. We ate it unseasoned—no salt, pepper, butter, or lemon—and yet it holds a place in my memory as one of the grandest feasts of my entire life.

The following morning Jim and I determined to hike back through the bush to our vehicle. We were in desperate need of supplies, something more substantial than canned asparagus and more reliable than catching the odd fish on Jim's popeye. The trail out to the highway was easy to follow because of an old telephone wire that ran between the lodge and Chester LaForest's farmhouse. In many places the wire lay on the ground underneath fallen trees but still could be seen most of the way. I don't know how we missed it on our trek into the camp three days before. We found the exact spot where we had taken the wrong trail and turned our two-hour hike into a twenty-four-hour ordeal.

Upon reaching the Volkswagen, Jim and I drove straight to Fabre, then down to the public wharf on Lake Temiskaming to check the ice. We were pleasantly surprised to find the docks free of ice. Also a narrow channel of open water existed about a hundred feet wide running south down the lake along the shoreline. Jim was exuberant. "If that channel is open all the way to the lodge, we could load the tri-hull with enough food and supplies to last a month and be back to the camp in half an hour."

"It would sure beat carrying a week's worth of grub on our backs down that trail again," I agreed.

We returned to town to see if the twenty-foot tri-hull could be ready to go within an hour or two. Jacques, the proprietor of the filling station, was just getting ready to close up shop for an hour-long lunch break. "I'm very sorry," he apologized, "but the motor on your boat burned up last fall when the man who was watching your camp forgot to put oil in it. I can get the parts and have it running in about two weeks."

"Two weeks!" I said incredulously. "We need a boat this afternoon, Jacques."

"No problem," he winked as he turned and disappeared into a shed behind the garage. For several minutes, Jim and I could hear Jacques grunting and cursing as he knocked over boxes, flung used tires against the wall, and scattered odd pieces of snowmobiles, chain saws, and outboard motors everywhere.

"Certainly Jacques is not going to find a boat in that pile of rubble," Jim quipped, as a bent axle and a rusty tire iron came flying through the doorway.

"Doubtful," I replied. "Even a canoe would have a hard time fitting in a shed that small. I'll bet he's just searching for a set of keys. He's probably going to lend us another launch while he repairs ours."

"Ah ha!" roared Jacques as he staggered out through the doorway, carrying a big black bundle of rubber which looked like an enormous inner tube bound up with twine. "Here is your boat," he grinned, dropping it in the dust at our feet. Then, with a wild gesture, he pointed to an air hose coiled up on the garage wall and exclaimed, "I will pump it up for you right now, and away you go down Lac Temiscamingue."

Jim and I stared blankly at one another while Jacques leaned over and cut the twine with a pocketknife, then proceeded to kick the bundle with his work boots. Slowly but surely, after a series of powerful kicks, the bundle unraveled in the shape of a very flat boat. Next, he walked to the side of the garage, grabbed the air hose, and returned to inflate it. When he pressed the hose to the valve, there was a high hissing sound, as a compressor inside the garage started to hum. Momentarily, the vessel began to take on a familiar form; it was a seven-foot-long dinghy with an inflatable floor and sides that came together at the front to form a bow. The transom was also made of rubber but had a piece of hardwood planking to which a small outboard motor could be attached. And I do mean small. Anything larger than a four horse would have been much too powerful for the dinghy. After searching the garage, the smallest thing we could find was a six- horsepower Evinrude. "You will be all right with a six horse," Jacques exclaimed. "Just don't run her wide open. That could buckle the boat in the center. Remember, it's only rubber." How could I forget?

Jim and I walked next door to Mr. Pellerin's general store and stocked up on fifty pounds of canned goods, bacon, sugar, flour, bread, milk, and a couple dozen eggs. That was all we figured the boat could handle, along with the two of us plus the motor and five gallons of gas. The groceries, motor, and gasoline went into the back seat of the Volkswagen, and the inflated dinghy we strapped on top.

"Good luck, Yankees!" Jacques yelled as we pulled out of the filling station and headed west toward the public wharf on Lake Temiskaming. Twenty minutes later the boat was in the water, loaded with supplies and ready to go. "You run the motor," I said to Jim. "I'll sit near the bow and try to balance this load between us." As we pushed off from the docks, Jim gave the starter cord a pull and turned the throttle wide open. Immediately, the boat surged forward and began to shake, jump, then buckle in the middle. The load in the center started to rise upward, while both the bow and the stern were pushed downward. The force of the motor on the weak, inflatable transom was too much for the boat to bear and water came pouring over the bow in front and spilled into the stern from behind. "We're swamping!" I yelled to Jim as he quickly killed the motor. Fortunately, only a couple of gallons had come on board, but we had to bail it out bare-handed. The water was like liquid ice. Our joints and knuckles ached after we scooped up a dozen handfuls. Jim shook the water from his frozen hands and buried them under his armpits. "Somehow we've got to keep the bow and the stern from diving down when we accelerate. If we can't travel at least three-quarters speed, we'll never make the lodge before nightfall, and that's one experience I don't care to repeat."

"I'm with you, Hos. How about tying some rope between the bow and the motor housing. Maybe that will offset whatever force is causing the middle to buckle."

"It's worth a try," Jim replied, carefully idling back to the dock. While Jim continued to bail water, I hurried to the Volkswagen and retrieved the length of rope we had used to strap the boat on top of the vehicle. After passing one end through a metal grommet on the bow, I handed the other end to Jim, who wrapped it tightly around the motor housing and tied a stout knot with the loose end.

"We're ready to go," he called out, then yanked on the starter cord once again. I watched the rope grow taut with the bow and transom straining at opposite ends as Jim gradually accelerated to three-quarters speed. Thankfully, the rope held firm and kept both ends riding high and dry.

"Yahoo!" Jim hollered as the dinghy plowed down the narrow channel with the tree-studded shore on our left and the ice-covered lake on our right. I estimated our speed to be about seven or eight miles an hour as the wharf and the Volkswagen disappeared behind us, but it felt like we were on eagles' wings.

"Nothing will stop us now," I yelled to Jim. "At this rate, we'll make camp in a couple of hours."

Forty minutes later, when we rounded Pointe Martel, the narrow channel of water opened up into a broad bay that was relatively free of ice. We were still making great time. Jim steered the boat further out from shore in order to travel a straight line across the open water toward the next point of land. Here and there were large pieces of drift ice which had broken off from the main body of the frozen lake. Some were five or six times the size of our boat, causing us to weave in between or around them. "Let's just nudge one of those with the bow of the boat and see what happens," Jim shouted over the noise of the motor. Jim could be notoriously impetuous at times. It was a trait born of curiosity more than recklessness, and although I never encouraged the behavior, it was something I had come to accept as part of his nature. And besides, once an idea took hold and the wheels were set in motion, there was very little one could say or do to change Jim's mind, short of whacking him over the head with a board. On this occasion, I had no board. I just shrugged my shoulders and gripped the sides of the dinghy. Jim had already turned the boat directly toward a large, weather-beaten plate of ice. "Are you ready?" he cried. I nodded my head in resignation and agreed that "ramming the ice broadside" was the right thing to do. After all, I reasoned, two mules are faster than one when pulling a wagon over a cliff.

As we approached the ice, Jim accelerated slightly and began to laugh. I noticed the surface was covered with slush. Perhaps it was soft and mushy enough to allow us to pass through the center unobstructed. Maybe Jim was acting on a well-thought-out plan rather than an impulsive whim. If I was still harboring such hopes, they were summarily dashed to pieces when the bow made contact with the ice. Like a ship run aground on a reef, the boat slammed into the frozen plate, came to an abrupt halt, then was thrown backward and sideways with such force we nearly capsized. I grabbed at groceries and gear in an attempt to keep everything on board, while Jim tried to stabilize the craft as water poured over the stern. For a moment, I thought we were going down. Once the danger had passed, Jim looked up and sheepishly grinned, "It's not as mushy as it looks. From now on, I think we'd better go around." I did not dignify his statement by responding at all. Subsequently, we gave the pieces of drift ice wide berth as we continued down the lake.

The further south we progressed, the more open water we encountered. I kept glancing down at our map in an effort to keep track of the distance we had traveled from the docks at Fabre. "I'd guess we're almost halfway there. How much gas is left in the tank?" I called back to Jim. When he did not answer I turned to see what was wrong. Jim was looking over his shoulder at a big, black, formidable bank of clouds that was sweeping down the lake in our direction. Within minutes the sky turned from a dazzling blue to a dark and ominous gray.

"Batten down the hatches!" Jim cried, as the first stirrings of wind rippled the water around us. Immediately I scanned the shoreline for a cove or anyplace that might offer us shelter from the oncoming storm. There was nothing. As far as I could see down the lake, there were only vertical cliffs and rugged boulder-strewn shores that afforded little in the way of protection.

"We'll just have to ride this out and hope that the dinghy is up to the test," I said pessimistically. Jim began to angle the boat closer to shore when a furious blast of wind lifted his hat off his head and sent it skipping across the surface of the water. "You can forget about chasing after that!" I exclaimed as the hat disappeared behind one of the drifting ice floes. Fortunately, the wind was to our backs, and the boat was running with the waves, which were only a foot high due to the fact that the lake was still three-fourths covered with ice. Nonetheless, in a seven-foot dinghy, a one-foot-wave seemed substantial enough. My fingers soon grew numb from the freezing spray that whipped over from the side of the boat from the top of each wave as we hastened to narrow the gap between us and the edge of the lake.

By the time we had motored within fifty yards of shore, visibility was down to a few feet, and the storm had completely engulfed us. Escape was no longer an option. Stinging bits of sleet and hail descended on us like a swarm of angry bees, leaving small, red welts where they struck our hands, ears, and cheeks. The north wind continued to howl and scream, driving the boat before it further and further down the lake. For a time we were entirely at the mercy of the elements. The best we could do was to keep the dinghy straight and the wind to our backs to avoid taking on water. Eventually the sleet and hail abated, replaced by a cold, driving rain that penetrated every inch of our clothing and gear.

"Who would have thought operating a fishing lodge could be so much fun?" I said, turning to Jim, who was sitting in the stern with a scowl on his face and water dripping from the tip of his nose. He was not a pretty sight. His left eye was red and swollen, having been struck by a hailstone. His hair was matted with sleet and plastered to his head every which way. "Look on the bright side," I continued, "Things can't get much worse."

"Oh, yeah? We could be sinking!" he scowled pointing to the bottom of the boat where a steady stream of bubbles was rising up from a leak in the inflatable floor.

It was then I noticed how soft and limp the dinghy had become. When I pressed my boot down on the floor, instead of it springing back into place, there remained a depression, which immediately filled with water. The sides of the boat had also begun to sag, and the motor seemed to be riding lower than ever behind the transom.

"We'd better make land in a hurry or we might end up swimming," Jim warned. Once again I surveyed the shoreline for a place to get off the water. Two hundred yards in front of our bow, there loomed a stretch of rocky beach that appeared less steep and somewhat less treacherous than what we had encountered for several miles. "Straight ahead, Jim," I called out, pointing toward the beach.

Jim responded by turning the motor toward shore and increasing our speed. Immediately, the boat began to shake and buckle in the center as water poured in over the bow once again. "Slow it down!" I yelled over my shoulder while lifting my feet up off the floor in a futile attempt to keep my boots dry. By the time Jim was aware of the situation and cut back the power, the bottom of the dinghy had three additional inches of water in it There was no point in bailing, however; we would be on land in a couple of minutes.

The storm continued to rage as we pitched and rolled in the frothing, icy waves. Finally the boat drew within ten feet of the shore, and I jumped out into waist-deep water and dragged the bow up onto the rocks. The lake was bitter cold, but my legs were already so numb that it didn't make much difference, and I couldn't get any wetter. After tilting the motor up, Jim crawled from the back of the boat, and together we lifted and pulled the dinghy up until it was halfway out of the water. Then we both sank to the ground like a pair of drunken sailors. We were utterly exhausted.

For two or three minutes Jim and I just sat there staring at the dark, menacing, windswept lake. It had been a close call. "She's a mean, nasty, old witch," Jim muttered under his breath. "She tried to kill us."

I was too cold and fatigued to say anything. Reaching into the dinghy, I grabbed a mangled loaf of bread, ripped open the top, and stuffed a whole slice into my mouth. Then I turned and threw the package to Jim. He grunted appreciatively and followed suit. After eating several slices, I felt some strength return to my limbs. I stood up and began rummaging through the groceries. I wanted cookies. Somewhere in that load was a pack of Fig Newtons. When I found them, they were smashed into one big, pancake-shaped Newton. I started wolfing them down anyway.

Jim stood up and pointed south down the shoreline. "I recognize that next point. It's where we slept out in the rain four nights ago. We're only a mile and a half from the lodge."

"Sit down and have a Fig Newton," I smiled and held out the flattened package. "Your brain is cold and tired, Jim. The storm has muddled your thought process. You need a Fig Newton. They are fortified with protein and have natural sugar to stimulate your weakened mind."

"To hell with you!" Jim angrily sneered, pushing the package aside. "I'll bet you ten bucks that's the point we slept on four nights ago. And by the way, Fig Newtons don't have any protein."

"Sure they do, Jim. Last winter I dated a girl from Fresno, which happens to be the fig capital of the world. She told me how bees get stuck in the figs, then ground up and made into Newtons. Those little crunchy things in the center are actually bees. Pure protein. Have some."

Jim would not be deterred. He stepped into the boat and checked the gas tank. "It's still half full, and the lodge is right around that point. You can stay here and sleep in the rain with your Fig Newtons, or you can climb aboard. Either way, I'm leaving."

In the final analysis, I chose to climb on board and assist my partner in reaching the camp. He never would have made it without me. Although Jim is a skillful boatman, it was I who held a finger in the icy cold water and plugged the leak in the floor to keep the craft from sinking.

We proceeded down the lake for another mile, tossing about in the whitecaps. As it turned out, Jim was absolutely right. The next point we motored past was the very spot we had been forced to camp in the sleet and rain four nights earlier. A few minutes later, the lodge came into view. What a welcome sight! A sturdy log cabin nestled beneath towering spruce and pines, in a sheltered cove alongside the Kipawa River. For the first time, I understood why the mouth of the river was such a haven for weary travelers on a relatively inhospitable lake. It was the only place for miles in any direction that offered refuge and protection from the elements, especially a howling north wind. I smiled and took another bite of Fig Newton. It felt good to be home.

Jim in the rubber dinghy.

Dam
Update

Wednesday, June 17, 1998
Notre Dame du Nord, Quebec, 7:00 P.M.

Hydro Quebec officials, engineers, and consultant meet with a committee of individuals representing cottage owners on Kipawa Lake, outfitters, fish and game officials, local politicians, etc. I am seated next to Henry LaForest, a longtime friend who does an admirable job of translating for me. I asked an HQ official why we, the only people who actually reside on the Kipawa River, were never informed concerning their project or invited to previous meetings. He said Hydro Quebec was not aware of our presence. I thought to myself, "Not aware of four log buildings, a ninety-foot-long wharf, and a family of seven at the mouth of the river? Pity the poor fish, frogs, otters, loons, and ravens that also live along the river and will be affected by this project." We leave the meeting slightly more informed, yet vastly more apprehensive concerning their proposal. We are outnumbered and outgunned, but not yet out of the way.

Picture of Kipawa River Lodge, June 1998.

A great day fishing!

Chapter 4

THE ODYSSEY OF WEBSTER QUINCY SMITH

Fishing, my son, is like landing an important contract;
Consistency, perseverance, and punctuality
are the keys to success.
—Webster Quincy Smith

Winter finally released its icy grip on Lake Temiskaming on May 13. The previous afternoon a balmy south wind had begun to blow, and overnight the ice vanished. The next morning we awoke to summer. Suddenly there were leaves on every tree and mosquitos and black flies hatching out by the thousands. By midafternoon the temperature was eighty degrees. Spring had come and gone in a single day.

The river also underwent a dramatic transformation that morning. Ten miles upstream in the town of Laniel, somebody opened the flumes at the dam on Kipawa Lake, releasing more than 300 cubic meters of water per second. What had been a quiet, meandering stream the day before turned into a wild, raging torrent in a matter of hours. Jim and I stood on the deck of the cabin watching in awe as the river threatened to climb right out of its channel. The immense rapid adjacent to the lodge became a thundering cascade of whitewater, which created three-foot standing waves a hundred yards out into the lake. The power and force of the current were awesome. Pieces of driftwood the size of canoes and entire trees with roots still intact were swept downstream like so many matchsticks. I told Jim there was a hundred-foot waterfall called Grande Chutes, just a mile upstream from the camp, that would be absolutely spectacular with so much water pouring over its precipice. We determined to hike there within a few days and to explore the entire river by summer's end.

Now that the lake was free of ice, our first priority was to go back to Fabre, get the tri-hull out of storage, and return to the lodge with enough supplies and provisions to have the camp up and running by the first week of June. Jim had repaired the leak in the rubber dinghy, and I had found a small set of oars in the boathouse just in case we ran out of gas and were forced to row. Fortunately, the trip was uneventful. The weather was clear and the water calm all day long. We reached the wharf near Fabre at noon.

When we arrived in town, Jacques had the motor repaired and the tri-hull ready to go. We thanked him for the use of the dinghy, but cautioned him about lending it out for future voyages on Lake Temiskaming. "The next guys might not be as resourceful as my partner and me," Jim explained. "Should they get trapped in a hurricane with a leaky boat, you might never see them again."

"Ha, ha!" chortled Jacques. "You Yankees always are making a joke. Have a leak in a hurricane. Ha, ha! Very funny."

After loading the tri-hull with more than a thousand pounds of food and equipment, I stopped at the post office to pick up mail, and then we were on our way. The ride back to the lodge was a breeze. Even loaded, the big tri-hull cruised down the lake at twenty-five miles per hour. Jim drove the boat while I scanned through the mail. In a letter from Don Bair, we were informed that our first guest would be an important client of Don's insurance company, the purchasing agent for one of his largest corporate accounts. The man's name was Webster Quincy Smith. He had visited the camp by float plane on two previous occasions, and Don warned us that he could be "meticulous, demanding" and that he liked things to be just so. The letter described Webster as an "avid fisherman" who would spend all day, every day, on the water. It also said he would be arriving by boat on June 1 with his future brother-in-law, an Iowa farmer named Earl. We were to put them in the River Cabin, where they would be comfortably close to both the Main Lodge and the boat docks.

On the morning of Webster's arrival, a dense, low-lying fog had spread over Lake Temiskaming. A mile to the west I could vaguely see the tops of the tree-lined hills peeking through the mist five hundred feet above the Ontario shore. "Roll out!" I called to Jim. "Today we begin our careers as fishing guides, cooks, and bottle washers."

An hour later we had coffee brewing on the stove and pancake batter and bacon ready to throw on the griddle, when a small bass boat emerged from the fog out on the bay.

"Looks like our guests are right on schedule," Jim remarked as we walked out the door toward the docks to greet them. His choice of the words "right on schedule" was a precursor of future events.

As the boat neared the dock, a large man sitting in the bow and wearing a yellow mackinaw and a matching hat gave the order to "kill the engine." When they bumped up alongside the pilings he stood up and threw a rope to Jim. "Secure the vessel, son. I'll pass you some gear." I turned to Jim, who remained standing with the rope in his hand. He looked ready to laugh, so I jabbed an elbow into his ribs and told him, "Hove to, matey, and secure that boat, or I'll have you keelhauled underneath the tri-hull." Then I reached over and held out my hand to the man in the yellow slicker.

"I'm Webster Smith," he said, as all six-foot-six-inches of him stepped out of the boat. I introduced myself and Jim, then turned to the fellow in the stern, who was busily arranging odds and ends scattered about from their trip down the lake. Eventually he looked up with a shy but friendly smile and stammered, "H- H- Hi, I'm Earl. P- P- Pleased to meet . . . "

"Earl is engaged to my sister Mary Margaret," Webster interrupted. "They are to be wed in September. Earl and I decided that a fishing expedition would be a good opportunity to get acquainted."

Looking at Earl, who remained silently seated in the stern, fiddling with the gas line, I got the distinct impression that the "fishing expedition" was mostly Webster's idea and that Earl had been brought along because he owned a boat.

After unloading a small mountain of gear onto the docks, Jim placed several bags and suitcases marked "Webster" into a wheelbarrow and offered to accompany our guests to the River Cabin. Webster politely refused the offer and said he was anxious to start fishing. "Earl and I have a small wager on who will catch the first, the biggest, and the most fish. I intend to be the winner."

He told Jim to put his belongings in the master bedroom and Earl's "bag o' stuff" in the bunk room. He then turned, reached down into the boat, and hoisted an enormous object the size and shape of a steamer trunk, which he set on the dock with a resounding "thunk." It was his tackle box, a double-wide, multipaneled, six-tiered cornucopia of fishing tackle, the likes of which I had not seen before. After opening it up and proudly displaying the numerous shelves, panels, and drawers, Webster turned to Earl and said, "You'd better get cracking if you expect to win that bet." Earl calmly smiled and climbed from the boat holding a khaki-colored duffel bag in one hand and a heavy, wooden-handled fishing pole in the other. The pole had a broken tip with an ancient, open-faced reel held in place by several wraps of electrical tape. Webster virtually cringed at the sight of the thing.

"You're welcome to use one of mine," he offered as he opened an elaborate fiberglass case with the initials W.Q.S. emblazoned in silver on the top. Inside the case were half a dozen fancy rods and reels lined up according to thickness and length.

"Go ahead, Earl; take your pick."

"No thanks. I'll try my luck with old 'Mr. Ugly.' It belonged to my grandpa," Earl replied as he turned and followed Jim to the River Cabin.

"Don't be too long getting unpacked, or you'll lose the bet before you even get your line wet," Webster called after him. Then he selected one of the rods, attached a shiny silver-chartreuse lure to the line, braced his feet, and let fly a high arcing cast that sent the lure sailing halfway across the mouth of the river.

"Nice cast, Mr. Smith," I said, genuinely impressed.

"Just call me Webster. I'm on vacation, so let's drop the formalities, son."

"Okay, Webster. I guess I'll go in the kitchen and rustle up some breakfast."

"By the way, son, I've drawn up a schedule I'd like to follow for the next seven days." He handed me a piece of paper with an official letterhead that began 'From the Office of Webster Quincy Smith.' The schedule was typed in bold letters in the form of an outline and listed in minute detail the time he would arise, take his meals, go fishing, have a nap, play dominoes, and retire at night. There was even a half-hour block marked "free time" between 4:30 and 5:00 just before dinner each day. What amazed me most, however, were the first four lines which read:

May 31, 2:00 P.M. — Depart Indianapolis
June 1, 6:00 A.M. — Arrive Fabre, Quebec
June 1, 6:30 A.M. — Launch boat (Fabre wharf)
June 1, 7:30 A.M. — Arrive Kipawa River Lodge

I checked my watch. It was 7:55 A.M. Then I recalled looking at my watch as Jim and I were walking out the door to greet them. It was 7:27 A.M. when they came motoring out of the fog. Incredible! After making an eight-hundred-mile drive from Indianapolis and a ten-mile ride by boat down Lake Temiskaming, Webster had arrived at the lodge within three minutes of his calculated time. Then, as if reading my thoughts, Webster stated, "You will note that I pride myself on being punctual. Fishing for lake trout is like landing an important contract, son; consistency, perseverance, and punctuality are the keys to success. Don't you agree?"

"Yesiree, Mr. Smith, I mean Webster," I replied, suppressing an urge to salute and stand at attention. "We'll have breakfast on the table at precisely," I feverishly scanned the schedule, "at precisely 8:30 sharp, Mr. Webster sir, I mean Webster."

He turned and smiled with a grin so wide it hurt to look at it. "I like your style, son." Then he hauled back and let go another powerful, high arcing cast into the current at the mouth of the Kipawa. "This is going to be a great vacation so long as we understand each other."

I was in the kitchen flipping pancakes when Jim returned from the River Cabin. He was breathing hard. "You wouldn't believe how much gear Webster packed for a seven-day vacation. I made two trips with the wheelbarrow to get all his stuff to the cabin. The only thing Earl brought was one duffel bag. He gave me a pocketknife though. Seems like a nice guy."

When Jim saw the schedule that Webster had given me, he rolled his eyes and groaned. "This must be a joke. He can't be serious. What's this 'free time' business at 4:30?"

"I don't know, but I guarantee it's not a joke. And just in case you thought you knew everything about fishing, think again. Webster says fishing is like landing a big contract. The key to success is consistency, perseverance, and punctuality."

"No! He didn't say that."

"I'm afraid he did. And right now you'd better check the schedule and march down to the docks and announce that breakfast will be served in precisely ten minutes."

When Jim stepped outside, a golden shaft of sunlight came slanting through the open doorway. The entire room was cast in a beautiful bronze hue. The sun had barely crested the ridge across the river, and the fog was lifting. All indications were that a perfect day was in the making.

I looked through the kitchen window and noticed Earl standing next to Webster on the end of the dock with his fishing pole bent over double. "Must be a snag," I chuckled. Then the water started to boil and churn thirty feet in front of the pier. All at once, Earl began cranking on his reel as an enormous fish broke the surface, twisting and dancing on its tail. I dropped my spatula and lit out after Jim.

"Grab the net!" I hollered as I dashed through the doorway leading onto the screened porch. Jim was already out in front of me fifty paces racing toward the docks with a large landing net in his hands. I could see Webster jumping up and down, waving his arms, and yelling, "Hurry up, son, we need that net!" By the time I reached the end of the dock all three of them were bent over double peering down into the water. "I'll bet its twenty pounds if it's twenty ounces," Jim crowed.

"Nonsense!" Webster intoned. "I've caught enough twenty pounders to know one when I see it. That fish is not an ounce over ten." Suddenly line began zinging off of Earl's reel as the fish made a run for the bottom. "Keep your tip up and tighten your drag!" Webster ranted as he continued to jump and flail his arms.

Little by little, Earl retrieved the lost line. Several minutes passed before we got another glimpse of the big fish. It was a beauty, a huge, shimmering lake trout. After making two more frenzied runs into deep water, the fish began to tire, and Earl succeeded in bringing it up alongside the dock. Cautiously, Jim slipped the net underneath the trout and began to lift it out of the water. The instant the fish felt the enclosing net, it went wild. The lure popped out of its mouth as it flip-flopped and rolled, but Jim had the situation well in hand. He hauled the monster up onto the dock while everyone cheered and congratulated Earl. Everyone but Webster. He turned to Jim and said, "You're lucky it wasn't any bigger, son. You nearly lost it trying to get it into that net."

"He did not!" Earl countered. "That fish was barely hooked. The only reason it didn't get away was because he was so quick with the net. And it doesn't matter either way. I'm going to release it."

Webster looked stunned. "Release it?"

"That's right. You said yourself it's not all that big."

"It's huge!" Jim interrupted. "And you can't throw it back until I've weighed it." He set down the net and took off running toward the lodge to get his scale. Jim was unwilling to spend the rest of the week listening to Webster carry on about what a mediocre lake trout his future brother-in-law had caught. He wanted hard evidence to the contrary.

Earl reached down and cupped his hand under the trout's gills, then gently lifted it from inside the net. The bright morning sun had a dazzling effect on the magnificent fish. Its back was mottled green and gray but transformed to a brilliant silver along the sides. The belly was immense and as white as a pearl. The fins were pinkish-orange, and the tail fanned out like the wings of an enormous silver butterfly from which water dripped like a string of diamonds onto the dock. The eyes were translucent gold with tiny black opals in the center. Jim and I had fished every day for three weeks, but the largest thing we had landed was an eight-pound northern pike. It wasn't half the size or nearly as beautiful as Earl's fish.

Then I noticed the lure that had popped out of the trout's mouth. It was an old rusty daredevil with half the paint peeled off. And it was attached to the end of the line without a steel leader or even so much as a swivel to protect it. Most fish in Lake Temiskaming have teeth big enough to cut right through nylon line, no matter how heavy. "You're lucky to have caught anything with this," I said, holding up the line and the lure for closer inspection. Earl was obviously offended by my comment. He thought I was making a derogatory remark about the lure itself.

"That's Grandpa's lucky lure. He says that daredevil has caught more fish than any lure in Iowa, and I reckon he's right."

I was quick to agree, then explained how the use of a steel leader would insure that grandpa's "lucky lure" would remain in the family for a long time to come. Webster shrugged his shoulders, then turned and picked up his fishing rod.

Momentarily Jim came pounding back down the walkway swinging the scale in his hand. "This thing only registers up to twenty pounds," he said panting for breath.

"Don't worry, there's no way it's more than fifteen pounds," Webster chimed in, having increased his initial estimation by one-third. All eyes focused on the gauge as Jim hooked the scale onto the trout's lower jaw and raised it with both hands. The arrow bottomed out at twenty pounds and was straining for more.

"That's close enough to twenty for my curiosity," Jim smiled and shot a glance at Webster.

"Humph, I've seen bigger," he grumbled, as he turned and cast his line in the very spot Earl had hooked the big lake trout.

Earl carefully lifted the trout off of the scale and set it back in the water. With one hand under its belly and the other grasping the tail, he moved it gently back and forth allowing water to flow through its gills. Once he was sure the fish was fully revived, Earl released his grip and the trout disappeared with a swish of its tail. "That was exciting," he grinned. "We'll catch some more after breakfast."

Breakfast was served at 8:40 A.M. "Ten minutes behind schedule," Webster remarked as I walked from the kitchen to the dining room carrying a fresh pot of coffee and a platter of pancakes. "We'll blame it on the fish this time," he continued as he held out his cup for a refill. Beside his water glass, Webster had arranged an orderly row of pills. There were two blue pills, one red, three green, and four large white ones. All of them were consumed at intervals during the course of breakfast. The routine was repeated at every meal.

After breakfast, when Webster and Earl were out on the lake for their scheduled "10:00-12:00 A.M. Fishing Session," I carried some extra blankets and pillows up to their cabin. Laid out on a shelf near the fireplace were seven pairs of tennis shoes. Each pair was a different color, and all had tags with the various days of the week written on them. And sure enough, as the week progressed, Webster sported a different pair each day to match a designated outfit.

The rest of the week went pretty much "according to schedule." Webster was not one to deviate from the original plan. On Monday afternoon, I took the tri-hull to town and picked up four young law students whom Don Bair had sent up from Indianapolis to spend a week "fishing and playing poker." They were all quite close in age to Jim and me, and despite the fact that they wanted to be lawyers, we got along fine.

Tuesday was cold and blustery as three-foot whitecaps whipped across the surface of the lake, driven by gusty north winds. Regardless of the rough water and stormy weather, Webster and Earl remained committed to "the schedule" and stayed anchored in the mouth of the river throughout the day. Their persistence paid off. They caught several pike, two more big lake trout, and a pile of walleye. However, it seemed to gall Webster that his brother-in-law-to-be always caught the most and the biggest fish. Not that we would have known, except Jim was always on hand to greet them when they returned from fishing. After Webster's arrogant remarks concerning Earl's lake trout on the morning of their arrival, Jim could not pass up an opportunity to make note of who caught the biggest and the most fish each day, especially when it happened to be Earl. The situation was made even more unbearable because Earl was catching everything on a broken pole, using his grandfather's rusty old daredevil. Webster, on the other hand, had experimented with everything in his tackle box and lost about half of its contents to snags on the river bottom. When Earl magnanimously offered to lend him "grandpa's lucky lure," Webster stubbornly replied, "I have daredevils, thank you very much."

In fact, Webster had tried numerous daredevils of various size and color, but as Earl was heard to comment on more than one occasion, "There's just something about grandpa's lucky lure that fish can't resist." It was a phrase that Jim enthusiastically adopted for his own use as he continued to greet the two men every time they returned to the camp from fishing. It had an effect. As the week progressed, Earl grew more talkative and outgoing, while Webster became withdrawn, quiet, and taciturn.

34

On Saturday morning, the day of Webster Quincy Smith's departure, Lake Temiskaming was in a foul and ugly mood. When I got out of bed and peered through the window, the flag on the far end of the dock was blowing perpendicular to the pole, and whitecaps were rolling down the lake. The skies were filled with dark, menacing clouds from which a cold drizzle had begun to fall. After three mild days of relative calm, the temperature had plummeted overnight, and a howling north wind had returned. Conditions could not have been more treacherous for our guests, who would be heading directly into the worst of it in a craft built for bluegill fishing on a pond.

Breakfast was on the table when Webster and Earl entered the dining room at seven o'clock. After a brief "Hello and good morning," they sat down to eat in relative silence. Earl had already been down to the docks and loaded the boat with gear in preparation for a seven-thirty departure. I was waiting for either of them to broach the subject of weather and conditions on the lake, but other than "pass the cream and sugar," hardly a word was spoken. When they got up to leave, I told Webster the lake was extremely rough, and I was concerned about them making the trip back to Fabre alone in such a small boat. I suggested they wait for an hour while Jim and I got breakfast out of the way for the other guests and then we could escort them to town in the tri-hull.

Webster glanced at his watch, stepped over to the window, and took a brief look at the lake. "It doesn't seem too bad to me. I think we'll be on our way."

As we walked out toward the docks, I reminded them that in a north wind conditions would be much worse four miles up the lake when they rounded Pointe Martel. "Avoid the middle of the lake, and stay close to shore so you can land quickly if you get into trouble." Neither of them responded. I could only hope they were listening.

Earl climbed into the boat first and stowed his gear in a compartment near the stern. Then he strapped on a life jacket and tossed a second one to Webster. "Cinch it on tight. It might come in handy," he said in a very non-Earl tone of voice. Webster seemed a little put out. It was the first time he had worn a life jacket all week, and the only time Earl had spoken to him in a slightly brusque manner. Webster was not accustomed to being told what to do by anyone.

"Seems like a lot of fuss over nothing," he shrugged, then removed his slicker and tied his life vest in place. Replacing the yellow mackinaw back on top of the life jacket, he looked every inch an angry, six-and-a-half-foot hunchback.

Earl stepped to the back of the boat, pumped the gas line, set the choke, and gave the starter cord a quick pull. The small outboard popped and sputtered then settled into a steady idle. Webster climbed on board, placing all of his weight on one side of the deck, which caused the boat to tilt precariously. He nearly toppled into the lake, but Earl saved the situation by quickly sliding hard to starboard. When he regained his balance and composure, Webster nonchalantly perched himself high atop the fishing seat on the raised platform in the bow, a position which made the vessel even more unstable. I felt a sudden sinking in my stomach. "Good-bye and good luck!" Jim hollered as they pulled away from the docks and motored out into the bay. When they disappeared around the bend, the bow was already bucking into some very big water. The last I saw of Webster, he was climbing off the raised platform and crouching down low in the bow, holding his hat on with one hand and a safety line with the other.

"I hope they realize how bad it is and come back to camp and wait for a while," I muttered to Jim.

"Don't count on it," he replied. "Webster's determined to stay on schedule."

Forty-five minutes later we cleaned up the last of the breakfast dishes. The four law students were still in the dining room, sipping coffee and playing blackjack. One of them, who answered to the nickname of Buddy, leaned back in his chair, took a long drag on a cigar, and blew three perfect smoke rings above the table. "I can't believe those guys took off alone in weather like this. They're fools. It's good you advised them not to go. I'll defend you in court if they turn up dead." Buddy was grinning when he made the remark, but neither Jim nor I found much humor in it. We donned all the wet-weather gear we could find, then hustled out to the docks carrying blankets and a spare battery for the boat.

Other than a dark, nagging premonition, we had no reason for going into town that morning. The lake was getting rougher and the wind more powerful by the minute, so we filled the tri-hull with gas and prepared to head north.

For about three miles I ran the throttle wide open, letting the boat bounce and crash directly into the oncoming waves. The middle of the lake looked like a sea of tiny geysers as the wind blew foam and spray off the tops of the whitecaps that rolled and broke every few seconds. I steered the boat closer to shore, taking advantage of four small coves that offered relative protection from the wind between the lodge and Pointe Martel. Inside the coves, the water was choppy and turbulent, but nothing compared to what lay beyond the Pointe where Lake Temiskaming takes a northerly turn and opens up to receive the full force and fury of storms sweeping down from Hudson Bay. Once Pointe Martel is passed, there are no sheltered bays or estuaries for several miles.

Jim was standing up holding onto the windshield, keeping watch for logs and driftwood which are prevalent in the spring as the lake level rises from winter runoff. Debris was scattered all over the place that morning. Whenever he sighted something large enough to damage the boat or motor, he would point and call out "Log dead ahead!" or "Veer to the left!" On occasion, pieces of driftwood hidden in the swells appeared so suddenly he would order me to "kill the engine." That way we saved the prop and lower unit from damage, even though the bottom of the boat took a beating. When Pointe Martel loomed into view, I felt a tightness gripping my throat and chest. Beyond the Pointe, as far as I could see, the surface of the lake was an unbroken chain of towering whitecaps. Some of the waves crashed and broke onto the Pointe, sending flumes of spray into the pines that grew near the water. I scanned the shoreline between us and the Pointe hoping to see the little bass boat safely moored somewhere waiting out the storm. There was nothing but raw howling wind and dark rolling water.

As we rounded Pointe Martel, Jim and I braced ourselves for an onslaught. The first set of waves broke over the bow and sent a sheet of water running down the windshield, through the hatchway and around our feet. Immediately I decreased the power to half throttle and turned the tri-hull at an angle so we could quarter the waves instead of taking them head on. It was the only way to keep water out of the boat. The waves were staggering. We began climbing over swells and dropping into troughs that alternately blocked our vision or gave us a birds-eye view for miles ahead. Looking pale and drawn, Jim turned to me and said, "If Webster and Earl are still on the lake, they're goners." I had to agree. We were relatively safe in a twenty-foot tri-hull, as long as we maintained power and control of the wheel, but an overloaded thirteen-foot bass boat was a disaster waiting to happen.

For the next fifteen minutes we pressed head-on into the waves as Pointe Martel fell further and further behind us. Jim remained standing near the hatchway on the lookout for obstacles and debris. "I can't imagine they made it this far without capsizing or pulling off the water," he yelled. Unless they had crossed to the Ontario shore there was really no place for any craft, even the size of the bass boat, to make land without breaking to pieces on the rocks.

Three miles north of Pointe Martel, a small island appeared. I recognized it as the island directly offshore from a group of six cottages owned by locals in the town of Fabre. It was a small protrusion of land no more than fifty feet across, covered with rock and low-lying brush. In the center of the island was a beacon, mounted on top of a metal platform to ward off tugboats passing in the night towing log booms in their wake. The lea side of the island was one of the few places a small boat might seek refuge in a storm. I watched as we passed by, hoping to catch a glimpse of Webster and Earl tucked safely away in their tiny craft. At first glance, I saw nothing. Then, an object caught my eye several hundred yards beyond the island near the center of the lake. "Look there!" I motioned to Jim. He turned and stared in the direction I was pointing, but the object had disappeared.

"What was it?" he queried, holding his hand up to shield his eyes from the wind and spray.

"I'm not sure, but it wasn't driftwood. Keep an eye out in that direction," I said, pulling back on the throttle to slow down just a bit. When we crested the next big swell, the object reappeared momentarily and took on a distinctly familiar form. It was the bass boat beating into the waves, dead center in the most perilous part of the lake.

Immediately I changed course and steered due west. We were now running parallel to the swells, which enabled me to increase our speed without fear of taking on much water.

"What are they doing way out there?" Jim cried, shaking his head incredulously.

As we approached the bass boat, I could see Webster still crouched in the bow, furiously bailing water with a small plastic container. Earl remained at the helm, grasping the motor handle and trying to quarter the oncoming swells. Their tiny craft was dwarfed by the waves breaking and building all around them. Twice it disappeared into valleys between huge rollers only to reappear a moment later as they crested the following surge. Webster continued to bail frantically. Not until we were about sixty yards from starboard did they notice our approach. Suddenly, Webster jerked upright and began waving his arms and yelling as if trying to get our attention. Jim calmly gestured back to assure him we were coming to their assistance. When we were less than thirty yards from their boat, I motioned for Earl to cut into our wake and follow us to shore, rather than pull alongside and imperil both vessels. I was hoping to guide them into the cove where the six local cottages lay.

Webster continued to flail his arms and shout, while Earl proceeded to turn the boat in our direction. Everything seemed fine, when all at once he lost power and the bass boat slipped sideways into the oncoming waves. "Get down, Webster, get down!" Earl yelled, as the vessel began listing dangerously to one side. Jim and I watched in wide-eyed amazement as Webster dropped to his knees, grabbed hold of his seat, and prepared to abandon ship. It was like viewing a slow-motion movie. The first wave hit the little boat broadside and filled it to the gunwales with water. The next wave finished the job by lifting the starboard side high into the air, then dumping the entire craft upside down. The last we saw of Webster inside the boat, he seemed resigned to his fate. When the vessel began to tip, he calmly and deliberately held his nose with one hand, grasped the handle of his tackle box with the other, then relinquished himself to the cold, dark water.

The first person to resurface was Earl. By the time I turned the tri-hull around and was motoring in his direction, Earl bobbed to the surface and began breaststroking rapidly toward us. The shock of the forty-five-degree water was written all over his face. He was gasping and gulping for air as he swam alongside the tri-hull. Jim reached out and grabbed his arm and pulled him back to the stern where he was able to climb aboard over the transom. "I'm sure glad you guys came along when you did," he muttered through chattering teeth. "Twenty minutes later and we'd be dead."

For Webster, resurfacing took a bit longer. The buoyancy of his life jacket was somewhat compromised by the weight of his double-wide, multipaneled, six-tiered tackle box, which he had stubbornly refused to surrender to the lake. Furthermore, his size fourteen rubber rain boots had instantly filled with water and were weighing him down. When I saw his yellow rain hat emerge on the far side of the overturned boat, I knew Webster would not be far behind. Presently, he broke the surface blowing spray from his nostrils and mouth, looking like a great bewildered whale. It was obvious that Webster Quincy Smith was not accustomed to the rough treatment or lack of respect being shown him by Lake Temiskaming. He had the presence of mind, however, to grab hold of the bottom of the overturned boat and hang on tight as it continued to rise and fall in the passing swells. Fortunately, the boat had built-in flotation as well as a large pocket of air trapped underneath the hull to keep it afloat. In spite of the bone-chilling water, Webster made no attempt to swim to the safety of the tri-hull. On the contrary, he was pointing at various items floating in his general vicinity and shouting out orders. "Save that bag! Get that box! Don't let my suitcase sink!" I turned to Jim, who had leaned over the edge of the boat and retrieved a couple of tennis shoes. One was green and the other orange. With an impish grin, he held up the dripping pieces of footwear and muttered, "What a pity! Not only are they different colors, but they're both left-footed."

I carefully angled the bow of our boat within five feet of Webster and told him that only when he was safely on board would I attempt to recover his gear. "Oh, have it your way!" he blubbered in exasperation. Releasing his hold on the overturned boat, he held up his hands in a gesture of defeat. Jim and Earl each grabbed an arm and proceeded to haul him into the boat a few inches at a time. Once we had all six-and-a-half-feet of him on board, he lay motionless on the floor gasping like a giant yellow-tailed tuna who had no more fight left in him.

We retrieved most of the gear, with the exception of a bag of clothes that contained all seven pairs of his tennis shoes (minus one green and one orange) and the tackle box. Webster told us how he had doggedly fought to hang onto his tackle box, and probably would have succeeded, but the handle broke loose and it sank. Only then did he give up and surface for air. He opened his hand and showed us the broken handle, as if material evidence were required to verify his story. In his own strange way, the man had grit.

Rather than attempt to right the overturned vessel in the middle of the wind-tossed lake, we secured a heavy line to the bow and towed it the half mile to shore. It was slow, rough going. The waves continued to beat against the side of the tri-hull, while Earl's little overturned boat disappeared beneath the rollers from time to time. Twenty minutes later, we made land on a sandy beach in front of the six cottages. After dragging the bass boat into waist-deep water, the four of us climbed out of the tri-hull and waded into the lake. Reaching down and grasping the submerged gunwales, Jim and I lifted, while Earl and Webster pushed down on the opposite side. What would have been a daunting task in the middle of the lake was a simple procedure with us standing in shallow water. The boat flipped right side up with hardly a splash. At that point, Jim and I were as wet as Webster and Earl.

Earl was pleasantly surprised after checking the contents of his boat. The only thing missing was a twelve-volt battery used to power the running lights. The outboard motor had remained solidly clamped to the transom, and all of his personal belongings were still packed safely in their various compartments. Some of them were actually dry. Earl reached down behind the back seat; then grinning with delight, he held up a familiar object. "Looky here, Webster. Even grandpa's fishing pole and lucky lure survived that disaster. Pretty darn lucky, huh?" Webster's face turned crimson. His eyes rolled and his jaw began to quiver as if to say, " I would like to break that ugly pole in a thousand pieces and throw that stinking lure in the bottom of the lake!"

Earl and I caught a ride into town with one of the cottagers then shuttled his truck and trailer from the Fabre docks back to the cove. Jim and Webster stayed with the boats and spent a long, silent hour drying out clothing and gear. It was 10:30 A.M. when we winched the bass boat onto the trailer and said good-bye to our first guests. As Webster glanced at his watch, his final words were "Humph, two and a half hours behind schedule. At this rate, we won't make Indianapolis until two in the morning."

Jim and I tried to sound apologetic concerning the mishap and the delay to their schedule, but Earl would hear none of it. "We're alive, thanks to you guys. If you had not shown up when you did, we'd be fish food right now." He shook our hands, then climbed into his truck and fired it up. Webster was already sitting in the passenger seat, drumming his fingers on the dashboard and checking his watch every few seconds. He was not a patient man. As they pulled away from the cove and started up the hill, Webster turned in his seat and motioned for Earl to slow down. Then leaning out of the window, he held up his hand and began nodding his head in a curious manner, as if acknowledging something for the first time.

"What do you suppose he meant by that?" Jim ventured.

"I haven't a clue. He seemed to be looking more at the lake than at either of us." When the truck disappeared around the bend, I breathed a sigh of relief. Peace and tranquility had returned to the north woods.

Jim and I made one last trip to town that morning in the Volkswagen. I felt an urgency to call Don Bair at his office in Indianapolis and prepare him for what I expected would be a very negative report from one of his most "valued clients." When Don answered the phone, I could sense he was busy and somewhat distracted by voices and noise in the background. I got right to the point. As I recounted the episode of the nearly disastrous affair on Lake Temiskaming that morning, Don remained silent. When I finished, he softly chuckled, "It sounds like your day was a lot more exciting than mine. I'd say you did everything you could have under the circumstances. Webster and Earl are lucky to be alive. Now brace yourself. On Friday morning a whole motor home full of Websters will arrive from Chicago. Nine of them to be exact. At least now you know what to expect."

For the rest of the summer, Jim and I adopted Don's nickname for guests. We referred to them as Websters. "How many Websters are coming this week?" Jim might ask. Or, "Go tell the Websters it's time for breakfast," I would say.

The following Friday morning, I returned to Fabre in the tri-hull to pick up the "nine new Websters." When I pulled up to the public wharf, the motor home was already there. The group had been waiting for about twenty minutes. Eight of the Websters were milling about outside the vehicle, swatting mosquitos. Most of them were wearing patent leather shoes, double-knit slacks, and short-sleeve shirts. They looked like they were going to Myrtle Beach for the weekend, rather than a wilderness lodge. Already I felt uneasy.

Suddenly the door of the motor home swung open and out stepped a short, stocky, middle-aged man wearing camouflage pants, a red flannel shirt, and combat boots. He even had a hunting knife and flashlight strapped on his belt. I breathed a sigh of relief, not because I believed the man was necessarily more suited than the others to spend a week at a fishing camp, but only because he took charge in a way that the others understood and accepted. They moved aside as he marched toward the boat and held out his hand. "Hello, my name is Phil. Sorry if I seem a bit tired or cranky, but I drove the entire eighteen hours from Indianapolis while the rest of these bozos slept in the back."

I put Phil in charge of loading the boat. He assured me it would require two trips: one for the passengers, another for the gear. Meanwhile, I drove to town and made a quick phone call to Indianapolis to see if Earl and Webster had returned home safely. Don seemed surprised to hear my voice when he answered the phone. "They pulled in at about three o'clock on Tuesday morning," he said. "Webster called me that afternoon here at work. He was pretty upset about losing his tackle box and wanted to know if my insurance would cover it. The way he described it, the box and its contents had the value of a small home. But he also told me that the trip was the greatest adventure he had ever had. He said something about 'teetering on the edge of the abyss' and how alive he felt. He wants to return next summer with his fourteen-year-old daughter. As for Earl, the engagement is over. He dropped Webster off at his house Tuesday morning then headed west for his farm in Iowa. He called Mary Margaret from a rest stop somewhere in Illinois and told her he was sorry, but there would be no wedding. He said it would be unfair to expect her to adapt to the 'rigorous schedule' that farm life imposed on a person from the city. Then he hung up the phone and drove away. What do you suppose got into Earl?"

Three lake trout and a pair of Websters.

There was a momentary silence. I shifted the phone to my other ear and swatted a mosquito that was drawing blood about an inch upstream from my wristwatch. On the other end of the line, Don cleared his throat. He was waiting for me to respond. "I, I, I'm not sure what got into Earl," I stammered. "Perhaps he is struggling with an acute case of 'Chronic Common Sense Syndrome.' I observed various signs and symptoms in his behavior the minute I met him."

"I don't believe I've heard of such a thing," Don intoned suspiciously.

"It is a reoccurring disorder that affects Midwestern farmers in particular. Oftentimes, it lies dormant in its victim for years, then suddenly is triggered by a prolonged or traumatic exposure to an environment of excessive regimen. Earl seems to be unaware that he has the disorder. Or perhaps he is in a state of denial. You know the type, Don. Calm and content on the surface, completely oblivious to the seething cauldron of rage just waiting to erupt and boil over if exposed to a tight, restrictive schedule. Statistically speaking, anyone who contracts the illness, eventually dies. In most cases, however, they die happy and at peace with the world."

My answer seemed to satisfy Don. "Keep up the good work," he encouraged. "And don't let the Websters grind you down."

I said good-bye and hung up the phone. For a moment, I stood there thinking how fortunate I had been to have met Don Bair the year before on the Salmon River. In some respects, he is a lot like Earl—an ordinary man but an exceptional individual. Although Don is a successful insurance executive and a hardworking entrepreneur, I get the impression that somewhere in his past, he too has dealt with a less severe but equally fatal strain of "Chronic Common Sense Syndrome."

I was in a happy mood as I stepped from the phone booth into the bright, penetrating warmth of the late morning sun. Inhaling slowly and deeply, like a baby drawing its first breath, I filled my lungs with pure, sweet, northern air—the essence of life. A mile to the west I could see the glassy surface of Lake Temiskaming, untrammeled by even the faintest breeze. It was the kind of day I would come to hope for whenever transporting people up and down the lake. A perfect day—a day to celebrate life.

⚜ Dam Update

Friday, June 19, 1998
Kipawa River Lodge (Topping's Camp), 10:00 A.M.

Two consultants, Marcel and Pierre, have been hired by Hydro Quebec to study the impact their hydroelectric project will have on the human use of the Kipawa River. They want to assess the effect on kayaking and rafting in particular. Marcel asks me to fly with them in a helicopter up and down the river. He'd like me to point out its various rapids and describe the water levels necessary for running this river. "We can have a chopper here at your camp in forty-five minutes," he says. I agree to go.

It is a clear, magnificent morning when the helicopter lands on the grass behind the Main Lodge. A tall, young, nice-looking pilot named Stephan waves us aboard. I sit up front next to the pilot. Moments later we're off and heading upriver, skimming just fifty feet above the rapids. The river is about one-quarter full, running at about seventy-five cubic meters per second. Through a headset I describe various features of the rapids we pass over: Hollywood, Elbow, Grand Chute, Picnic, White Pine, and Big Zipper. The view is spectacular. Even after twenty-four years of living on its shores and kayaking its rapids, I sit in awe at the unique beauty of the Kipawa. The consultants seem equally impressed. Ten feet below the river's surface, we can clearly see each pebble and stone on its bed. They shimmer like opals, garnets, and emeralds, as rays of sun illuminate the glistening water below.

As we continue upstream over Log Jam and Island Rapids I notice a distinct increase in water level. Someone from the Ministry of Natural Resources has pulled the plug at Laniel, opening up the dam gates for tomorrow's kayak rally. When we pass over Broken Bridge Rapid, I point out the big, glassy-topped roller known as the Surf Wave. At certain water levels, five or six paddlers at once can ride its shoulder, playing and surfing almost effortlessly. Around the next bend, we fly over a series of rapids called Three Blind Mice and then Buttonhook, a long, fairly technical rapid. I can tell from the number of rocks now submerged in Buttonhook that the dam flow at Laniel is peaking at about 150 cubic meters per second. That flow should make for a fine rally.

Further upstream, at Tumbling Dice Rapid, a pair of kayakers are surfing some play waves and five more are approaching the gut-wrenching drop in Rock 'n' Roll. Two people have pulled their kayaks on shore just before the challenging drop to scout the rapids. "Certainly they will walk around that one," suggests one of the consultants through his headset.

I know what the paddlers might be thinking: *Are the river gods smiling today? Do I run right and do the bump and grind, or go left and hope that boat-eating hole will release me? Maybe I'll stay center and float over the shelf that tore my paddle in two last year. Why is my throat so dry? Come on, let's get moving before I talk myself right out of this.*

The two paddlers make a quick exit into the bush then reappear adjusting their spray skirts and cinching down helmets. They wriggle into their boats and paddle toward Rock 'n' Roll. We proceed upriver. I feel my pulse quicken, and wish I could join them. The river gods are smiling today.

People are hoisting kayaks from roof racks and pulling on wetsuits. It looks like the rally has begun a day ahead of schedule. The word must be out on the Internet: the Kipawa River is under siege.

Stephan edges the helicopter even closer to the water as a half dozen kayakers prepare to run the spillway—a screaming twenty-five foot drop down the middle of a glassy-tongued chute. Running this high-pressure outlet from Lake Kipawa to the river below is about as fast a ride as a person in a kayak is likely to find. At the bottom of the spillway, an explosion of whitewater boils and churns for about seventy yards out into the river. Some kayakers call this the Jaws of the Dragon.

I can see the paddlers faces as they rocket down the spillway. Their expressions vary from pale white fear to sheer exaltation. The last paddler grips his paddle like a spear, then raising his arms and clenching tight the fist of his left hand, aims the weapon in the direction of our helicopter. It seems a defiant gesture to the schemers of Hydro Quebec.

I know the guy in that boat. His name is Dave Pollard. Dave eats, sleeps, drinks, and breathes kayaking. Two or three weekends a year he drives eight long hours from Montreal to paddle this river. Dave had polio when he was three months old. The disease left him with a badly crippled left leg. But Dave was born with the heart of a lion. His discovery of kayaking ten years ago put him on a level playing field with everyone else. Unlike skiing, cycling, mountaineering, or other outdoor sports, kayaking depends mostly on upper body strength. Dave has mastered the art of paddling. Fellow paddlers are sometimes shocked when they see Dave strap himself into his boat with a diver's weight belt he has modified. But Dave smiles and says, "Don't worry, I can get out. Let's just say I am a lot more committed to a successful Eskimo roll." As I watch Dave set off over the spillway I think to myself that in a kayak having a limp is not much of a handicap. His boat leaps and dances across the top of the waves with the best of them.

Dave knows of Hydro Quebec's plan to divert more than half the flow of the Kipawa River down a canal and through a pipe to generate electricity. He also knows first-hand that the Kipawa is one of the precious few rivers left in the province that offers world-class whitewater in a remote wilderness setting. Dave's warrior antics before running the spillway reveal his deepest feelings about those plans. "Nothing personal," I assure my fellow passengers, "just one man's exasperation over the impending loss of yet another wild river."

While returning downstream toward the lodge, I notice an empty seat behind me in the chopper. "If there is room on the next flight, my wife would be thrilled to see the river from the air," I tell the pilot. "Of course," he replies with an ingratiating smile, "and your children as well." Stephan makes two more flights upriver with Pat and our daughters in the back seat and me as co-pilot. The consultants from HQ wait on the ground. Perhaps we are being schmoozed. Nonetheless, I like the young pilot—a man of action, not words.

Perhaps we are being schmoozed. . .

Blasting through Buttonhhook.

Chapter 5

DESCENDING THE KIPAWA RIVER

We're having an adventure, Fezzick, and most
people live and die without being as lucky as we.
—William Goldman

On August 9, 1975, Jim and I set out for adventure. Real adventure is seldom planned in advance or laid out in a travel guide. An adventure involves a certain amount of risk, and its outcome must not be too predictable. A trip to Disneyland is not an adventure unless you wreck your car on the freeway while traveling there. For true adventure, you do not buy a ticket and then stand in a line.

At 6:00 A.M., we loaded two sleeping bags and a can of beans into an old cedar-strip canoe and headed south down Lake Temiskaming. We paddled for five miles then pulled out at a small stream that according to legend was the path followed by Algonquin Indians from Lake Temiskaming to Kipawa Lake. The Kipawa River is actually the main artery between the two lakes, but there are many treacherous rapids along its ten-mile course, including Grande Chutes, a hundred-foot waterfall one mile upstream from the lodge. The Algonquins avoided the swift current and the waterfall by taking the alternate route commonly known by present-day canoeists as the Indian Portage. We began the first leg of the portage, struggling uphill for half a mile through a dense growth of birch and tag alder. I began to wonder if we were on the right track. Our canoe, an eighteen-foot, square-stern, cedar-strip vessel, was not designed for portaging like contemporary plastic and aluminum models. As we hoisted it onto our shoulders and started uphill through the brush, Jim muttered a couple of French words he had learned from Jacques, the local mechanic who had whacked his knuckles on a motor they were fixing. After two hours, we arrived at a clear, shallow lake surrounded by low-lying hills blanketed with spruce, fir, and poplar. Happy to be rid of the burden, we slid the heavy canoe into the water. As we dipped our paddles and pulled, we could see every pebble and rock shimmering in the depths twenty feet below.

We crossed to a narrow inlet that opened up into a larger lake, at the far end of which stood an ancient, dilapidated cabin. The door was open, so in the spirit of the North, we entered and sat down at a homemade table. For lunch we dined on cold, canned beans. Nailed to a log above the cabin door was a current trapline number, and underneath on a shelf was a journal with several entries. The trapper's name was McKenzie and by the location of his cabin and the words in his journal it was evident he enjoyed solitude. He summed up his entry of March 25, 1973, with this sentiment: "L.P. stopped on his way to town this afternoon. He had caught several beaver— all he wanted was to talk."

Beyond the cabin was another lake, which we crossed in less than an hour. Then a second lengthy portage took us to Kipawa Lake. Now we had to decide whether to set out onto Kipawa Lake or paddle down the Kipawa River to the lodge. Kipawa Lake branches out into five major channels with over a thousand miles of shoreline. Our food supply had been fairly well exhausted at lunch, so we chose to head down the river and run some rapids.

On the first section of the river we portaged a rapid that had a treacherous drop of about twenty feet, with several jagged rocks sticking up like alligator teeth in the water below. The next two miles were comprised of smaller rapids, which we ran successfully. At mile four, with our confidence building, we stopped to scout another large rapid, which was significantly longer and more technical in nature than any we had previously run. We considered making another portage, but the day was getting late, and the longer we looked, the more we thought we could pull it off. "Can't be much worse than what we've already done," I calculated. "Let's have at it then," Jim replied.

In retrospect, I believe our success upstream had made us a bit overconfident. In recent years I have run that rapid many times in a kayak, and I now realize how slim our chances were in an open cedar-strip canoe. Today that rapid is known to kayakers as Buttonhook. About halfway down in the middle of the river sits a large dome-shaped rock that must be navigated on the right; then immediately thereafter one must paddle hard left to avoid a deep hole of turbulent water near the bottom. Jim and I knew the course we had to run to make it through successfully, but we were not fully aware of the limitations of our boat, or of ourselves for that matter.

With Jim in the stern and me in the bow, we pushed out into the current, which quickly pulled us past the point of no return. The first two waves hit us hard, and we took on some water. All was going as planned until a third wave turned the canoe sideways, and the current pulled us straight toward the large rock. We dug in our paddles with a vengeance, but the powerful current had already pulled us off course. The canoe floated broadside into the rock; then, with a loud bang, it broke in two and surrendered itself to the river.

I do not know how long I stayed with my half of the boat, but it was nowhere in sight when my head finally broke the surface of the water. The current had dragged me downstream right through the center of the turbulent hole we had hoped to avoid. Eventually I floated into an eddy, climbed out on shore, and began searching the river for Jim. After a tense moment, I heard him yell from upstream, where he was standing in the middle of the river on top of the dome-shaped rock that had scuttled our canoe. At the instant our canoe broke in half, Jim had made a desperate leap and landed safely on the rock. He was still dry above the knees. Raising his paddle triumphantly over his head, he began to strut and crow like a rooster. The crowing stopped however as he realized that to get back to the lodge he must descend from his lofty perch and be baptized by the river to atone for his display of arrogance. By the time Jim swam back across the current and crawled up onto the rocks at my feet, he had assumed an air of genuine humility. "Any sign of our paddles or sleeping bags?" he sputtered as water dripped from his beard. "Nothing," I replied. "It all belongs to the river god now." After one last, futile look at the rapids, we turned away empty-handed and headed toward home.

The sun was a huge, golden sphere on the western horizon, but with five miles of dense bush and rocky shoreline between us and the lodge, there was precious little time for gazing at sunsets. We tramped downriver through woods as silent and still as a January graveyard. Our own ten-foot-long shadows were marching in step right behind us darting in and out between the trees like phantoms mimicking our every movement. The only sound was the buzz of mosquitos swarming around our heads and the sloshing of water in our spongy boots. When daylight disappeared we became quadrupeds, tripping over deadfalls and crawling on our hands and knees like a pair of lost dogs.

An hour after dark, Jim and I staggered into the lodge, removed our wet clothing, and dropped, bone-weary, on top of our beds. With blistered feet, mosquito bites on our heads, and hunger gnawing in our stomachs, we agreed that the day had indeed been an adventure. We had explored the Kipawa River.

Hydro Quebec consultants running the spillway.

Into the "Jaws of the Dragon."

⚜ **Dam Update**

Saturday, June 20, 1998
Laniel, Quebec, 9:30 A.M.

One hundred kayakers converge on the Kipawa River for the twelfth annual rally of the Northern Ontario Liquid Adventure Club (NOLAC). They have come from Toronto, Montreal, Windsor, Thunder Bay, Rouyn, Timmins, Sudbury, and points in between for some of the best whitewater paddling in eastern Canada. And to show solidarity in their opposition to Hydro Quebec's proposal to divert the Kipawa River.

Newspaper reporters from Laniel and Temiscamingue are on hand to interview people and take photos of paddlers descending the spillway into the river. The kayakers know that the media is watching so they go down the chute backwards, sideways, in pairs, a few upside down (although not by choice), and even on a boogie board. The scene at the dam is a whitewater circus, a kayaking carnival, a perpetual parade of paddlers.

The last boat over the spillway is an eight-man paddle raft guided by Doug Skeggs, one of NOLAC's founders. The raft is filled with HQ consultants and members of a committee who are studying the social impacts HQ's proposal will have on the region. We want them to experience the Kipawa River firsthand. They are in for the ride of their life. I capture their expressions on film as they come flying down the spillway into the Jaws of the Dragon. After paddling for a day on a river of such great historical significance, through wilderness and down rapids that have evolved over ten thousand years, if the people on board the raft have no qualms about diverting the water down a man-made canal, there is little more we can say or do. The river speaks for itself, but is anybody listening?

The Main Lodge and a beach full of canoes, 1935.

Chapter 6

THE DUGOUT CANOE

They Shoot Canoes, Don't They?
—Patrick McManus

Two weeks after the sinking of our cedar-strip canoe, I began to truly mourn its loss. At the camp there were four motorboats ranging in size from a fourteen-foot aluminum skiff to a twenty-foot fiberglass tri-hull, but for anyone who enjoys the serenity of paddling a wooden canoe on a mirror-smooth lake, a motorboat is a poor substitute. The noise of exploding pistons and the smell of exhaust tend to detract from the experience of wilderness.

One afternoon while we sat on the wharf with fishing poles in hand, I lamented out loud to Jim, "If only you had steered our canoe more to the right of that rock, we could be out on the lake paddling now instead of marooned on this dock. For all your years of experience, you sure didn't turn out to be such a hot-shot paddler."

Jim, who had also been mourning our lost canoe, was quick to respond. "As I recall, it was you who quit paddling and just sat there like a pole-axed pig waiting for the rock to break us in two."

"Well, as long as we're trading insults," I replied, "at least I stayed with the ship until it went down, instead of jumping onto the rock like a scared rabbit and abandoning my partner to his fate."

"If I'm not mistaken, partner, you were trying to jump ship long before I was, but your foot got stuck underneath the thwart, and you nearly tore your boot right off trying to get free of that boat."

I could see our conversation was going nowhere. Jim could never remember the facts as they actually happened. Leaning back against the flagpole, I closed my eyes and dreamed of paddling the old cedar-strip silently across Lake Temiskaming.

After awhile Jim stood up and began walking down the dock. He paused partway, pointed to a large pile of driftwood at the edge of the river, and said, "If you really miss that old canoe so much, you could always hollow out one of those drift logs and make a dugout. A dugout is an honorable vessel. Perhaps building one could make you a decent canoeist."

Jim's words stirred me to action. Within an hour, I had sharpened an axe and was chopping away on one of the old drift logs.

The logs were actually the property of the Upper Ottawa Company, who for nearly a hundred years had been dragging timber in massive booms behind tugboats up and down Lake Temiskaming. Some of the logs occasionally escaped from the booms and drifted on the lake until they were retrieved by the company or run over by unsuspecting motorboats. We called those fugitive logs deadheads or sinkers. They were usually waterlogged just enough to float undetected about an inch below the surface, waiting for some innocent boater in his leisure craft to come racing along and punch a hole in the bow or tear the outdrive from the stern. There was seldom any warning. Just a sickening thud that usually rendered a vessel helpless and left its occupants bailing water or attempting to paddle to shore. Jim and I had reckoned with sinkers and deadheads on numerous occasions.

When Jim saw me chopping away on the big log, he ambled over and said, "That log you're mutilating belongs to the Upper Ottawa Company. That's their stamp on the other end. They might have something to say about you making it into a canoe."

"Well, it was your idea," I said, stepping down to the opposite end of the log and removing the mark with a stroke of my axe. "Now the log belongs to us, which is only right since it has been lying here cluttering up our beach all summer."

For three days, I made slow progress chipping away at the damp wood while Jim occasionally watched from a distance. On the third afternoon he approached quietly and gave my work a thorough examination. For five minutes he circled the log, making profound utterances like "Hmmm, well well, my oh my."

Eventually, he sat down on one end of the log. "The native Kwakiutl used fire to hollow out their canoes," he pointed out. "You might save yourself some time and a few blisters to do likewise."

"Well, thanks for the advice, Kimasabe, but I tried that yesterday. This wood is too wet to burn. I think I'll just continue using the method our forefathers in Utah perfected."

"What method was that?" Jim queried.

"The one where my ancestors worked all day, while yours sat on their keisters making useless suggestions."

"Well, someone has to be the brains behind this operation. Otherwise you'd still be out on the dock sulking over the lost canoe."

Eventually Jim took an active interest in the project, and after two more days of chopping, we had the log hollowed out to a thickness of about two inches. Next we designed and carved a shallow keel along the bottom, then trimmed the ends so they tapered to a modest point. After caulking a few small cracks with pine resin, we decided the craft was ready for its maiden voyage.

Jim and I were surprised at the weight of the dugout when we tried to carry it down to the water. We were unable to raise it more than a few inches off the ground. Even though we had hollowed it out, the old log still weighed several hundred pounds. We finally succeeded in moving it down to the beach a few feet at a time on log rollers.

Before the final launch, we held an informal ceremony where we toasted our achievement with a bottle of ginger ale, then christened our boat The Deadhead. Jim concluded the ceremony by throwing the empty bottle at the side of the vessel, but it bounced off and smashed on a nearby rock.

"I hate to sound pessimistic, Jim, but that could be a bad omen. Perhaps the dugout is going to sink like a rock."

Jim laughed, "That would be a good omen. If it sinks we'll be rid of it. If it floats we will probably have to leave it out on the lake because it's too heavy to haul back up on shore. Then we'll have one more deadhead to contend with. I hope it sinks."

We gave the dugout a final shove, and it entered the lake with a tremendous splash. A couple of gallons of water poured over the bow, then it tipped dangerously to the left and over-corrected to the right before coming to a halt. The dugout was afloat.

Jim insisted that since I had done most of the chopping I deserved to take the first ride in the dugout.

"Thanks, old Buddy," I grinned, "but you were the brains behind this operation. You deserve the honor of taking the first paddle."

Both of us could see that there were only about five inches of freeboard on either side of the dugout, and we had our doubts as to what might occur when a passenger climbed on board. Even empty, the dugout floated precariously low in the water. Finally we agreed to flip a coin. The loser would go first. Jim flipped. I lost.

While Jim balanced one end of the vessel, I cautiously climbed aboard. I experimented with several different positions, but the wobbly nature of the craft left no alternative to just sitting flat with my legs extended out in front of me. Fortunately, the weight I added to the vessel had little effect on the amount of freeboard. There were still about five inches showing above waterline.

"Bon voyage, and don't forget your paddle," Jim shouted as he pushed me out from shore.

The paddle was a crude, homemade device I had carved from a two-by-ten-inch board, using a machete. It was six feet long with a bulky blade at either end, similar to a kayak paddle only four times as heavy. Though not real effective for paddling, it turned out to be a helpful counter balance whenever the vessel tried to turn upside down.

From his vantage point on the dock, Jim said the dugout appeared to "glide smoothly over the lake like a birch bark canoe." From my vantage point, however, the description was somewhat different. "It plowed ponderously through the water like a garbage scow in a typhoon."

The craft responded poorly to acceleration, but after a prolonged effort with the unwieldy paddle, I gained considerable momentum only to discover that the dugout responded even worse to slowing down. I was on a collision course with the dock, alongside which rested one of the aluminum boats. Attempting to avoid a mishap, I began to back paddle, which nearly tipped me over but did little to decrease my speed. In desperation, I tried to turn the vessel by making a couple of power strokes, which is how I learned that the dugout had another inherent flaw—it couldn't be turned. I slammed headlong into the aluminum boat, creating a large V-shaped dent in its side.

I could hear muffled laughter coming from Jim as he approached the scene of the accident. "It doesn't look too bad," he remarked after surveying the damage to the aluminum boat. "A few good whacks with a wooden mallet and she'll be back in business."

"I'm happy to hear that, Jim," I said climbing from the boat and handing him the paddle. "Now, let's see how an expert maneuvers this log."

Jim fared about the same as I had. He had difficulty making turns, and when he tried to paddle in a straight line, the dugout constantly veered off course to the left. As far as stability was concerned, he compared it to "walking a tightrope in a windstorm, blindfolded." Upon returning to shore still upright, he said he was glad to have had the experience, but in all honesty he would never set foot in the vessel again.

In spite of the numerous problems we encountered on its maiden voyage, I was not quite ready to give up on the dugout. It occurred to me that perhaps our expectations had been too high. After all, it was only an old tree trunk we had hollowed out to see if we could travel in relative peace and quiet from one point to another without getting wet. From a noise perspective, the dugout was a great success, probably the quietest vessel ever to ply the waters of Lake

"It looks a lot like a coffin," said Jim.

Temiskaming. Eventually, as I learned to deal with its idiosyncrasies, I had to admit that the dugout fulfilled its basic objectives. It was an honorable, if not perfect, vessel.

Three weeks after its maiden voyage, on a clear, calm night in August, I told Jim I was going to spend the night on Lake Temiskaming, sleeping in the dugout. "Go right ahead," he said. "I'll tell your family you died doing what you love best—being a fool."

I prepared the dugout by lining the bottom with a Hudson's Bay blanket folded several times to use as a mattress. For a pillow Jim suggested I take a bright yellow life jacket with one of the straps tied to my wrist so he could retrieve my remains for the next of kin. For a cover, I used another blanket folded in such a way that it could not dangle over the edge into the water. A sleeping bag would have been a warmer alternative, but I had to admit that if the boat capsized, getting out of a sleeping bag might be complicated.

When everything was in order, Jim accompanied me out to the docks to bid a final farewell. I crawled aboard the dugout, then lay down and pulled the blanket over me to show him how perfectly everything fit. "That's marvelous," he said. "It looks a lot like a coffin. Maybe we can save some money on your funeral by using it for the casket."

When I pushed off from the docks, a big yellow moon was shining through the trees on the hill across the river. "Don't worry about me, old Hos. I'm going to sleep like a baby in a cradle tonight. See you at breakfast. Just rustle up something simple like sausage, eggs, and blueberry cream cheese croissants."

As I paddled out toward the middle of the lake, I noticed something unusual about the moon. It was shrinking in size, but not in the way that it normally does as it climbs higher from the horizon. Its bottom edge was slowly disintegrating as if it were being eaten by hordes of hungry termites. By the time I reached the center of the lake the man in the moon was nearly gone. By then, of course, I realized I was witnessing a lunar eclipse. But to have it occur so unexpectedly and to view it from a dugout canoe in the middle of Lake Temiskaming was an unforgettable experience.

Within an hour the eclipse was total. All that remained of the moon was a faint sliver of light reflecting from behind the earth's shadow. In the absence of moonlight, the stars and constellations were brilliant. Orion stood poised, holding his sword aloft, ready to fend off the attack of Taurus the bull. But with all his attention focused on the charging beast, the great warrior was unaware of Scorpio approaching from the south with his long, deadly tail coiled and ready to strike. Suddenly from out of nowhere a huge meteor with a glimmering tail flashed across the sky and pierced the monster through its middle. To me it seemed marvelous. To Orion it was just another night on the job—another universe saved.

As the moon began to reappear, I wondered if Jim had seen the eclipse. Gazing out across the water towards the mouth of the river, I noticed tiny lights flickering in the windows of the lodge half a mile away. The scene was vaguely reminiscent of something from my childhood. It reminded me of a miniature trading post that was part of an electric train my neighbor had in his basement. The train set, an elaborate creation built on three pieces of plywood, had tracks running through towns and villages, over mountains and valleys, and even stopping at a cattle yard and coal mine. All the kids in the neighborhood competed for a chance to be the engineer or the conductor, but for me there was only one place that held any allure. On the far side of the mountain, a long way from the town, in an isolated corner of the board was a small trading post on the edge of a lake. The train only passed by it on rare occasions when the conductor decided it was time to deliver some goods or pick up some timber and coal. I was the lucky kid who got to run the trading post. It became my permanent and exclusive residence whenever we played with the train. I sometimes wondered why nobody else ever wanted that job. I certainly wanted no other.

As I lay floating in the dugout with the moon and stars overhead and the wilderness all around, I thought about that little trading post and how I would pretend it was my home. Even as a boy I imagined that a place like the lodge on the Kipawa River really existed. I had seen images of similar places at the movies, on television, and in books and magazines. During the summer of 1975, those images had become a reality, a reality that was even grander and more magnificent than the dream. Living in the north woods on the shores of Lake Temiskaming had exceeded all my expectations.

In mid-September Jim and I closed up the camp and prepared the boat for the last ride of the season. We had decided, somewhat reluctantly, that it was time to return to school and work on our degrees. University had always been an important goal for each of us, although it sometimes seemed we were doing it at the expense of a greater education. With the autumn leaves changing, the air turning colder, and the tourists migrating southward in droves, perhaps we should have remained in the north to learn what it was they were fleeing. Most places become more beautiful as they get less crowded.

In the final analysis, however, it was not just the pursuit of higher learning that prompted our return to civilization. For several weeks we had received letters from a couple of young ladies whose acquaintance we had made the previous winter. As the days of August waned and the fall nights grew longer, there came a sudden restlessness. Once the decision to leave had been made, it was only a matter of hours until we had boarded up the windows, loaded the boat, and headed south with the tourists and the geese.

Jim and Scott reluctant to leave.

Dam
Update

Saturday, June 20, 1998
Kipawa River Lodge (Topping's Camp), 7:00 P.M.

After the last of the kayakers are off the river and the raft has bounced and jostled its way down Hollywood Rapid, we hold a meeting with Hydro Quebec officials, consultants, and committee members. They have come to the lodge to explain their proposal to kayakers attending the river rally. It goes over about as well as Custer's meeting with the Sioux at the Little Big Horn. We can agree on nothing. Even terminology is a stumbling block. HQ engineers refer to Kipawa Lake as Kipawa Reservoir, because in 1912 the level was raised fifteen feet when the gates at Laniel were installed to control flooding. Kayakers maintain it is a lake because it was carved out of the Canadian shield ten thousand years ago by retreating glaciers at the end of the ice age. A twenty-foot dike does not a reservoir make.

The kayakers refer to the proposed, man-made canal as a "diversion of the Kipawa River." According to HQ, as much as 80 percent or more of the water that annually goes down the Kipawa would now run down their canal and into a pipe to turn their turbines. Nonetheless, HQ officials cringe at the very mention of the word diversion. "We are not diverting anything," says an engineer. "We are simply reestablishing outflow from Kipawa Reservoir through three distinct channels into Lake Temiskaming. All the water still ends up in the same place."

"That is ludicrous," cries a man at the back of the gathering. I recognize the voice even before I identify the face. It is a paddler known simply as Farmer. He hates double-talk and mincing of words. "The Kipawa River is the only natural outlet between Kipawa Lake and Lake Temiskaming. It is neither a canal nor a channel of outflow, and I'm leaving." With that, he stood up and marched to the lake and paddled his kayak out into the last rays of sunshine.

At that moment, the meeting began to deteriorate. Peter Leonard, the man in charge of the HQ delegation, tried to salvage something. "Please understand, Hydro Quebec is a nonprofit organization. Yes, we produce hydro-electric energy, but only under circumstances where we can improve the surrounding environment, not damage it or destroy it."

Peter Karwacki, one of the founders of NOLAC, had also heard enough. "You've already created a negative impact on this river by spraying fluorescent orange paint on the rocks, hanging your tags on trees, and driving metal stakes along the shoreline, and I don't like it!" With a look of utter contempt, Peter stomped off toward the beach to join Farmer paddling on the lake. Soon thereafter the meeting dissolved. I explain to Mr. Leonard that diverting the Kipawa River is not like shutting down someone's favorite fishing hole where they can simply go into the next bay or even to the next lake and find something similar. "In all of Quebec and Ontario there are only a handful of places that offer the quality of whitewater paddling found on the Kipawa River. If this is lost, one must travel hundreds of miles to find anything similar." Mr. Leonard acknowledged that we had a wide gulf to bridge.

63

Pat and Scott   Wedding Day   May 5, 1976

Chapter 7

THE WEDDING FEAST

By all means marry;
If you get a good wife,
you'll become happy;
If you get a bad one,
you'll become a philosopher.
—Socrates

Among the ancient traditions of the Cree Indians is a belief that when a marriage is consummated by the couple eating the heart and liver of a bear, many strong sons shall come forth from that union. I explained the ritual to my new bride as we loaded the boat in preparation for her first trip down the shores of Lake Temiskaming to the lodge in May 1976. Pat and I had been married less than a week and she, having been raised in the golden valleys of central California, did not put much stock in the customs of the Northern Cree. I implored her to be open-minded, but she just smirked and said, "You can eat all the bear guts you want, Honey; just don't expect me to cook them up for you." I told her not to worry about cooking them because, according to ancient custom, the organs must be devoured raw, immediately after the kill, to have any effect. She was not impressed and reminded me of a promise I had made before we were married. I had assured Pat that bears would not be a problem around the camp. I told her that despite numerous hunting expeditions the previous year, Jim and I had seen only a few tracks and not a single bear.

Pat and I had met a year-and-a-half earlier out on the west desert of Utah. She was eighteen and building a lean-to from sagebrush, pinion boughs, and juniper bark, a task which was part of a wilderness survival course we were taking at the university. One evening, after a strenuous daylong march through rugged terrain, Pat offered me an ash cake straight from the coals of her fire. It was a simple gesture on her part, but for me it kindled a flame that has never died.

That semester I was living in a tent on the banks of the Provo River, a choice which had little to do with the survival course and everything to do with a personal aversion to student housing and apartment dwelling. Living in a tent just five miles upstream from the university was quiet and comfortable, but it left a dubious impression on some of the girls I had dated. Pat, however, was less judgemental and acknowledged that my tent was a step up from a primitive lean-to. It has since been my opinion that a person who has lived happily in a cave or a lean-to can be content almost anywhere.

By the light of the west desert moon, while cooking ash cakes and horsetail tea, I recounted stories to Pat about the cabin on the Kipawa River some twenty-five hundred miles to the northeast of Utah. In time I asked her to accompany me there. Perhaps it was true love, or maybe my tales of Canada merely sparked her sense of adventure; at any rate, she accepted my invitation. We were married in Salt Lake City on May 5, 1976. The next day we departed for the north woods.

We journeyed east for nearly a week through America's heartland in a Datsun pickup truck with a small camper shell, which we had traded for the old Volkswagen bug Jim and I drove the previous summer. After retracing the route our pioneer ancestors had taken from the Mississippi River to the Great Salt Lake, Pat and I turned north and crossed into Canada between Lakes Huron and Michigan. Arriving in Fabre, Quebec, on May 12, we loaded the boat and prepared for the twelve-mile trip down Lake Temiskaming. Under a clear, blue sky, with a gentle north wind to our backs, we traveled past steep, rugged hills blanketed with pines, maples, and poplars. The sun had cast an amber glow on the massive, lichen-covered cliffs rising up from the water, and Pat noted that the only sign of civilization was a small abandoned cabin near Pointe Martel about five miles north of the Kipawa River.

When we rounded the final bend and the lodge came into view, Pat's expression was a mixture of excitement and anticipation. After traveling for several miles along rough, inaccessible shoreline, the sight of the small protected bay, where our house of logs stood surrounded by the tallest trees and greenest grass in all of Quebec, was a pleasure. Before stopping at the docks, I maneuvered the boat into the mouth of the river so Pat could appreciate the immense rapids and feel the force of the current as it pushed the boat out into the lake.

When we neared the docks, I pointed out the boathouse, the Main Lodge, and the River Cabin. Then, as I directed Pat's attention toward the icehouse, a black bear ambled out through the doorway to see what all the commotion was about. Apparently the animal had spent a quiet winter sleeping in the small log structure and was disturbed by the noise of our motor. He pawed the ground a couple of times, then headed out behind the lodge as though he owned the place.

I looked at Pat a bit sheepishly, then grabbed my rifle as we stepped out of the boat and walked cautiously down the dock. We approached the corner of the building and I checked the chamber of my rifle to be sure it was ready. Pat was mumbling something about the tranquil valleys of California and what a prevaricator she had married, so I stopped and said, "Pat, we are the luckiest of all people. This is the perfect opportunity to assure ourselves of many strong sons while lending credence to ancient Cree tradition at the same time."

We stepped out from behind the corner of the lodge and saw the bear still pawing at the ground several yards away. The animal caught our scent and made a deep woofing sound, then turned and rushed in our direction. As the bear gained momentum, I dropped to one knee and raised the gun to my shoulder. All at once everything seemed to be in slow motion. The movement of the bear and the touch of the rifle stock on my cheek felt strange and unreal. How I had time to notice the bear's powerful shoulder muscles rippling underneath its shiny black coat of hair is impossible to explain. That dreamlike moment was suddenly shattered by the blast of the rifle as I pulled the trigger. The bear did a complete somersault before coming to a halt a short distance away.

As we carefully approached the animal, Pat asked if I was sure it was dead. "Look at the eyes," I cautioned. "If they are open and still, he is dead. If they are moving or closed tight, watch out!"

I set about the task of skinning and cleaning the bear but was disappointed to find the bullet had pierced the animal directly through the heart, thus threatening our chance of verifying Cree tradition.

"Cheer up," Pat said. "Let's just be thankful we are skinning the bear rather than him skinning us."

I found the liver still intact, but Pat would agree to eat some only if we fried it up with bacon, onions, and lots of ketchup. I felt that to be a breach of Cree tradition, but she had her way. Nonetheless, it turned out to be the sweetest, mildest, most tender meat we had ever tasted.

That evening after dinner I went to work stretching the bear hide and preparing it for tanning. First I tacked the heavy, wet skin to the back of the boathouse door by pulling the nose, tail, and four legs as far apart as possible and driving small nails about every six inches all the way around the hide. In order to scrape the excess fat and meat from the hide, I left the skin side exposed to the air with the hair side against the wooden door. I needed both my crescent-shaped skinning knife as well as a large butcher knife for scraping the hide. By pounding a small block of wood onto the tip of the butcher knife I created a sort of draw knife that could be held on both ends and pulled evenly across the hide. It worked perfectly for fleshing.

Once the hide was relatively free of fat, I salted it down with a pound of Morton's table salt. Two or three pounds would have been preferable, but other than a half-filled shaker that Pat was guarding inside the kitchen, the Morton's was all I had. The salt is important because it eats away at whatever fat is missed by the scraping knife and also holds the hair to the hide for years to come.

Finally, before turning in for the night, I cracked open the skull of the bear and removed the brain. The Cree and numerous other Indian tribes have used brain as a tanning agent for centuries. It cures and softens a hide as well as any chemical process in use today, and almost as if Mother Nature had intended it so, every animal's brain is sufficient in size to tan its own hide. Although I had never brain-tanned anything larger than a badger skin, I knew that it would outlast a factory-tanned hide by many years.

The following morning when Pat complained about the plastic bag full of bear brains in the refrigerator, I told her how optimistic I was about our future as parents of many strong sons. She smiled and reminded me that medical science had proven the sex of a child is determined by its father, not by the ancient customs of Indians. Many years later, after the birth of our fifth daughter, I came to the conclusion that Cree tradition, though untested by modern science, might very well be valid. Perhaps the fate of our many strong sons was indeed sealed by the bullet that pierced the heart of that bear.

⚜ Dam Update

Saturday, June 20, 1998
Kipawa River Lodge (Topping's Camp), 9:00 P.M.

At the conclusion of the meeting with Hydro Quebec, kayakers hold their own meeting to form an association to be known as "Les Amis de la Rivière Kipawa" (Friends of the Kipawa River). The meeting is attended by representatives of paddling groups from Montreal, Toronto, Thunder Bay, Timmins, Rouyn, and Temiscamingue. Jose Mediavilla, the man who pioneered the initial descent of the Kipawa River by kayak in 1974, is also in attendance. The newly formed group (ARK) decides to make no agreements with Hydro Quebec concerning water levels or special releases for kayaking. It is much to soon for that. Hydro Quebec's approach seems to be that the diversion is a done deal and all that remains is to iron out a few wrinkles with the kayakers, fishermen and cottage owners. ARK will approach the project as nothing more than a proposal—a proposal that is environmentally destructive, economically marginal, politically unpopular, and socially unacceptable. We must question the results of every study and every action paid for or taken on behalf of Hydro Quebec. We will attempt to involve Federal Fisheries and also check into the Navigable Waters Act. Perhaps a move to have the federal government declare the Kipawa a national heritage river to protect both the ecological and historical significance of the waterway would be appropriate.

Daniel Marinier, newly elected president of ARK, has learned from the mayor of Laniel that Hydro Quebec is in the process of buying the dam at Laniel from the federal government for the price of one dollar. If they succeed, in the future kayakers will have to ask for water releases from the same entity whose proposal we are presently hoping to thwart. "We are in bed with the devil," says Doug Skeggs.

"Better the devil we do know than one we don't," interjects Felix Martel, referring to the private project waiting in the wings should HQ decide to back away from their proposal. Felix is the president of D'Eau Vive, a whitewater paddling group out of Montreal. He has dealt with H.Q. before and believes that if the project is economically viable there will be no stopping it. The best we can do is cut a deal for water releases. Daniel Marinier confirms that H.Q. is already pressing him for a specific number or level of cms (cubic meters per second) that would be acceptable to paddlers for running the river on certain weekends. Doug Skeggs, Ken Timmins, myself, and other NOLAC members believe that negotiating for cms levels or water releases at this stage is to surrender our premise that no dam should be built, no water diverted. Kayaking is now a secondary issue. Our primary concern is protecting the ecology and integrity of the Kipawa River.

Jose Mediavilla has the final word. "Twenty-five years ago when I was exploring the river, I never imagined there would someday be a road, hiking trails, picnic tables, or a viewing platform at Grande Chute. Even finding a remote fishing camp here at the mouth was a surprise. And now this talk about diverting the water to a different place to make electricity, then giving some of it back on weekends to kayak or to fish in . . . it sickens me. We are not dogs waiting to be thrown a bone! I do not want to make a deal with the devil. We have nothing to gain and everything to lose."

Chapter 8

FRESH MILK FOR THE FORT

Our forefathers had civilization inside
themselves, the wild outside.
We live in the civilization they created,
but within us the wilderness still lingers.
What they dreamed, we live,
and what they lived, we dream.
                                    —T. K. Whipple

1679–1900

I had lived at the lodge for less than a year when I became very curious about its history. While planting a garden, I unearthed three rusty axe heads and a tarnished belt buckle. While walking through a dense section of woods, I came upon an eight-foot-high chain link fence that ran between the trees for fifty yards then abruptly ended. On top of a hill, about a mile from camp, I stumbled upon a freshwater spring with an elaborate concrete basin and a roof of corrugated tin. These and many other strange and unusual discoveries fired my curiosity to know the history behind the lodge and its former occupants.

From local residents in Fabre I learned that Temiskaming is an Algonquin Indian word meaning place of deep water. Although in some areas the lake is less than a mile wide, it is ninety miles in length and depths of over eight hundred feet have been recorded. Unlike many shallow lakes in the region which were scoured out by retreating glaciers at the end of the Ice Age, Temiskaming was formed by a deep rift valley that filled with water from the melting ice cap. The lodge is located halfway up the lake on the eastern shore where the Kipawa River flows in from the interior of Quebec. Lake Temiskaming, which is the present-day boundary between the provinces of Quebec and Ontario, is also the source of the Ottawa River, the main artery used by

Fort Temiskaming and the old mission across the narrows. Photo taken in 1887. Photographed by Robert Bell/National Archives of Canada/PA-163895

Indians and fur traders traveling between Montreal and James Bay during the seventeenth, eighteenth, and nineteenth centuries.

As early as 1679, French Canadian coureurs-des-bois, or fur traders, established a post on Lake Temiskaming at a small island near the mouth of the Matabitchewan River. The post was relocated nine years later after most of its residents were massacred by marauding Iroquois from the south. The new post, built at the narrows just south of present-day Ville Marie, Quebec, became known as Fort Temiskaming.

In 1686 a French military expedition led by Chevalier de Troyes and Pierre d'Iberville made a journey from Montreal up the Ottawa River, along the length of Lake Temiskaming, then north to Hudson Bay, where they successfully attacked an English post at Moosonee. Undoubtedly, the expedition made camp at the Kipawa River and replenished their water supply before pushing on to the post at the Matabitchewan.

In 1795 Fort Temiskaming became part of the recently formed Northwest Fur Company, based in Montreal. For twenty-five years the aggressive new firm competed for furs with that well-established firm of gentlemen adventurers, the Hudson's Bay Company of England. In 1821, after years of bitter struggle and bloodshed, the two great rivals merged, and Fort Temiskaming became the property of the Hudson's Bay Company.

The first person to record an exploration of the Kipawa River was a Catholic priest named Louis Charles de Bellefeuille. In 1837 he traveled to Kipawa Lake to establish a mission for the Algonquin Indians there. His route took him from Lake Temiskaming up the Kipawa River, where he wrote of the great waterfalls and giant pots or "marmites de géants" along the sides of the river. Some of the pots he found were large enough to bathe in, with water over four feet deep. The pots, which are still visible today, were formed by fist-sized stones that became lodged in small crevices and holes along the river. Over many centuries, the turbulence from the fast-moving water washed the stones in a circular motion, grinding and polishing deep, smooth holes or "pots" in the riverbed.

The journals of Father de Bellefeuille portray a man who combined a love for God and religion with a deep appreciation for nature. He wrote poetically of the birds and animals and referred to the area around Kipawa Lake as his "cathedral in the forest."His life of service, dedication, and adventure ended just one year after his journey up the Kipawa River. He died of typhus in 1838.

In the early 1860s, while the Civil War was being fought in the United States, a French Canadian named Grenier came to the mouth of the Kipawa River and cleared the trees from several hectares of land. The property was then acquired by an English Canadian named Humphrey, who had already established a lumbering depot near present-day Haileybury, about thirty miles north on Lake Temiskaming. In 1865, Humphrey employed two brothers, John and Bill Burns of Kilarney, Ireland, to farm, cut timber, and generally maintain the property. The fate of John Burns is unknown, but his brother Bill spent the next fifty years living at the mouth of the Kipawa River.

Bill's closest neighbor, Stephen Lafricain, was in charge of a small Hudson's Bay Company store at McMartin's Point, on Lake Temiskaming, twelve miles south of the Kipawa River. In 1873, Lafricain left the employ of the Hudson's Bay Company and moved to a point fifteen miles north of the lodge where he set up a homestead near present-day Fabre, Quebec. The river and large bay in that vicinity still bear his name.

During the winter of 1873 Frère Moffette, a Catholic priest from a mission in Mattawa, Ontario, began a one-hundred-mile trek over the ice of the Ottawa River with a charge to deliver four milk cows to the people commanding the post and mission at Fort Temiskaming. He had at his disposal a sled and two strong horses, but they were of little significance compared to the valuable bovines that would provide the Fort with the luxury of fresh milk. The horses and sled were merely sent on the trip so the milk cows could take turns riding over the ice and snow without the risk of overexerting themselves.

The first two days of the journey went well, and after traveling twenty miles, Frère Moffette spent the night at a camp in South Temiskaming. On the third morning he set off under sunny skies, but at midday a freezing north wind came roaring down from Hudson Bay, and the temperature plummeted to well below zero. By nightfall he had made just six miles and was forced to make camp on the icy, windswept surface of Lake Temiskaming.

The following morning he pressed on toward the Kipawa River in the face of howling winds that drove ice and snow through the seams of his clothing. The milk cows began to balk and showed signs of weakening, but much to the relief of Frère Moffette, the sturdy horses kept plodding into the eye of the storm. He covered ten miles that day in spite of the harsh weather but was still eight miles short of the camp on the Kipawa River where he had been told he could depend on the hospitality of Bill Burns for some food, shelter, and friendly conversation. As he made camp again on the ice, Frère Moffette fed the last of the hay to the worn-out milk cows while the two hungry horses watched from a distance. All they got for their labors were some kind and apologetic words from the priest.

During the long, cold night, the storm finally blew itself out. The following morning dawned clear but freezing cold, and the milk cows refused to walk or even rise to their feet. The runners of the sleigh were frozen fast to the ice, but at the sound of the good brother's voice, the faithful horses leaned into their traces until the sled broke free. The reluctant cows, having been tied to the back of the sled, had little choice but to stand and follow or be dragged by their necks over the frozen lake.

Late that afternoon Frère Moffette was pleased to hear the roar of the rapids, which signaled his arrival at the Kipawa River. Disappointment prevailed, however, when he reached the camp and found it had been abandoned for the winter. With the realization that over twenty-five miles of ice and snow lay between him and Fort Temiskaming and with no food for his weary animals, Frère Moffat felt destitute. He searched through the empty camp, then offered a fervent prayer that his mission might not end in failure.

Shortly thereafter he felt inspired to climb the hill just north of the river. Floundering through waist-deep snow, he pulled himself along by grabbing branches and limbs until he arrived at a clearing half a mile from the lake. On the far side of the clearing stood a small log barn. He tried to enter, but the door was blocked and nearly buried by heavy drifts of snow. With the aid of a rope hanging from the roof, he scaled the front of the barn and entered through an opening in the loft. There he found the answer to his prayer. Several small piles of hay had been left behind by Bill Burns, who had departed a couple of months earlier. After shoveling the snow away from the barn door, Frère Moffette gathered up just enough hay in his arms to entice the animals up the hill and into the shelter for the night. It was not the indolent milk cows who received the first bite but rather the two faithful horses, who had worked so hard to bring him to a safe haven.

The next day he resumed his journey over the frozen lake, covering the final twenty-five miles by nightfall. That evening when the men at the Fort saw Frère Moffette approaching from the south, they fired a salute and gave him a welcome cheer. For the first time in 185 years, there was fresh milk at Fort Temiskaming.

AMAZING! — because it's REAL.

No picture ever
more lavishly prais-
ed by the press! "Un-
forgettable,"
says The New York
Times. "Excitingly,
entrancingly real,"
The Evening Post.

"THE
SILENT
ENEMY"

A Paramount Picture

Actually filmed in the pri-
mal wilds! Romance, peo-
ple, beasts beyond civilization. "Stands shoulder-to-
shoulder with 'Chang' and
those other epic spectacles
which come all too seldom,"
says The New York Ameri-
can.

ROYAL

Silent Enemy movie poster.

Chapter 9

ON-LOCATION MOVIES

The past is only the present become invisible and mute;
and because it is invisible and mute,
its memoried glances and its murmurs are infinitely precious.
—Mary Webb

1900–1930

There was a time when I believed history was an accumulation of facts stuck between the covers of a book. However, on July 23, 1976, I met a piece of living history in the form of an eighty-four-year-old trapper named Zepherin Fleury from Ville Marie, Quebec.

I did not find Zeph in a rest home rocking in a chair. In fact, he found me when at ten o'clock in the morning he came motoring into our bay in a small aluminum boat. His seventy-seven-year-old wife sat in the bow calling out directions to make sure he could see the dock and not run aground on the rocky point just beyond. "To the right, Zeph, more to the right!" she yelled, but the old man, with a look of grim determination, drove straight past the dock and maintained full speed until the bow of his boat came to a jarring stop on our beach. As she climbed from the boat, the woman complained, "He drives a boat the same way he drives a car, by sound and not by sight."

The man, who introduced himself as Zepherin Fleury, was over six feet tall with a shock of white hair and the laughing blue eyes of a twelve-year-old. He told us the story of how he had first come to the Kipawa River during the winter of 1910. His brother had died in an accident, so eighteen-year-old Zeph walked over the ice for twenty-five miles from Ville Marie to report the sad news to his father, who was working at Lateurs Mill six miles south of the lodge. When he arrived at the lodge, the caretaker would not allow him to proceed because the ice was dangerously thin around the mouth of the river. In his heavy French accent, Zeph told me the caretaker was known simply as "old man Bilbourne."

I asked Zeph how long Bilbourne had lived here and if he knew any other information about old-timers associated with the camp. He said Bilbourne had been here a very long time and was married to the sister-in-law of the owner, a French Canadian named Filteau. Zeph told us his father had first visited the camp in 1905, when he purchased a sleigh, a team of horses, and a large bull from old man Bilbourne.

At the time I met Zeph, I knew little of the lodge history prior to 1920. Years later when I discovered the details of the first settlers, John and Bill Burns from Ireland, who came here in 1865, I realized that Bill Burns was the same "old man Bilbourne" that Zeph met in 1910. It seemed incredible that after forty-five years the same man was still caretaker on this site, and yet almost nothing is known of Burns or what he experienced while living at the mouth of the Kipawa River.

It is likely that Burns was both a farmer and lumberman, depending on the season. In the spring and summer he cut hay for his animals, and during the fall and winter he cleared land and cut timber for the J. R. Booth Lumber Company. Such work was typical for most early settlers on Lake Temiskaming, who found it difficult to make a full-time living as farmers because of the limited growing season. After the first heavy frost, men often worked the fall and winter as lumberjacks, a job which offered them only seasonal work but guaranteed a cash flow. The two life-styles complemented each other because the more land that was cleared of timber each winter, the larger the area available to farm in the spring.

In 1918, after the death of Bill Burns, twenty-six-year-old Zepherin Fleury and his nineteen-year-old wife came to the lodge to be employed as caretakers. Filteau was still the owner, but he offered to sell the entire property to Zeph for one hundred dollars. Zeph was interested, "but in those days one hundred dollars was a fortune."

When Zeph first visited the property, the only living quarter was a small shack that Bill Burns had built many years before. Filteau allowed Zeph to build a cabin, which he promised would be his for as long as Filteau owned the property. Zeph built "a substantial cabin," but three years later in 1921, Filteau sold the property to a man named Fred Arnott. I asked Zeph where he had built his cabin, hoping to discover if any of the remains might still be visible. He pointed to the front room of the Main Lodge where Pat and I live, and said that was his old cabin. We were delighted to learn that our fifteen-by-twenty-foot bedroom was the "substantial cabin" built by the Fleurys in 1918. It was their home for more than ten years. Since then the Main Lodge has more than quadrupled in size with the addition of a kitchen, dining room, bathroom, screened porch, and laundry room. Zeph told us with great pride how he had dug the cellar, laid the rock foundation, then notched every log of what is today our bedroom.

Zepherin and Madame Fleury in front of the cabin they built in 1918.

Zeph and his wife stayed on as caretakers for Fred Arnott, who named the lodge Tim-Kip and advertised it as "an ideal setting to shoot on-location movies." The film and motion picture industry were still in their pioneer stages, but between 1923 and 1930 at least five movies were made at the camp. The most notable film was *Snow Bride*, starring Alice Brady, a well-known actress in the twenties, and Lefty Flynn, an American football player turned actor. The production company was Cosmopolitan from New York City.

Other films included *Indians Before Civilization*, *Capitaine*, *American Medium*, and *Silent Enemy*. Of those five movies, I have seen only a videotape reproduction of *Silent Enemy*, which Henri LaForest from Fabre, Quebec, obtained from the American Film Institute. The movie, produced and directed by Douglas Burden, is really a social commentary about the once proud and mighty Ojibwa Indians before they encountered the white man. It was filmed near the end of the silent movie era. Instead of subtitles, the voice of a narrator describes the action, plot, and other events as the story unfolds.

The movie received great reviews from the critics. The New York Post compared it to *Chang*, one of the most successful historical films of the twenties. The Wall Street Journal called it a "striking picture," and the New Republic maintained it was "the only significant film to be produced in this country for a long time."

However, in spite of good reviews, the movie was a failure at the box office. Perhaps it was too educational to compete with the new "talking movies" that were sweeping the country. Also, Paramount Pictures backed out of its promise to promote the film for Douglas Burden.

Long Lance and Chief Yellow Robe in a scene from *Silent Enemy.*

Interestingly, not long after *Silent Enemy* began to appear in movie theatres, it was learned that the actor who portrayed the warrior

Baluk and was purported to be a Blackfoot Indian chief from Alberta called Chief Buffalo Child Long Lance, was actually a reporter from North Carolina named Sylvester Long. It was also alleged that Long was of Negro descent. During the 1920s, it was culturally unacceptable for a black person to appear in a movie in the United States, and there followed an attempt to boycott the show in certain parts of the country. Another star, Chief Yellow Robe, was in fact the grand nephew of Sitting Bull, who led the Sioux against Custer at the Little Big Horn.

Most of the movies filmed at the lodge were made over a two-year period, depicting life in Canada during the various seasons. There was no trick photography and no special effects, such as Styrofoam snowstorms on an indoor stage where actors and crew could work in comfort.

Zeph recalled that in January 1926 actress Alice Brady arrived on the set by dogsled from Laniel, Quebec, during a snowstorm with the temperature twenty-five degrees below zero. Zeph had the ingenuity and physical prowess to double as a stuntman and movie-set technician. When the scene called for a team of horses and sleigh to fall through the ice, it was Zeph who cut the large hole, then hitched up the horses and drove the team into the freezing water. When they needed a full-scale blizzard, it was Zeph who thought of turning the airplane backwards toward the set and shoveling snow into the churning prop to create a veritable hurricane of ice, wind, and snow for the scene. In another movie where a man was shot on top of a cliff and fell to his death below, there was no provision made for the obvious blood and gore that would accompany such an event. In fact, the victim appeared more asleep than dead as he lay at the bottom of the precipice until Zeph produced a bottle of ketchup which he applied generously to the unlucky victim's body in an attempt to make the scene a bit more dramatic, if not realistic.

The leading actors in the movie *Indians Before Civilization* were Elmer Reuben and Lou Cote. On that set there were also 280 native Indians, 25 black bears, 15 deer, 2 cougars, and a bull moose named Big Bill. Zeph told us how they constructed several cages and corrals from chain link fencing to hold the animals. Although nothing they built could contain Big Bill, the large moose was enticed to remain near the camp by a daily handout of food. In the end, however, Big Bill learned the meaning of no free lunch, when he was killed with a flint-tipped spear by the warrior Baluk (Long Lance) in the filming of *The Silent Enemy*. Zeph recalled, "That old moose did not die easy." With the spear sticking out of his chest he rose up and knocked Long Lance

81

right on his back. But to the credit of Long Lance, who had written his will before performing the dangerous stunt, the Indian Warrior got up and charged right back and killed the moose.

During the summer of 1927, Zeph befriended a couple of young Ojibwa boys whose parents were working as extras in the film *Indians Before Civilization*. Neither boy spoke much English or French. Nonetheless, they followed "Uncle Zeph" around the camp each day as he went about his work.

One afternoon while Zeph was stacking firewood behind the lodge, the boys approached him holding a couple of mongrel pups. They had found them underneath the cabin porch. The pups were part of a litter that Madame Fleury's dog had given birth to earlier that spring. Clutching the little curs to their chests and chattering wildly in Ojibwa, they seemed to be telling Zeph that they wanted the animals as pets. "Go right ahead. They're yours," said Zeph, gesturing for the boys to take them. Grinning from ear to ear, the dark-eyed youths turned and vanished into the woods.

An hour later Zeph noticed a thin line of smoke snaking up through the trees some distance upriver from the camp. "Fire upstream!" he yelled, grabbing a shovel, then racing off in the direction of the smoke. Several men followed, carrying axes, shovels, and buckets. When he broke out of the trees alongside the river, Zeph found the two Indian boys sitting by a fire roasting something on a couple of sticks held over the flames. It smelled pretty good.

Suddenly Zeph felt his jaw go slack as he noticed two small brown and white hides stretched out neatly on a flat rock next to the fire. As the other men began to emerge from the woods, one of the boys turned toward Zeph with a huge smile and offered to share some of his "roast pup." Zeph's initial shock turned to anger. He began to scold and berate the "little savages" for "killing and roasting their pets." When the youngsters saw how distraught and angry Zeph had become, they retreated to the far side of the fire mumbling in Ojibwa. Fortunately, one of the Indian elders was present to clear up the situation. After a brief conference with the two youngsters, he turned to Zeph and said apologetically, "There has been a misunderstanding Monsieur Fleury. These boys never asked to have these dogs for pets. They simply asked if they could have them for dinner."

Zeph recalled another incident that involved a dog the following winter. He and a friend built a small fishing shack on skids and pulled it out onto Lake Temiskaming about two hundred yards from shore. They chopped a hole in the two-foot-thick ice and spent a couple of hours every morning catching ling. "Ling," explained Zeph, "are odd-looking creatures that have the head of a catfish, but much uglier, and the tail of an eel, only more slippery." Ling are seldom caught during the summer months, but in the wintertime they are everywhere. Zeph would say, "They're not much to look at, but they're good eating if you catch 'em when it's cold."

After several days of catching ling, Zeph was asked by some of the production crew from the film *Silent Enemy* to take them out fishing. Zeph agreed but insisted they each cut their own ice holes. The next morning Zeph and half a dozen men marched out on the ice toward the fishing shack carrying axes, augers and picks. While Zeph stepped into the shack to light the small wood stove for warmth, the others began chopping and drilling through the ice. Half an hour later a chap named Harvey, who was one of the crew chopping ice, suggested going back to the camp to obtain a stick of dynamite, "to make one big hole, instead of six little ones." Everyone agreed. None of them had imagined what a chore drilling through two feet of ice would be. Besides, Harvey was an "explosives expert," hired by the production company to create "special effects." He knew all about dynamite.

By the time Zeph had the fishing shack warmed up and was in the process of landing "a nice big ling," Harvey came walking back out on the ice. He had the dynamite in hand and a dog named Blackie lapping at his heels. Harvey's initial attempt to light the dynamite proved futile. A gentle but steady breeze had been blowing across the ice all morning long, making it almost impossible to strike a match and ignite the fuse. The crew gathered around Harvey in an effort to block the wind. Soon Zeph stood nervously alongside the shack shifting his weight from one foot to the other. Once the fuse was burning, everyone jumped clear and Harvey reached back and hurled the dynamite as far as he could in the direction of the holes they had been chopping in the ice.

"That's when the trouble began," Zeph explained. Blackie, who was about one-third Collie and two-thirds retriever, took off after that dynamite as if it were a wounded rabbit. He scooped it up in his mouth, and true to his breed, began loping back toward the fishing shack, where the group of men were now yelling at the top of their lungs. Their uninhibited display of enthusiasm only seemed to encourage the dog. Wagging his tail, Blackie bolted toward the group, which suddenly broke ranks and scattered to the four winds. While some of the men screamed obscenities, others yelled out commands, "Bad dog, Blackie! Roll over boy! Play dead, Blackie!"

The fact that the men ran helter-skelter in all directions probably saved them. Blackie became confused as to which of them he should follow or obey. Never in the dog's memory had a group of men become so excited over an object he had retrieved. Fortunately for Blackie, Zeph had dropped the big ling at the doorstep of the fishing shack before running for cover. In the ensuing melee, with the fuse burning ever so short, the dog sighted the fish and determined it was the greater prize. Dropping the stick of dynamite at the doorstep, Blackie grabbed the ling in his jaws and lit out after Zeph, who had slipped and sprawled on the ice a short distance away. Upon seeing the dog's approach, Zeph thought the end was near. He scrambled to his feet and turned to make one last-ditch escape effort but was leveled by a thundering "Kaboom!"

With his ears ringing and his senses blurred, Zeph looked around expecting to see "pieces of Blackie raining down from the sky." To his utter amazement, the dog was standing not ten feet away wagging his tail, holding the ling firmly in his mouth. "Good dog, Blackie," Zeph cried out as splinters of plywood floated down from the heavens. The dog dropped the ling in front of Zeph, then gave him a big fish-breath lick on the face. In return, Zeph threw his arms around the dog's neck and laughed for joy.

Several minutes passed before Zeph felt steady enough to get back on his feet. Wobbly-kneed, he walked to the place where the fishing shack once stood. Five of the men had regrouped, forming a somber huddle around the edge of a large opening in the ice. The water was filled with wood chips, splinters, and odd pieces of mangled fishing gear. Someone was missing.

"Where's Harvey?" queried Zeph, looking from one solemn face to another. "I thought I saw him right before the explosion went off."

"You did," answered one of the men with a smile. "He just kept running straight toward the camp. Now that he's made a big enough hole in the ice, he figures to get a head start rebuilding the shack."

Between 1920 and 1925, Zeph built the River Cabin, which is still in use today. He also constructed a large three-bedroom cabin on the hill directly north of the Main Lodge. I asked him if he had an explanation for the small, sturdy shed behind the River Cabin with walls, floor, and ceiling made of heavy concrete. Our best guess had been an elaborate root cellar or sauna house. He laughed and said the structure was built to protect the valuable rolls of film that had been shot and needed to be safely stored until they could be shipped out for developing. In the event of a forest fire, tornado, or other disaster, the film at least would be preserved.

During the prohibition years of the early twenties, Zeph made weekly trips by boat to a special "medicine" store in Temiscamingue. Each man at the camp was allotted just one bottle of "medicine" per week, so Zeph always took a rather lengthy list of nonexistent camp employees. In this manner, they built up a substantial reserve to last the long, lonely winters when a person frequently came down with cabin fever and needed some cheering up.

In the months between freeze-up and spring thaw, Zeph also made weekly trips to the mouth of the Montreal River to get the mail. He would pull a small sled seven miles each way over the ice, wearing skis or snowshoes depending on the conditions.

One afternoon while returning from the mail run, Zeph thought he saw a large dog out on the ice, but when he drew nearer, he found it to be a timber wolf chewing on a deer it had recently killed. The wolf ran off as Zeph approached, so he dragged the carcass of the deer within sight of the lodge, then laced it with strychnine. The following day when Zeph checked the deer carcass, he found the frozen body of a huge timber wolf nearby. He carried the wolf into the lodge to thaw out by the fire so it would be easier to skin; then he went outside to gather some wood. When he returned, he found that his wife had tied and chained the frozen animal to the bedpost. Mrs. Fleury was taking no chances with her two-year-old child in the same room in the event the wolf revived once it thawed out.

In the early nineteen hundreds, the main source of transportation on Lake Temiskaming was by steamboat or paddle wheeler. The largest and most notable ship, the Meteor, was 120 feet long and made biweekly trips between north and south Temiskaming. Its maiden voyage was in 1887 and its final run in 1923.

The building of railroads brought an end to the era when people would anxiously wait near the wharves and docks to board the ships or welcome home travelers. According to Zeph, the railroads actually isolated small ports and outposts like the camp on the Kipawa River. With no roads or rails linking them to the outside and the loss of passenger service by boat, a person could easily find himself stranded for days at the mouth of the Kipawa River. There were still many smaller ships and tugboats pulling log booms up and down the lake, but to catch a ride on those, a person had to ferry out from shore and board the boats after asking permission. If the vessel was headed south with a boom full of timber, which could trail for nearly a mile behind the tug, a traveler might find he could have walked or swum to his destination faster than he had traveled by ship. The tugboats continued towing log booms past our home on Lake Temiskaming until 1979, when the transportation of logs by trucks became more economically and environmentally sound. We waved good-bye to the crew of the tug P. J. Murer in July 1979 after they unloaded gas and propane at our docks on their final trip down the lake.

Saying good-bye to the P. J. Murer on its final trip down Lake Temiskaming.

While making the movie *Capitaine* in 1929, Zeph was involved in an accident that resulted in the death of a friend. They were shooting a scene that called for a boat to be caught in the river current and swept over the hundred-foot drop at Grande Chute. To make the scene more realistic a dummy was placed on board the old boat, then pushed out into the river directly above the falls. The boat hung up, however, on a logjam just before the chute. One of the stuntmen who was a strong swimmer volunteered to go out and try to dislodge the vessel so the scene could proceed. Around his waist was tied a safety line, which Zeph and two other men on shore held in the event the fellow needed assistance. The swimmer reached the boat without incident. However, when he dislodged the vessel and it swung clear of the logjam, he found himself trapped on the downstream side of the launch, which by then was dropping over the falls. Zeph and his companions held tight to the rope, but when they finally retrieved the man, he had died of a broken back. It was a somber group that carried the victim back downstream to the lodge. The following day they placed the body on a tugboat headed south to the town of Temiscamingue.

Not long after the filming of *Capitaine*, the movie production business declined. The stock market crash of 1929 in the United States and the Great Depression that followed sent shock waves throughout Canada as well. Zepherin Fleury, his wife, and two children were forced to leave their home on the Kipawa River and seek a livelihood elsewhere. As Zeph described the years of struggle and hardship working as a trapper, miner, and lumberjack, I noticed the smile never left his face. Somehow I got the impression the hard years held as many good memories for him as the easier ones. Zeph Fleury is one of those rare but indomitable individuals who at age eighty-four had the same passion and joy for living he had when he was twenty. He is a true survivor, whose courage and hopes for the future are as bright as his memories of the past. I am grateful to Zeph, not just for the knowledge and information he shared about the lodge, but especially for his contagious optimism and love for life that affects everyone in his presence.

Many years have passed since the day the Fleurys motored into our bay on Lake Temiskaming. Recently, while visiting Ville Marie on business, I was amazed to hear that Zeph was still alive at age ninety-seven and living in Rouyn, Quebec, where he and his wife reside in a rest home. I am happy to report, however, they did not go there willingly. It seems that in his early nineties, with failing eyesight, Zeph was still driving his car around Ville Marie, much to the distress of the local authorities. His wife, who had never learned to drive but still had clear vision, would sit close to him on the front seat, shouting, "To the right, Zeph, more to the right!" as they meandered through the streets of the village. Perhaps the local inhabitants feel safer now that Zeph has been retired from their streets, but for me the town of Ville Marie will never be quite the same.

Daniel Reid Topping with golf trophy.

Chapter 10

THE LOST TOPPING TREASURE

*Men spend their lives adding and subtracting and dictating
letters when they secretly long to write sonnets
and play the fiddle and burst into tears at the sunset.*
—Brenda Ueland

1930–1975

In 1931 when Fred Arnott could no longer attract movie producers to the lodge, he decided to open a youth camp for the sons of wealthy American families. One of his first clients, a teenager from New York named Dan Topping, immediately fell in love with the lodge in the wilds of Canada. Dan had already traveled extensively with his mother, Rhea Reid Topping, an heiress to a fortune worth millions in the steel and tinplate industry. But of all the places he had visited, nothing quite compared with the remote and rugged beauty of the wilderness around Lake Temiskaming.

When he returned for a second summer in 1932, Dan wrote home to his mother and said he would rather live on the Kipawa River than anyplace else in the world. At that time Rhea Topping became a bit concerned. At a very young age Dan had developed a fascination for the free-roving life of the cowboys that he had seen in western movies. He had accumulated all the cowboy paraphernalia, including spurs, boots, woolly chaps, a pair of six-guns, and a Stetson hat. Now he was writing letters expressing a desire to live in the wilderness of northern Quebec.

The following day Mrs. Topping informed Dan's younger brother Bobby that they would be making a trip to Lake Temiskaming. Their mission—to rescue her wayward son from his crazy notion of living in the wilderness. Bobby, whose real name was Henry J. Topping after his father, received his nickname from brother Dan when just a baby. Dan, a mere toddler himself, had difficulty pronouncing the word baby when referring to his little brother. It always came out "Bobby," and eventually the nickname stuck.

At age eighteen Bob Topping was already an accomplished pilot who had flown cross country several times. He owned a Sikorsky, one of the world's first float planes. It could take off or set down on either land or water. The Sikorsky was built by the same company that developed some of the earliest helicopters. The plane's fuselage was shaped like a boat and had a single bulky engine mounted on top of the wing, which ran directly over the cockpit. There were pontoons hanging down from either side of the wing, and a landing gear that extended from both sides of the fuselage. In this odd-looking craft the dignified Topping matriarch, wearing a fashionable calf-length dress and a bright, flowery hat, flew to the wilds of northern Quebec.

Bob Topping's Sikorsky.

When the plane descended on the mouth of the Kipawa River, Bob thought it would be fun to do a little barnstorming. Rather than merely landing at the docks, he made several low-flying passes directly over the camp while tipping the wing just enough to afford his mother a breathtaking view of the rapids flowing into the lake. The effect of this aerial feat was twofold. It announced their arrival to brother Dan and left his mother with the distinct impression that the lodge on the Kipawa River was no ordinary place. After setting down on the surface of the lake Bob taxied the Sikorsky toward the docks, while Rhea continued surveying the shoreline, watching for her eldest son. When she saw the look in Dan's face as he ran out to greet them, she knew she had a problem. She had come to Canada to convince young Dan that his love for the wilds was merely an infatuation that would quickly pass once he returned to New York City. But after spending two days at the lodge, Rhea herself had fallen under the same spell the Kipawa River had cast on her son. As for Bob, he loved anyplace that gave him an excuse to fly his plane. In the end, Rhea Topping determined there was only one solution to her dilemma. She bought the entire place from Fred Arnott for five thousand dollars and gave it to her sons for a present. For the next thirty years the lodge become known as Topping's Camp or Chez Topping.

The name Topping became synonymous with money, movie stars, professional sports, and other aspects of society that the average person could only read about in newspapers and magazines. It was especially intriguing to the local residents of Fabre, Temiscamingue, and Ville Marie, who were struggling through a depression and then a world war, to see people with wealth, fame, and fortune come and go as they pleased. Several locals were grateful to gain employment from the Toppings as cooks, maids, carpenters, and caretakers.

One of the first changes to occur at the camp was the construction of a large boathouse to store the thirty-foot Chris Craft, which they named Tops IV and used to travel up and down the lake. The River Cabin became the summer home of Rhea Topping. Two bedrooms, indoor plumbing, and a stone fireplace were added to the structure. Dan took charge of the three- bedroom cabin halfway up the hill, in which he also installed a fireplace, indoor plumbing, and a beautiful hardwood bar which ran the width of the living room. The cabin was christened Club 21, in honor of the famous nightclub that the Toppings frequented in New York City.

The Main Lodge became known as The Waldorf, and was used for cooking and dining as well as living quarters for the maids and caretakers. Dan would often greet his guests as they stepped from the boat or float plane by gesturing toward the Main Lodge and saying, "Welcome to the Waldorf in the wilderness." On the opposite side of the Main Lodge and near the river were constructed stables to house horses, tack, and bales of hay.

Rather than share Club 21 with brother Dan, Bob decided to build his own cabin. He picked a site on top of the highest hill, with a spectacular view of the lake, then designed the building himself. It had a large rectangular living room with the grandest fireplace on the property. A bedroom extended from each corner of the living room, and a bathroom was built between two of the bedrooms. The first time Bob saw his new cabin from the window of his float plane high overhead, he noticed its tortoise-like shape and christened it The Turtle.

The Topping boys spent money lavishly and led colorful, fast-paced lives. At age twenty-two, Dan, in partnership with quarterback John "Shipwreck" Kelly, bought the Brooklyn professional football team.

Dan Topping, "old man," and John "Shipwreck" Kelly.

Dan was also a top-rate golfer and won several championships. He was married six times, most notably to ice skater Sonja Henie. Henie, a

Sonja Henie and Dan Topping.

Norwegian three-time gold medalist in Olympic figure skating, made millions with her own ice follies, and starred in a half-dozen motion pictures.

Bob, who also had several wives, married actress Lana Turner in the 1940s. Lana visited the lodge on occasion, but only after the Toppings built a tennis court, which lent a certain cultural distinction to an otherwise rustic setting.

Bob Topping and Lana Turner.

In 1945, Dan Topping, along with partner Del Webb, bought the New York Yankees baseball team. In the twenty years he was owner, the club won fifteen pennants and ten World Series. Dan was criticized by some in New York City for the controversial firing of stalwarts Casey Stengel and Yogi Berra in the early 1960s. However, in the towns of Fabre and Temiscamingue, Quebec, he is fondly remembered

Sonja fishing.

by the youths, who received old uniforms, bats, and baseballs every spring from the Yankees' previous season.

During the late 1930s the Toppings installed seven miles of telephone line from the lodge out through the bush to Chester LaForest's farm. Albert Lavallee, who was caretaker from 1940 to 1967, would ride his horse Nellie along the line every week to check for fallen trees and branches that might obstruct communications.

I have talked with Albert several times about the Topping era, but whenever I ask more than a few questions, he gets weary-eyed, points to a considerable dent on top of his head, and says he cannot remember. The dent is where he was accidentally kicked by old Nellie. Albert is

93

a man of few words, but on one occasion he talked of an incident where Mrs. Topping came to spend a winter at the lodge.

In her later years Rhea Topping became less enamored with traveling the world and spent more and more time at the Kipawa River. When she arrived to spend her first winter at the camp, she found that her son Dan had recently installed a very expensive, but noisy, gas-powered generator to provide the lodge with electricity. When the single-minded Mrs. Topping heard the "abominable sound" emanating from that machine, she decided the camp needed peace and quiet more than it needed electricity. She told Albert to dismantle the noisy contraption and haul the "whole mechanical shittery" out onto the ice of Lake Temiskaming. When the spring thaw arrived in late April, Rhea celebrated as the pile of wires and steel sank to the bottom of the lake. Once again, she was content to spend her evenings reading by the soft and silent glow of a kerosene lamp.

Rhea Topping and Baby Dan.

One afternoon while I was visiting with Albert, he made a vague reference to a lost treasure. Apparently Rhea kept a heavy, locked metal box in the attic of one of the buildings. Nobody knew what the box contained, but whenever she left the camp for an extended length of time, Mrs. Topping would have Albert hide it in a location known only to the two of them.

According to Albert, one year after their mother died Dan and Bob Topping came to the lodge in search of the box. For several days they looked through buildings and searched underneath foundations but in the end came up empty-handed. They interrogated Albert as to the whereabouts of the box, but the old caretaker just pointed to the dent in his head and replied, "I cannot remember."

During the 1950s the Toppings made very few trips to the Kipawa River. After the death of Mrs. Topping, conditions at the lodge in Quebec began to decline. For several years Albert Lavallee, in his role as caretaker, had the place to himself. He lived in a small shack at the base of the hill where Bob Topping had built the Turtle Cabin. For months at a time, nobody entered the four spacious buildings that were filled with beautiful furniture and rare antiques. Roofs started to leak, walls began to rot, and weeds grew up around the buildings and throughout the tennis court.

In 1961 Topping's Camp was sold to John and Edith Dean. John had been an executive with Eatons of Canada and wanted the lodge as a retirement home. When he first arrived at the camp, he was amazed to find the place so completely furnished. The beds were all made up and covered with Hudson's Bay blankets. There were dressers full of fancy clothing, cupboards stacked high with expensive china and silverware, and inside the closets were dozens of fishing poles, rifles, shotguns, and other valuable items that seldom accompany a purchase of real estate. It was almost as though the previous owners had suddenly died and the next of kin were never notified.

John and Edith Dean renamed the lodge Deanwood, but to local residents it was, and still is, the Old Topping Camp. For six years the Deans, with the help of the aging Albert Lavallee, worked hard to try to restore or at least maintain the property. But old age and poor health soon caught up with them all. In 1967 the Deans moved back to their home in Toronto, and Albert to his shack behind the cemetery in Fabre.

When I met Albert in 1975, he was sitting on a stump in front of his shack staring out at the gravestones in the small cemetery. At age seventy-seven he had known most of the people buried there. The community of St. Eduard de Fabre officially became a town in 1890, and still has less than five hundred people today. Even in a place that small, Albert Lavallee is something of a loner, a man living on the fringe of society. Other than myself and the dog at his feet, I have never seen him talking to anyone. He has not been ostracized by those around him, he simply chooses to be alone. When he does talk, it is mostly about old Nellie, who died many years ago. To hear his stories, one would think Nellie was a person rather than a horse. Albert found it easier to communicate with animals than people. He rode Nellie over every trail, hill, and valley between Fabre and the Kipawa River. He knows that area and its occupants better than any living soul, but the secrets of the land and the knowledge of many past events are locked forever in the depths of his aging mind. Time rolls on and seasons change, and much of the "Old North" that Albert grew up in will die with him.

In 1968 an Ohio company, Geupel Construction Corporation, bought the lodge from the Deans. They hired Madame and Wilford Bourgeoise from Fabre, as cook and caretaker for their "corporate retreat" in northern Quebec. The camp became a private vacation resort for friends, family, and employees of the company. By 1974, however, the Geupel Corporation's interest in the lodge began to wane, and once again the camp was up for sale.

At that time I was a guide on the rapids of the Salmon River in Idaho. On one of my trips was a businessman from Indianapolis who spoke repeatedly about a lodge of incomparable beauty in the wilderness of northern Quebec. Don Bair stated on numerous occasions that he would "buy the place in Canada" if he could find somebody interested in living there and managing the operation. When he told me the rapids on the Kipawa River were as wild as anything he had seen on the Salmon, I became very interested. Two months later I boarded a float plane in North Bay, Ontario, which flew Don and me to the mouth of the Kipawa River.

When we landed at the lodge, with its magnificent view of the rapids flowing into Lake Temiskaming, I felt, as did Rhea Topping, the lure of the Kipawa River. The question, however, was not whether I would come to live on the Kipawa River but rather for how long. After many seasons, the question is still unresolved. But every morning as the sun's rays come dancing through the mist on the river and cast a golden glow on the hills of Ontario across Lake Temiskaming, the question seems less significant.

Chapter 11

THE STORM

Cannon to right of them,
Cannon to left of them,
Cannon in front of them
Volley'd and thunder'd;
—Alfred Lord Tennyson

I have never been to war or had my courage tested in battle, but on three occasions I have survived a journey in an open boat through an electrical storm on Lake Temiskaming. Though hardly "The Charge of the Light Brigade," the rapid and often unpredictable descent of a storm over deep water has given me a profound respect for the power of nature.

The first and most memorable incident was in August 1977 while returning to the lodge from an afternoon in town on a day that had been sunny and mild. I was traveling alone in a fifteen-foot fiberglass boat about three miles south of Maiden's Bay when conditions began to deteriorate rapidly. The skies behind me turned black and sinister, and a violent, northwest wind whipped the surface of the lake into a frenzy of whitecaps. I considered turning back toward town, but putting my bow into the wind would have been risky. Lake Temiskaming offers few safe harbors or protected bays, so I decided to try to outrun the storm by continuing south with the throttle wide open.

I was sitting up high on the back of the boat seat, which offered greater visibility over the windshield when the rain hit. It started as a few large drops but soon turned into a solid curtain of water. Within seconds I was soaked to the bone. Thunder began to clap in the distance, but with the wind to my back I believed I could stay out ahead of it. When I rounded the bend at Pointe

Martel, the skies grew even darker, and I felt a strange eeriness crowding in around me. There was a slight lull in the wind and rain, but rather than calm my fears, I knew for a certainty the worst was about to come. As I looked back over my shoulder, the sky overhead exploded. A tremendous bolt of lightning parted the air directly above the boat and sent me sprawling onto the floor. The accompanying thunder left my ears ringing and my head swimming. For a moment I thought I had been hit. My entire body shook and convulsed as I attempted to raise myself from the floor.

Gradually my head began to clear, and I realized my left hand was still clutching the steering wheel as the boat continued racing through the storm. My right hand meanwhile groped instinctively for my baseball cap, which had fallen from my head. Looking around, I noticed my hat in the back of the boat flopping around like a fish out of water. Powerful gusts of wind kept picking it up, threatening to carry it overboard into the lake. All at once I became obsessed with the need to retrieve my hat. It was all that separated the top of my head from the bolts of lightning that continued to strike and flash on every side. In a state bordering on hysteria I reached and strained for that small piece of cloth and nylon, convinced it would save me from a swift and violent destruction.

I dared not release my grip on the steering wheel for fear of losing control of the boat. On the other hand, stopping or slowing down for even an instant was inconceivable with lightning flashing on either side. I was not going to give Mother Nature a standing target even for the sake of recovering my hat. Yet without it the situation seemed hopeless. I felt like a soldier who had lost his rifle, running from foxhole to foxhole while the enemy blazed away.

At one point while attempting to regain my hat, I noticed an unsettling phenomenon. Small charges of electricity were dancing at intervals between the poles on the boat's battery. It appeared to coincide with the lightning strikes and caused the hair on my neck and forearms to stand up on end. With renewed effort, I stretched towards the back of the boat. In one frantic moment a powerful gust of wind lifted my hat out over the transom, then just as quickly another blast pitched it back onto the floor almost within reach. Extending my leg, I was able to press the toe of my boot down on the hat's visor. Slowly and cautiously I worked it toward me while the boat pounded through the waves and the tumult raged all around.

Once my hat was firmly in place, I felt like a knight cloaked in armor. Bring on the tempest, let the fury rage—nothing could harm me now. I regained my perch up high on the back of the boat seat and drove through the storm undaunted. Thereafter, when the lightning flashed or the thunder roared, I just grinned and pulled the brim of my hat a little bit lower. With a smugness born of some indescribable confidence in a baseball cap, I raised a fist toward the heavens and defied the lightning to strike me now. It is a difficult thing to explain, but ask any mariner who has piloted a

vessel through a violent storm and he will confirm my theory. The task is less formidable while wearing a hat.

When I arrived at the lodge, I found Pat and four-month-old April lying on the floor next to the bed. Initially, as the storm approached, they were out on the screened porch watching the black wall of wind and water rolling across the lake. Within minutes the storm enveloped the camp and rain came sluicing in through the screens, so they retreated to the safety of the bedroom. Once inside, Pat observed an immense bolt of lightning strike the flagpole out on the docks. Then, almost simultaneously, a small window above the kitchen sink flew open and a visible charge of electricity jumped along an exposed wire between two light sockets. Seconds later, Pat noticed the downy, blonde fuzz on April's head standing straight up. She quickly wrapped the baby in a blanket, then the two of them lay down on the rug by our bed. "I could actually feel the electricity in the room," she recounted.

The fury continued to vent its rage for nearly an hour. I struck a blaze inside the fireplace and we sat and watched the retreating storm to the accompaniment of Tchaikovsky's 1812 Overture. Perhaps Tchaikovsky composed that number while observing a similar tempest. It is music so alive with howling wind and roaring thunder that even now I find it impossible to listen to—without wearing a hat.

"I could actually feel the elecricity in the room."

Dam Update

Monday, June 22, 1998
Temiscaminque, Quebec 7:00 P.M.

The meeting held at the Temiscamingue Recreation Center included Hydro Quebec officials, engineers, and consultants. Also in attendance were members of ARK (Les Amis de la Riviere Kipawa), Henri LaForest representing the cottage owners on Kipawa Lake, and a half-dozen other committee members as well.

The meeting had an austere beginning. A Hydro Quebec official stood up and welcomed everyone. He then made mention that a member of the press (a reporter from the local newspaper) was present at the meeting. He went on to say, "We do not feel it necessary at this juncture to have the media present. We hope to keep our discussions as constructive and nonpolitical as possible." The Hydro Quebec official then invited the reporter to leave. Even more amazing, the man stood up and left without protest. So much for freedom of the press in Temiscamingue, Quebec.

When my turn came to speak, I voiced my concern that no one on the committee was representing cottage owners on Lake Temiskaming who were going to have a dam built in their backyard. A Hydro Quebec official said that they could not see how constructing a dam on Lake Temiskaming would affect cottage owners enough to warrant representation on the committee.

"But how will they know what effect it will have unless they are informed of the project? A few who have found out about the proposal have driven their boats twenty miles to my camp to sign the petition. They seemed as shocked as I was not to be told about a project that directly impacts the fisheries, aesthetics and value of their property."

Speaking on behalf of the members of ARK, Doug Skeggs made an appeal concerning the intrinsic value of the Kipawa River: "It would be a gross mistake to rush ahead with any proposal that would permanently damage or alter the delicate ecosystems and the important, historical significance of the river." When he asked one of the consultants specific questions about fish habitat, microecosystems, and shifting sand and gravel bars that would be greatly impacted by the diversion of water, he got a rather caustic response from the Hydro Quebec official. "Mr. Skeggs, we consider your position on this committee as representing the interests of kayakers from Ontario. We welcome your questions insofar as they pertain to whitewater rafting and kayaking. However, we ask that you keep the focus of your questions within that frame of reference. We do not see you and your organization as one primarily concerned with the ecological and environmental aspects of the river."

For a moment the silence in the room was deafening. I could hardly believe what had just been said. Skeggs was quick to pick up the gauntlet.

"Sir, I am a Quebecer by birth. My wife was also born in Quebec. Our family owns a cottage in Quebec, and I resent the inference that I am here merely as an Ontario kayaker. I work for the Ministry of Natural Resources. Even if I never paddle a kayak again, my primary concern is for the ecological and environmental preservation of the Kipawa River. I have paddled rivers all over the world from Quebec to India and I want to tell the members of this committee that what stands to be lost here is a priceless gem. There is inherent value in allowing water to flow unrestricted down the natural and historical course of a river. That value cannot be measured in kilowatt hours alone. If I or any other member of our organization is to be excluded from asking questions of an ecological or environmental nature, then what is the point in us being here? Furthermore, what is the point in holding these meetings if certain areas of discussion are off limits? Now may I proceed with my questions?"

For a moment I wondered if the Hydro Quebec official would dismiss Doug like he did the newspaper reporter.

"Very well," he shrugged, "but we are running late, so please be brief."

Where is the press when you really need them?

Doug Skeggs running the "Tail of the Dragon" in Hollywood Rapid.

Chapter 12

TRACKING TIME ON TEMISKAMING

All is as one day with God,
and time only is measured unto men.
—Alma 40:8
Book of Mormon

One sunny afternoon in October 1977, I said to Pat, "Let's go to town and eat some greasy, truck-stop food, watch a cheap, mindless movie, and breath some smoggy air before the effect of this pristine wilderness kills us!" I was mostly concerned for our baby daughter April, who had spent the first six months of her life breathing pure, unpolluted air and drinking fresh, toxin-free springwater. Knowing how detrimental the effects of these things could be for the uninitiated infant, it seemed wise to acclimate her system gradually to the rigors of civilization.

For three weeks we had lived in complete isolation, with no guests or visitors and not even the occasional passing of a canoe or fishing boat. I had accidentally let my watch run down, and Pat had not worn one for months, so as we approached town we made a little wager on who could best estimate the time. Pat played it smart (as usual), and after I said 4:00 P.M., she guessed 4:01. We congratulated ourselves when we checked the clock in the post office and found it was 4:20. "Why don't we just throw our watches away and go by the sun?" Pat suggested. "It seems to work about as well as your Timex."

Our next stop was the Fabre garage, where I asked Jacques, the mechanic, if he had some lug bolts to replace a couple that had broken on the rear wheel of my truck. He had none in his shop but promised to have some sent down in the morning from Ville Marie. I told him that would be impossible, for the next day was Sunday, and nothing in

Quebec stays open on Sunday. He gave me a strange look and said, "Today is Friday, Monsieur. Tomorrow is Saturday, and on Saturday we can have beaucoup lug bolts."

At first I thought it was Jacques who was missing a lug bolt or two, so I checked next door with the grocer, who showed me a calendar which confirmed Jacques was right and I was wrong. Then the grocer asked me if indeed I had forgotten what day of the week it was. I looked Mr. Pellerin straight in the eye and said, "Of course I know what day of the week it is, but my silly wife thinks today is Saturday."

When I returned to the truck and asked Pat if she knew what day of the week it was, she laughed and said, "I just found out from the grocer's wife that today is Friday and not Saturday. I felt pretty dumb at first, but in the end I convinced Mrs. Pellerin that it was you who didn't know what day it was." As we drove out of town past the post office, I acknowledged we could no longer boast about being off by just twenty minutes on our estimation of the time. We had been off by twenty-four hours and twenty minutes, which was not much to brag about. At least we had gained a day instead of losing one.

That incident reminded me of my youthful aversion to clocks. During the long days of summer, my brothers and I would escape into a deep gully behind our house in Utah where we became cowboys and Indians, legions of infantry, and knights of unquestionable valor. Nobody cared about the time of day. We were too busy chasing outlaws, fighting enemies, and rescuing fair maidens in distress. Our only defeats were suffered at the hands of a clock when at seven each night our mother called us home to bathe and get ready for bed. The clock became our greatest enemy. It had the power to enslave our entire legion. It reduced us from gallant knights to groveling knaves.

Life on the Kipawa River is like being a kid again. Time is not measured by the hands on a clock or the days on a calendar. There are no schedules that tell us when to get out of bed, fix breakfast, or go to work. Each day is so packed full of living one forgets time altogether. We do not look forward to holidays or weekends as escapes from the drudgery of the workweek. Monday morning is the same as Saturday evening on the shores of Lake Temiskaming. We do not feel like we are beginning a mad race each week that ends with the sound of a horn on Friday afternoon.

Our memories are not of Thanksgiving Day parties or Fourth of July picnics but rather of the day lightning hit our flagpole, the time our sauna house burned down, the night a porcupine fought with a skunk underneath the cabin, the morning a baby merganser appeared on the beach and we put it in the kitchen sink and fed it minnows all afternoon. We remember the bear that punctured our inflatable raft with its claws, the thirty-pound lake trout that lived in the bathtub for three days, the raccoon that approached our campfire with a plastic peanut butter jar stuck on its head, and the snake that ate three frogs in five minutes. And who could forget the time we treated a gunshot wound from a hunting accident, or the leg that needed stitching when a chainsaw slipped, or the third-degree burn from the sauna stove, or the dozens of porcupine quills we pulled from a husky's mouth and nose.

April and Jenny giving Katie a bucket bath.

There are memories of people like the lady from Chicago who found petrified moose tracks in the rocks across the river. We told her they were nothing compared with the petrified trees full of petrified birds singing petrified songs on the other side of the lake. There were hunters from New Jersey who shot a cardboard black bear behind a farmer's barn in Fabre. "It wouldn't die!" they insisted. "We shot it fifteen times, but it just remained there in a frozen stance." And a boy from Detroit who said he would climb a big tree if a bear ever chased him. We told him Quebec bears are so smart they would catch two or three beavers to chew down the tree and get him anyway.

There was a man from New York who wanted to know what time the northern lights came on at night so he could wake up and observe them at the designated hour. We told him that would be no problem because Lake Temiskaming has a five-hour echo and when he

105

retired to bed at ten that evening, if he stood on the docks facing west and yelled at the top of his lungs, "It's time to get up and see the northern lights," the echo would return at precisely three in the morning and wake him up when the aurora borealis was at its peak.

Then there was the owner of the local welding shop who helped my daughters with their science project, which was to research and study the food chain. He dumped a bucket of fish guts out in the field behind his shop then waited for the weasels and martens to "come pickin'." After he dispatched about "a dozen of the varmints," some crows and buzzards arrived on the scene, so he dispatched them too. The next morning three racoons and a fox were "workin' on the pile," so he added them to the collection as well. Then he took a picture of the whole pile and taped it to a piece of cardboard under the heading "Food Chain From Top to Bottom" and proudly presented it to my daughters.

Life is seldom dull on the Kipawa River.

❧ Dam Update

Saturday, July 4, 1998
Kipawa River

Today I paddled the river with Tom Brown and a group of friends from Sudbury, Ontario. Skies were clear, wind was out of the northwest, temperature was in the 80s F, and the river was running at about 70 cubic meters per second (cms). A perfect day.

Tom Brown works for the Ontario Ministry of Environment and has a private business called Paddlesafe. He offers canoe and kayak courses with an emphasis on safety and rescue. Tom also has a degree in fisheries biology. He commented, after observing two separate pairs of loons, a great blue heron, and a pair of mergansers (fish-eating ducks), that the Kipawa is very much a "live river." And because it is the main link between Kipawa Lake and Lake Temiskaming, Hydro Quebec should perform thorough and extensive studies on its fisheries for at least an entire year before a decision is made on diverting the water. "The mouth of the river is quite likely an important spawning ground for walleye and possibly even trout. At the very least, it is one of the major feeding grounds for many species of fish in Lake Temiskaming, especially when the current is high."

A happy fisherman, with a 25 lb. lake trout.

I concur with Tom. People drive their boats from as far away as New Liskeard, Ontario, and Temiscamingue, Quebec (forty miles either direction), to fish the mouth of the river, especially when the current is high.

Chapter 13

THE WHISTLER OF THE NORTH

There's a race of men who don't fit in,
A race that can't stay still,
So they break the hearts of kith and kin
And roam the world at will.
—Robert Service

Late one night in June there came a strange whistling from out on Lake Temiskaming. It was past midnight, but Pat and I were still up, reading by the light of a kerosene lamp in the kitchen of the Main Lodge. The whistling began faint and low like a breeze through the pines, but as it grew louder I could detect a certain melody. I laid my book down and asked Pat if she could hear somebody whistling out on the lake. When she raised her head to listen, the sound faded away.

I continued reading, but after a few minutes I heard it again. It was the sound of someone whistling an unfamiliar tune; it seemed both lonely and far away. The tone was deep and rich, and for a moment it sounded like several people whistling at once, but then it faded again altogether. "Pat, I heard someone whistling out there," I said. She reminded me we were ten miles by boat from the next cabin and said, "If you heard anything, dear, it was probably a loon, and if you hear it again then perhaps you are a bit loony." She continued reading while I listened once more for the sound, but after a long silence I concluded my mind had played tricks on me. It was preposterous to think anyone would be out on Lake Temiskaming in the middle of the night whistling songs to himself.

I read for another twenty minutes, and then from the corner of my eye I saw a shadow move outside the kitchen window. I sat staring outside the glass, then watched Pat nearly jump from her chair as three distinct knocks sounded on the cabin door. In the four years we had lived on the Kipawa River, we seldom had unexpected visitors, and when they did appear their arrivals were usually announced by the sound of a boat or airplane engine, never by a knock on the door in the middle of the night. I picked up the lamp and walked cautiously to the door as a thousand thoughts raced through my head. I turned the knob slowly and opened the door to one of the strangest spectacles I have ever encountered.

On the doorstep was a thin, barefoot man wearing a large slouch hat, a homemade vest, and ragged leather pants. He had long, fiery red hair that hung to his shoulders, and before I could say hello, he walked into the cabin and headed for the kitchen. I told him to make himself at home as he sat down at our table without saying a word. He surveyed the kitchen, then peered down the darkened hallway toward the dining room, but said nothing as he took in the scene at hand. He had a thick, drooping mustache that matched his tangled red hair, and green, catlike eyes which never stopped moving. When I asked him his name, the sound of my voice seemed to startle him. After a long silence, he cleared his throat and said, "People call me Whistler." For quite awhile he offered nothing more, but at least I had a clue for the strange noise I had heard earlier out on the lake.

Pat rose from her chair and asked him if he would like some hot chocolate or coffee. He nodded yes, but once again the sound of her voice seemed to have a strange effect on him.

I proceeded to ask him more questions and found his reluctance to answer was due not to a lack of good manners, but rather to a lack of practice in conversing with people. He had spent the previous three summers paddling a twelve-foot canoe around northern Canada and his winters were spent holed up in abandoned cabins and deserted mining camps. It appeared we were the first people the redheaded hermit had seen or spoken to since the previous fall when he found himself frozen in on a lake north of the Des Quinze River. He had spent the winter there in an old maple shack, and when the spring thaw arrived, he set out down the Des Quinze, which flows into the north end of Lake Temiskaming.

He told us he often traveled at night because after dark there was seldom wind or rough water on the lakes and rivers. He also preferred sleeping in the day when he could crawl under his overturned canoe and feel the warmth of the sun radiate through the aluminum hull.

When I asked him his age, he looked a bit puzzled; then he asked me how old I was. "Twenty-seven," I replied. He smiled and answered, "I'm about that old too!"

Whistler said he was traveling south toward Ottawa to sell his canoe and rejoin society. He expressed concern about becoming a total stranger to the human race. Just two days before, he had received some odd looks from a couple of fishermen when he paddled toward their boat for a bit of friendly conversation. As he approached, they suddenly pulled up anchor and took off as though they had seen a ghost. They were in such a hurry that they left their minnow bucket hanging over the side of their boat and the line it was tied to snapped as they sped away. He retrieved the bucket from the water and found a stringer of fish attached to one end of it. He held it up and waved for them to come back, but that only seemed to hasten their retreat. So he kept the fish and figured it was just nature's way of sharing her bounties with one of her own. Fresh pickerel were a welcome change from his usual fare of bannock cakes and herbal tea.

After visiting for two hours, I invited Whistler to spend the night in our cabin, but he insisted on paddling across the river and sleeping under the stars. He thanked us and walked outside, but returned momentarily with an unusual proposition. "I know it is late, but if you care to join me, there is a show just getting started out over the lake that could prove to be one of the season's best performances." I detected a slight hesitation in Pat's step as we walked toward the door, not knowing what to expect from his invitation.

Outside, Whistler was pointing his canoe paddle behind the lodge at the hill where beams of light from the aurora borealis were dancing on the horizon. "Conditions are right for a real show tonight," he said. "But we'll have to paddle out on the lake to see the whole thing." I looked at his small six foot canoe, then suggested we take our cedar-strip boat instead.

As we motored toward the center of the lake, I watched the sky come alive with shimmering columns of light, the likes of which I had never seen before. When I stopped the motor and gazed up at the heavens, the northern lights had extended across the sky from one horizon to the other. Using life jackets for pillows, we lay down on the boat seats and enjoy the performance.

There were luminous clouds of green and blue that faded then reappeared, while undulating shafts of pink and silver light descended toward the lake then retreated back into the heavens. Then from the bow of the boat came the mysterious whistling I had heard out on the lake earlier, but now it was strong and clear, coming from the red-haired stranger just a few feet away. It began as a low, deep whistle, then climbed to a high, unearthly pitch which was rejoined by the lower sound, as though two or three people were whistling at once. The different notes had a perfect harmony, and he could duplicate the sounds while breathing in or out, which allowed him to whistle at long intervals without halting for air. The tunes were his own compositions, but they had a certain wildness that made them seem as natural to the surroundings as the call of a raven or cry of a loon. And yet the melodies were human and passionate, sometimes sad and lonely, other times cheerful and serene.

Finally the lights in the sky began to fade, and we returned to the lodge for some rest. As I climbed into bed, I could still hear the whistling out on the water. True to his word, the stranger paddled across the mouth of the river to set up camp by himself.

I awoke late the next morning, and while lying in bed staring at the rafters on the ceiling, I heard the whistling start up again. I peered out the window and saw Whistler perched naked on the rocks about 150 yards away on the other side of the river. Sitting with his knees pulled up under his chin and the long unkempt hair on his shoulders, he looked like a whistling Neanderthal man. When Pat leaned over to see what had caught my attention, he suddenly stood up and plunged into the lake for his morning bath. Pat was pleased to see he was bathing. Her pleasure was somewhat diminished, however, when he climbed out of the water and put on the same greasy vest and leggings he wore the night before. It appeared Whistler was a man of simple tastes, very few needs, and just one set of clothes.

Whistler paddled back to the lodge that afternoon for a visit. I asked him how long he planned to stay at the Kipawa River. He just shrugged and said he would stay until it was time to move on. Other than the change of seasons, time had no importance to him. When he said he was on his way south to Ottawa to rejoin society, I had assumed he had a certain date in mind for his arrival, but when pressed for an answer, he simply replied, "Maybe late this year, or early next."

Whistler and I spent several days tramping the woods and paddling the lake together. We hiked to Grande Chutes and dove from a thirty-foot ledge into the bottom of the waterfalls.

One stormy afternoon when a powerful north wind had raised large whitecaps on the lake, we paddled out in his canoe and spent a couple of hours surfing in the waves. A few of the swells were so large

I felt sure we would capsize, but Whistler was a master paddler, and we hardly took on water.

When he walked in the woods, nothing escaped his attention. Whistler knew the names of every plant, insect, and animal. One evening on the back porch, he and our two-year-old daughter April were investigating some small yellow flowers they had picked behind the lodge. They were so intent that I asked them what was so interesting about the flowers. They showed me how each one had dozens of tiny aphids moving around on its petals.

We invited Whistler over for dinner one evening, and as he walked past the mirror in our bedroom, he stopped suddenly and stared into the glass. I guess it had been a while since he had seen himself in anything except the reflection of a lake or river. He ran his fingers through his long red locks, made a few strange faces, then shifted his hat and turned away as though he had seen enough to last him for a couple more years.

At midweek Pat and I asked Whistler to join us for a drive into town to pick up supplies. By then we had grown accustomed to his appearance, but the natives of Haileybury, Ontario, were unprepared for the shock. Heads turned and vehicles slowed as we walked down Main Street. One lady whom we approached on the sidewalk suddenly grabbed her child and disappeared into the Laundromat. All this went unnoticed by Whistler, who was preoccupied with the sights and sounds of the city. He strolled barefoot past shops and windows, whistling a jovial tune, his long red hair flowing in the breeze.

On a clear, cool night, exactly one week after Whistler arrived at the lodge, Pat and I were again up late reading in the kitchen. It was just past midnight when we heard a knock at the cabin door and this time were not surprised to find Whistler standing on the porch. I invited him in, but he said he had merely paddled over to say good-bye. Earlier that afternoon Pat and I had been speculating that he might stay the rest of the summer. But now the moon was full and the sky was clear, with the promise of a morning north wind which would push him south toward Ottawa.

Whistler was a patient man. Rather than paddle into the wind or even travel on a calm day, he would wait for a tail wind to push him where he was headed. He was not one to try to conquer nature. He had lived in the wilds long enough to know that a person who attempts to battle the elements will inevitably lose. He seemed content with the notion that Mother Nature is generally kind to those who are patient and willing to accept her on her own terms. But to those who are reckless or indifferent, she can be ruthless and brutal.

We walked out to the docks to say good-bye, and Pat handed him a bag full of cookies and bread. He gave us each a hug then stepped lightly into his canoe and headed south. We watched and listened as he paddled out on the moonlit lake, whistling those haunting, lonely tunes. As he disappeared around the point and the last few notes faded in the distance, I had the feeling we would never see him again. Perhaps because he was too much of a vagabond and wanderer to go back to a place where he had already been. For several weeks afterward, I found myself speculating where he might be. It was hard to imagine the red haired recluse on the streets of Ottawa or Toronto.

In early August we traveled north to New Liskeard, Ontario, to attend a bluegrass festival, which had already been in progress for a couple of days. I asked the lady in charge about the performances of the first two days and what had impressed her the most. She talked about a couple of fiddlers and a promising young banjo player, and then she mentioned a strange occurrence of the previous night. A large crowd had gathered for an impromptu session of fiddling and guitar picking. About a dozen artists had already performed, and there was a lull in the activity with no one on stage. From the back of the crowd walked a wild-looking man, who wore a slouch hat and had flaming red hair hanging down to his shoulders. He climbed up on the stage, and everyone noticed he carried no instrument. When he picked up the microphone and held it to his mouth, many people thought he was going to sing. But what came from his lips was a deep, low whistling sound that rose to a high unearthly pitch, then was joined by other notes as though three or four people were whistling at once.

For fifteen minutes the red-haired stranger held the crowd in silent awe as he whistled a medley of unfamiliar tunes. When the whistling stopped, there was a roar of approval and a call for an encore. His second rendition, another strange but beautiful tune, was also received with a great round of applause. When he finished, he quietly bowed and without a word disappeared into the crowd. No one had seen him since, although several people had inquired as to who he was and where he had come from.

As she finished her story, the lady looked at me and said, "You probably think I'm making the whole thing up, but it's true. Just ask anyone else who was there." I smiled, then told her I believed every word. His name was Whistler, he came from the north, and for a week that summer he lived with us at the Kipawa River.

Many years have passed since Whistler visited our home on Lake Temiskaming. There have been several changes in our lives, including the addition of four more daughters. Their favorite bedtime story is of the wild, red-haired whistler of the north, who years ago came paddling down the lake one night in June. For our girls, it is just another story like Alice in Wonderland or Little Red Riding Hood. But for Pat and me it is much more than just a story.

Sometimes late at night, when the moon is full over Lake Temiskaming, I stand at the cabin door listening to the breeze out over deep water. And on rare occasions when the air is cool and the wind is just right, I hear that strange, lonely whistling from out of the north, and I wonder where Whistler is paddling tonight and on whose door he might knock before morning.

Chapter 14

THE SAINT JOHN'S DISASTER

They that go down to the sea in ships,
that do business in great waters;
These see the works of the Lord,
and his wonders in the deep.
—Psalm 107:23, 24

On June 11, 1978, four chestnut war canoes set out from the south end of Lake Temiskaming on the first leg of a 525-mile journey north to Moosonee on James Bay. Each canoe carried six or seven young men between the ages of ten and fifteen, plus one adult instructor, all from the St. John's School in Claremont, Ontario. There was a great deal of excitement and enthusiasm within the group, for this was the culmination of a year's study and training at the Anglican school.

The morning was sunny and warm, with a gentle breeze rising out of the south. The young men had all made at least one extended canoe trip before and, with the wind to their backs, they had traveled almost twenty miles by noon. When they stopped for lunch, the group had already passed Ottertail Creek, where they had initially planned to camp their first night.

The leader of the expedition was a tall, athletic man named Richard Bird. At age twenty-nine, he was an experienced sailor, a private pilot, and an associate professor of economics and mathematics at Queen's University. He was also a veteran of several long canoe trips with St. John's school. As the group sat on a rocky bluff eating their lunch, Bird congratulated them for the progress they had made, then announced that they would proceed another ten miles and make camp near the mouth of the Kipawa River. As they strapped on their life

117

jackets and returned to their canoes, Bird and the other three leaders determined it would be best to cross to the Ontario side of the lake, which appeared to offer more protection from the increasing wind and waves. It was a logical decision because at that location Lake Temiskaming is only a mile wide and it makes a dogleg to the northwest, which adds considerable distance for a group traveling on the Quebec shore.

Bird, the most experienced member of the expedition, was steering the lead canoe as they initiated the crossing. He was followed by instructors Peter Cain and Mark Denny. Both men had several years of canoeing experience in northern Ontario and Manitoba. The last canoe, guided by Neil Thompson, the least experienced of the leaders, began to fall behind and eventually developed problems. By the time they reached the middle of the lake, Thompson's boat was turning sideways, floundering between the waves, and nothing he could do seemed to correct the problem. The vessel began to take on water, and the entire crew found itself in a very dangerous circumstance. Thompson held up his paddle as a signal of distress to the boats ahead, but suddenly his canoe slid sideways into a deep trough and capsized between the waves.

When the boat overturned and dumped its crew into the choppy water, the young men realized for the first time how cold the lake actually was. The water temperature was a bone-chilling forty-five degrees Fahrenheit. Just six weeks prior to the trip, Lake Temiskaming had still been covered with two feet of ice. After the initial shock passed, Thompson tried to turn the canoe upright but found it impossible. The weight of the gear lashed between the thwarts acted like a ballast. He admonished the boys to hang onto the boat and wait to be rescued, but when he turned to see if help was on the way, he was dismayed to see Mark Denny's canoe had also capsized just a hundred yards away. Both groups were now in the same desperate situation.

Neil Thompson felt a numbness creeping over his body and, realizing the hopelessness of staying with the canoe, he told the boys they must try to swim for shore. Shaking and shivering, the young men were very hesitant to leave the boat and swim, but Thompson assured them they would not drown with their life jackets tightly secured. Thompson paired up with the smallest boy, Tom Kenny, and began to swim. In their weakening condition they made slow progress, and eventually Kenny just stopped. At that point Thompson could no longer feel the cold, and he was overcome with fatigue. He fought off the urge to sleep, but he lapsed in and out of consciousness and then remembered nothing. When he awoke an hour later, he found himself lying alone on the rocky Ontario shore.

When Richard Bird and Peter Cain became aware that the other two canoes had capsized, they paddled directly to shore and unloaded some gear and a few of their people. With their loads substantially lightened, they returned to Mark Denny's canoe and shuttled five of his crew to safety. Bird returned to rescue the remaining three people, but capsized when too many tried to board his canoe at once. As Peter Cain approached in the only canoe still afloat, he found Bird, Denny and their seven young crewmen hanging onto the side of the overturned boat. Bird told Cain to go in search of Thompson and his crew and leave them to try and swim. For twenty-five minutes they attempted to push their overturned canoe into the wind and waves until Cain returned and began to tow the whole group toward shore with a rope. After proceeding a short distance, Mark Denny, who was almost delirious after having been submerged in the cold water for a long period of time, swam up alongside and successfully boarded Cain's boat. Once inside, however, he stood up, rendering the craft dangerously unstable. In the stern Peter Cain was yelling, "Sit down, Mark, sit down!" but the canoe tipped perilously to one side, then as the crew tried to correct by leaning the other way, it dumped them all into the lake. Now the entire group was faced with a life-and-death situation.

Richard Bird grabbed hold of young David Cunningham, who had reached a state of total exhaustion, and they began the long swim to shore. There was pandemonium as some of the boys cried for help and others set off swimming with Peter Cain, who yelled encouragement at various intervals. Peter, a stout, powerfully built man, took hold of one of the weaker boys to assist him to shore, but after swimming partway he became very distressed by his decision to leave the canoes. Several boys were still clinging to the overturned vessels and calling for help. He looked back and saw his exhausted friend Mark Denny tying himself and another young man to the bow of a boat. Both were too tired to swim. He realized then how slim was Denny's chance for survival, but perhaps no worse than his own as he continued to battle the wind, waves, and mind-numbing water.

Mike Mansfield, a heavily built young man, had been swimming in the freezing water since capsizing in the third canoe with Mark Denny. As he struggled toward shore, he came upon three of his smaller classmates, who had lost all hope and had ceased to swim. He asked them to join hands, then led them in singing a hymn which helped to raise their flagging spirits. However, there was little he could do for them in their weakening physical condition except to continue swimming toward shore with the promise that should he succeed, he would try and return with help. For several minutes thereafter he could hear them bravely singing the words of the hymn until their voices grew faint then faded.

After pulling David Cunningham for a distance, Richard Bird became irrational and considered stopping to rest for a time, but he knew such action would result in certain death. He forced himself to continue swimming and eventually made it to shore, where he carried the Cunningham boy to safety. At first the young man was too cold to move or even speak, so Bird laid down on top of him in an attempt to give him some warmth. But soon he heard cries for help, so he covered the boy with some life jackets that had been dropped nearby on shore and set off to see what other assistance he might offer.

As he struggled along the edge of a small bay, Richard Bird encountered three people floating helplessly within seventy yards of the shore. He entered the icy water three more times and pulled each of them to dry land. Then he called to some of the boys who had initially been dropped off safely and instructed them to begin mouth-to-mouth resuscitation on their three comrades, who by then had ceased breathing. For half an hour the young men tried to revive their friends, and in one instance they detected a pulse and saw one of the boys move his eyes momentarily, only to lapse back into a state of lifelessness. They failed to understand at the time that their friends had not died of drowning or lack of oxygen but rather from hypothermia; a prolonged exposure to cold that lowers the body temperature to a point beyond which it is capable of recovering without some external source of heat.

In the weeks following the tragic accident on Lake Temiskaming, when every major newspaper in North America had something to say about the worst drowning incident in recent memory in Ontario or Quebec, the real killer, hypothermia, escaped mention in almost every account. But to those of us who found the survivors and recovered the bodies, the fact that each victim had died from hypothermia and not from drowning was eminently clear.

As Richard Bird walked back toward the place he had left David Cunningham, he was relieved to see that Peter Cain and some of the boys had also survived the swim to shore. When they reached Cunningham, they found Neil Thompson, who had miraculously endured a very long and intense exposure to the icy water. After a brief rest they rejoined the others in a makeshift camp about twenty minutes away.

Prospects for the group seemed pretty grim when the final count was taken. Of the thirty-one members on the expedition, there were ten people missing, three people dead, and eighteen survivors huddled at the foot of a rugged cliff on the isolated western shore of Lake Temiskaming. With nightfall fast approaching, they had no food, shelter, or any means of communication or transportation to the world outside. To reach the nearest points of civilization at Temagami, Cobalt, or Temiscamingue would mean a trek of more than forty miles through dense bush and rough terrain during the peak of the black fly and mosquito season. Of the eighteen survivors, Kevin Black and Frazier Bourchier were missing, their twin brothers and Scott Bindon's older brother Dean was last seen with Mark Denny tied to an overturned canoe as it drifted north with the wind and the waves.

One of the four St. John's chestnut war canoes.

ST. JOHN'S SCHOOL OF ONTARIO

IN MEMORIAM

BARRIE NELSON		TODD MICHELL
JODY O'GORMAN		TIMOTHY PRYCE
DEAN BINDON	MARK DENNY	OWEN BLACK
TIMOTHY HOPKINS		THOMAS KENNY
DAVID GREANEY		ANDREW HERMANN
CHRISTOPHER BOURCHIER		SIMON CROFT

The St. John's school symbol. A wooden replica now hangs from a tree as a memorial at Whistler's Point across the river from the Kipawa lodge.

Chapter 15

SEARCH AND RESCUE

Then they cry unto the Lord in their trouble,
and he bringeth them out of their distresses.
He maketh the storm a calm,
so that the waves thereof are still.
—Psalm 107:28–29

The following morning dawned foggy and cold in the survivors' camp. The boys from St. John's had spent the previous night fighting off hunger, fatigue, and hordes of mosquitos. There had been moments of anguish and despair over the loss of friends and classmates, but at the same time there had been a tremendous display of courage, faith, and prayer that held the group together.

Four miles north on the opposite side of Lake Temiskaming, Pat and I had just finished cooking breakfast for some guests at the lodge when the sound of a helicopter caught our attention. As the noise grew louder, I walked to the door and was surprised to see a chopper, with skids rather than pontoons, making a determined effort to land in our backyard. There was little space to set down between the trees and our clothesline, so I quickly lowered the line, giving the pilot just enough clearance to land.

The pilot, twenty-eight-year-old Gary Smith, had been flying south toward Ottawa when through the fog over Lake Temiskaming he noticed two canoes turned upside down in the water near the Quebec shore. He hovered down closer and was shocked by the sight of two lifeless bodies floating alongside the canoes. When he tried to report the incident on his radio, he was unable to make contact with anyone. The dense fog and foul weather were blocking the air waves. Having no place to land, he traveled south for twelve miles, where he passed over our camp at the mouth of the Kipawa River. Smith noticed the 160-foot radio tower in the grassy area behind the lodge, but decided there was not enough room to make a landing, so he continued down the lake.

He had proceeded just one mile when the startling sight of two more overturned canoes and three more bodies came into view. At that point Smith realized the gravity of the situation and returned to the lodge determined to report the incident. He carefully maneuvered his helicopter down between the trees and made a perfect landing right outside our back door.

After telling us what he had seen, Smith asked if we had any radio or telephone communication with the outside. I told him there was none, that the big tower behind the camp had been out of service for a couple of years. I suggested he fly north about twenty-five miles to the town of Ville Marie and inform the authorities there about the situation. As Smith climbed back into his chopper, I prepared to go by boat in search of survivors. I grabbed a coat, some blankets, a few first aid supplies, and proceeded south down the lake. The fog was still very thick, but in less than a mile I spotted the two canoes and three bodies that Smith had seen from the air.

Judging by the size of the canoes and the age of the victims, which I estimated between ten and fifteen years, I knew there were others involved in the accident. For five minutes I signaled and called from the boat, but there was no response.

It struck me then how quiet and unreal the whole situation was. An eerie silence had fallen on the surrounding forest, where even the normal chatter of birds and squirrels had disappeared, and there was no trace of wind to rattle the leaves or stir the surface of the lake. The air felt heavy and stagnant, and I found myself straining for breath as though someone had placed a blanket over my head. Suddenly I felt an instant of panic, an overwhelming urge to cry out and hear a human voice break the silence. I yelled at the top of my lungs, but even my voice echoing from the overhanging cliffs had a hollow and empty ring to it.

From the time I was very young, I have always loved solitude. I never found it lonely to sit by the edge of a stream or on top of a hill with nothing but my thoughts for a companion, but there in my boat, staring through the fog at the three lifeless boys floating in Lake Temiskaming, I felt as though I were the only living soul on earth.

After studying the situation for several moments, I had the strong impression that there must be survivors. Gary Smith had reported two similar canoes with two other victims about ten miles north, so it seemed likely any survivors would be somewhere in between. As I headed north, I scanned the shoreline but saw nothing unusual until I arrived at the other two canoes. It was the same tragic scene I had just left behind. The canoes were lashed together with a long bow line, then tied at opposite ends of the boats were two more victims. One was a boy who looked about fifteen, and the other a young man in his early twenties. Like the first three victims, they seemed all too much alive, with their eyes open and their heads supported well above the water by life jackets.

I called again for survivors, but hearing no response, I decided to cross the lake and continue to search the Ontario side. As I reached for the key to start the motor, I heard another boat coming down the lake. Presently there appeared from the fog a red, tri-hulled cruiser with four policemen on board from the town of Ville Marie. When Smith had landed his helicopter in town and reported the incident to those in authority, there had been some confusion at first, but soon they rallied to action.

In the eyes of some, Ville Marie is a town of no small significance. It boasts four thousansd people, one Kentucky Fried Chicken franchise and, every summer on the third weekend of July, a boat race. On that gray day in June when a helicopter descended on the sleepy village and reported a canoeing accident, nobody was quite prepared for a full-scale disaster.

There was an immediate need to launch a search and rescue operation by air and water, but the authorities in Ville Marie had no planes, helicopters, or boats, and their five patrol cars would be of little use in searching an area with no roads. They enlisted Gary Smith and his helicopter to continue to search by air. They sought out the most capable boat in town, which belonged to the owner of the hotel, who was at that time away on business. The hotel owner's wife gave permission to the police to take their new, twenty-two-foot, inboard/outboard cruiser out on the lake to survey the situation.

It was that boat which pulled up alongside me on Lake Temiskaming that morning. On board were four very excited policemen all talking at once in French, which I hardly understand when just one person talks very slowly. As it turned out, their English was no better than my French, but after a few minutes, I began to ascertain the drift of their questions. "Had I heard there was a drowning? Did I know of any victims? Could I show them where to look for those victims?" I pointed over the bow of my boat toward the canoe and two bodies floating in the water about fifty yards away. Suddenly the questions ceased, and all was quiet as each man focused on the scene before him. Although they had been told by Gary Smith what to expect, the stark reality of coming face to face with the young victims took a minute to sink in.

We placed the two bodies in the bow of their boat, then, rather than search for survivors, they insisted I show them where the other three victims were located. They could hardly believe it was over ten miles away, and by the time we arrived at the other canoes they seemed very confused. I was the most baffled of all, however, when they put the other three bodies in the front of their boat and started back to town as though that was the end of the matter. I asked them if they intended to help search for survivors, but either they did not understand or simply believed there were none.

As they prepared to leave, the fog began to shift and I felt a strong wind coming out of the north from the direction of Pointe Martel. The twenty-mile section of Lake Temiskaming between Ville Marie and the Kipawa River is particularly treacherous in a north wind. I have seen it form three-foot whitecaps in front of our camp, but five miles north when a boat passes Pointe Martel, the waves get much larger. The nearly fatal incident with Webster Quincy Smith and Earl just three years earlier loomed large in my memory. Hardly a season passes without some unsuspecting fisherman or canoeist having a close call along that section of the lake. I told the four policemen of my plans to search the Ontario shore for survivors, then I cautioned them to stay near the Quebec shore particularly north of Pointe Martel. They gave me a look of indifference, then headed north, confident that their vessel was equal to anything Lake Temiskaming had to offer.

I turned south and crossed the lake to continue the search alone. When I reached the middle of the channel with its tumult of churning whitecaps, I thought once more about the four policemen and the size of the waves at Pointe Martel. The idea that man can do battle with nature or conquer the elements is a ridiculous notion. One can struggle, fight, and scream until he is blue in the face, but it will not change the outcome. Nature will do its own bidding and never give man a second thought. Sometimes the best a person can do is try to determine which course nature is taking, then align himself on a similar path and go along for the ride. I have known people who have survived the forces of nature, but none who have conquered them.

After searching the other side of the lake for over an hour, I returned to the lodge with two of the victims' canoes in tow. When I arrived at the docks, Gary Smith had just landed his helicopter and he had some encouraging news. While flying about three miles south of the lodge, he had seen smoke rising from some trees on the Ontario shore. Hovering down close, he observed several life jackets hanging on a tree, then two or three people standing on the shore waving for help. He tipped his machine to the right and left to acknowledge they had been sighted, then returned to the lodge. Gary was not sure of their numbers, but he told me to expect a boatload of possibly seven or eight survivors.

With extra gas and a few blankets on board, I traveled across the lake in a southwesterly direction, quartering waves that were still three feet high. I reached the Ontario shore near Nagel Bay, then turned directly south for two miles, where I saw three more victims floating in a small inlet.

With four canoes and eight victims accounted for, it hardly seemed possible there might be seven or eight survivors as Smith had reported seeing from his helicopter. I continued past a rocky point and noticed yet another victim along the shore. It was a boy in his early teens, but rather than floating in the lake, he had reached land and pulled himself out of the water, only to die a few feet away on the beach.

One mile north of Grand Encampment Bay I saw smoke from a campfire, and a tree covered with bright orange life jackets. Beneath the tree was a man standing on a large rock waving me in. It was Richard Bird, the leader of the ill-fated expedition. He was still holding out hope and asked me if I had found any other survivors, in particular one of the leaders, a grown man in his twenties. By this time three or four young men were approaching from out of the trees, so I answered him in a whisper. I told him I had found a man in his twenties plus eight other victims, but no survivors. A momentary look of grief and despair shattered his countenance, but he covered it quickly, then took a deep breath and informed me there were three more victims plus eighteen survivors in their camp. It was then I realized that what appeared to be a pile of wet clothes underneath a piece of semitransparent plastic at the base of a cedar tree were the bodies of three young men. There was still one person unaccounted, for but little hope of finding him alive.

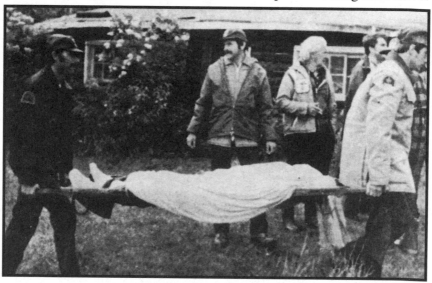

Bird asked me to say nothing of the nine victims I had seen until we transported the survivors to safety. He mentioned that three of the boys had missing brothers and in two of the cases they were twins. I told Bird I could transport only half the group back to the lodge at a time and would need to make two trips. He assigned eight youths and one adult to board the launch. I recognized one of the boys as the twin to the first victim I had found that morning. He stepped into the boat and asked if I had found his brother, who looked and dressed just like him. I tried to sound optimistic and said we were still searching, but it was a hard lie to tell; the mental picture of his twin floating lifeless in the water was still clear in my memory.

Immediately I set a course for the Quebec side of the lake to avoid the four bodies I had seen along the Ontario shore. Some of the boys were so relieved at having been found that they began asking questions about how fast my boat could travel, how far it was to the lodge, and how many extra beds were available there. One of the leaders, Peter Cain, thanked me as we approached the camp, and they all seemed relieved to get their feet back on dry land again. I returned with the other nine survivors in less than an hour, and by dusk they were all safe inside our cabin drinking soup and hot chocolate near a roaring fire. We recovered the thirteenth victim just south of the survivor's camp and shortly thereafter returned to the lodge with the entire group accounted for.

That night, as the eighteen survivors sat close together in our dining room, we confirmed what by then must have been obvious—there were no other survivors. The few boys who showed outward signs of grief were comforted by Pat and our guests from Indiana. Our guests, the Martins and the Hamiltons, had been very helpful in a situation that for them began as a quiet fishing trip to Canada and ended in a very traumatic experience.

For some of the boys, the night they spent at our lodge was the first time they had slept in almost forty hours. But for leaders Richard Bird, Peter Cain, and Neil Thompson, sleep did not come easy. We talked until the early hours of morning about the accident and how well each individual had performed in the face of extreme danger and grievous loss.

One aspect of the ordeal had just begun for the instructors when early the next morning a squadron of float planes descended on our camp. Like bloodhounds on a fresh track, there were reporters from Toronto, Montreal, Detroit, and New York City, all racing each other to get their stories and pictures in the newspaper first. Some of the television networks brought in crews with video cameras so the incident could make the six o'clock news on Tuesday night.

That entire morning and for the next three weeks, Bird, Cain, and Thompson relived each tragic event a hundred times as they fielded questions from reporters and gave detailed accounts of their actions at the coroner's inquest in Ville Marie. Although the coroner's report found no justification for pressing criminal charges, it was highly critical of St. John's and certain aspects of the expedition. The inquiry noted that the trip leaders had received little or no sleep the night before while the group traveled in vans from Toronto to the launch site. Neil Thompson, the twenty-year-old sternsman and sole survivor of the fateful number four canoe, had never steered a canoe before. Some of the boys were nonswimmers. However, each was wearing a certified life jacket at the time of the accident. There was an absence of emergency plans, and the leaders had also failed to anticipate the dangerously cold water temperatures. In reference to the St. John's tradition of "expecting boys to act and behave like men," the inquiry concluded: "We feel that for boys from twelve to fourteen years of age, this entire expedition constituted an exaggerated and pointless challenge."

Nonetheless, most of the boys who survived returned to the school the following year. Many parents who had lost a son continued to support St. John's and credited the school with having given their sons renewed optimism and a greater opportunity to succeed. Pat and I were fortunate to have met some of the parents at the inquiry in Ville Marie. Parents of the survivors and victims alike were kind and gracious in their manifestations of gratitude for the assistance we had rendered. If only we could have done more! Though devastated by the loss of their sons, four of the parents made a visit to the lodge in mid-September. Two of them asked to be transported to the scene of the accident, where they spent a quiet, reflective hour observing the lake and the surrounding hills. It was a magnificent autumn day. The frost-nipped maples, oaks, and poplars were ablaze with crimson and gold beneath a cloudless azure sky. The entire panorama was mirrored in breathtaking detail on the glassy surface of the lake, like an enormous upside-down painting.

"This place is so beautiful and serene," said the grieving mother as she marveled at the rugged cliffs towering above the survivor's makeshift camp. "It is more like a cathedral than the scene of a horrible tragedy."

For that particular couple, the journey down Lake Temiskaming had been a pilgrimage of sorts, a chance to actually see the now infamous passage known as deep water where their son had spent the final hours of his life. It was a time of healing and closure as well. In a gesture of faith and humility, the man turned to his wife and said, "We did our level best in raising our son. I have no regrets. He is in God's hands now."

I am intrigued at how society and the legal system reacts to an event like the accident on Lake Temiskaming. We often judge a situation knowing few or none of the facts. We bring in people who were nowhere near the event and listen to their opinions on what should have been or what might have happened. We try to reconstruct the incident in detail to satisfy our sense of justice and duty. It must be human nature to resolve every issue and answer every question, especially when the question concerns loss of life. We insist there be a reason for everything that happens. We search for guilt or innocence even in matters where neither apply. We demand a final statement of right and wrong before putting the matter to rest. Many people find it difficult to accept that life itself involves an element of risk. They want to eliminate risk and feel in control of every situation, but with nature a person can control only how he reacts to a situation. A man cannot change the direction of the wind; he can only turn his back to it.

It is easy to look back on the accident and speculate about what might have happened had the group made some different decisions. It is simple enough to blame the instructors, the equipment, the weather, or even God himself, but that does not alter the final outcome. When I talked with the boys and their leaders during the day and night following the accident, I came to the conclusion that there were no villains, only heroes, on that windy afternoon on Lake Temiskaming. When the group came up against the ultimate test, there were many acts of courage and selflessness on the part of several individuals. People who find themselves in a struggle for survival often forget those around them and watch out only for themselves. Such was not the case with the group from St. John's School.

On the morning of June thirteenth, as the eighteen survivors prepared to leave our camp and travel by float plane to the outside, we asked them to sign our guest register. Many in the group wrote words of praise and gratitude for the assistance we had rendered. But next to the name of young Mike Mansfield, who had helped and encouraged several of his classmates in swimming to shore, there was a reference to a verse in the book of Psalms. That night as I read through their comments once again, I became very curious and opened our

Bible to the passage in Psalms. The words I found there, though written thousands of years ago, left a deeper impression on me concerning the accident on Lake Temiskaming than all the opinions, theories, and speculations brought forth by those investigating the incident in the months that followed. That scriptural message is a tribute to the character, courage, and faith of the young men and instructors from St. John's School.

They that go down to the sea in ships,
that do business in great waters;
These see the works of the Lord
and his wonders in the deep.
For he commandeth,
and raiseth the stormy wind,
which lifteth up the waves thereof.
They mount up to the heaven,
they go down again to the depths:
their soul is melted because of trouble.
They reel to and fro,
and stagger like a drunken man,
and are at their wits' end.
Then they cry unto the Lord in their trouble,
and he bringeth them out of their distresses.
He maketh the storm a calm,
so that the waves thereof are still.
Then are they glad because they be quiet;
so he bringeth them unto their desired haven.
Oh that men would praise the Lord
for his goodness, and for his wonderful
works to the children of men!
—Psalm 107:23-31

Chapter 16

WILD NEIGHBORS

Life consists with wildness. The most wild is the most alive.
As the wild duck is more swift and beautiful than the tame,
give me for my friends and neighbors wild men, not tame ones.
—Henry David Thoreau

Our nearest neighbors, Jake and Harley Helm, were wild men. If not for them I might never have heard a full account of what happened to the four policemen and five victims traveling in the boat toward Pointe Martel on June 12, 1978. The Helms arrived on the shores of Lake Temiskaming early in the spring of that year. Their worldly possessions included a 1967 Pontiac GTO, two cases of whiskey, a chain saw, and a piece of paper that said they had permission to homestead a tract of land at Pointe Martel five miles north of the lodge. They had migrated from Oregon, a state which they dearly loved but for various reasons felt compelled to flee.

The Helm brothers were in their mid-twenties and even though they claimed to be brothers, nothing in their physical makeup would lead a person to draw that conclusion. Jake was tall, blond-haired, blue-eyed, and thin as a fence post. Harley was of medium height and build, with red hair, devilish green eyes and an enormous hatchet-shaped nose covered with freckles. At times Jake referred to his brother as "Eaglebeak," which always drew the same caustic response from Harley, "You talkin' to me, Stickman?" I regretted mentioning the fact that they did not look very much like brothers. When I did, Harley's face broke into a maniacal grin and he said in a high, raspy voice, "Same father, but different mothers. Jakey boy's a bastard. He's my brother of another mother."

One trait that Jake and Harley had in common was an unfettered love for whiskey. Like true soldiers of fortune, they believed that anything could be accomplished with a chain saw and a case of whiskey. They spent the month of May laying a foundation wall for their cabin by stacking short logs like cordwood and setting them into cement. Their progress was slow but steady, as long as they had enough whiskey to help them forget the scourge of black flies and mosquitos that plague the north woods every spring. But when the supply of whiskey dwindled, so did their enthusiasm to continue hauling sand, cement, and water up the steep rocky hillside to where they were building their cabin.

When I passed Pointe Martel every week in my boat, I would stop and see how the Helm brothers were doing and offer to pick up any supplies they might need from town. The only things they ever requested were whiskey, beer, wine, and more whiskey. My offer to bring bread, milk, and eggs was usually met with scorn. Whiskey would do.

A short distance from their cabin site stood an old dead spruce, which they called the whiskey tree. Over the years the tree had been reduced to a snag about twenty feet high with dozens of tiny protruding stubs, which were all that remained of the branches. Every time they drained a bottle of whiskey, Jake or Harley would climb the tree at great peril and push the empty bottle onto the end of a broken branch. Initially they had set a goal to complete the cabin by the time each dead branch was adorned with a whiskey bottle. However, by the first of June, with only four dead branches left undecorated and a large amount of foundation yet to finish, I suggested that perhaps their original goal was a bit lofty. They were quick to agree and revised their goal to something that favored the whiskey at the expense of the cabin.

Off to one side of their construction site the Helms had made a crude lean-to. "Temporary housing," explained Jake when he gave me a tour one afternoon. It consisted of four tall corner posts with four large pieces of transparent plastic draped between each post. For a roof there was nothing but sky.

"We like lotsa sunshine during the day and the stars at night," hooted Harley, who was standing next to an immense pile of firewood yanking wildly on a chain saw cord.

Inside the structure they had built a wobbly set of bunk beds from scraps of two-by-fours and plywood. Underneath the lower bunk was a badly mangled can of pork and beans which had not been opened in the customary fashion, but oozed tomato sauce from several puncture holes in its sides. I asked them if they had been using the can for target practice.

"Hell no! We don't even own a gun," cried Jake. "Night before last a bear got into here and tore our camp to pieces lookin' for food. Me 'n Harley both sat on the top bunk hollerin' but that just made it mad. It kept rootin' around til it had its fill, then left."

At first the story seemed doubtful. When Jake and Harley went on a drinking spree, anything was possible. With enough whiskey, even a racoon might transform into a bear in their estimation. Then Jake showed me a shredded piece of plastic with several muddy paw marks that were unmistakable.

All at once Harley cursed and dropped the chain saw, which had refused to start. He ambled over to where Jake and I stood, then spat a long, dark line of tobacco juice that hit the plastic and splattered all over the paw prints. "On its way out o' here that damn bear stepped right in the coals of our fire, then lit out like a burning cat. It knocked down a corner post, flattened our table, and run right through the back wall without so much as a thank you or good-bye. We spent all morning fixin' the place up."

Hoping to get a better look at its tracks, I walked down the hill in the direction the bear had headed. In the mud at the side of a small stream were several clear footprints. It was a good-sized bear. The track measured seven inches long and five across. I noticed the imprint of the large toe on the outside of each print—exactly opposite that of a human foot.

As I prepared to leave, Harley asked to borrow my twelve-gauge in case the bear returned. The thought of him waving my shotgun around in the dark after downing a pint of whiskey seemed like a recipe for disaster.

"I'll try and remember to put it in the boat next trip up the lake," I hedged. "In the meantime, Harley, don't store any food inside the lean-to and keep your fire burning at night."

Four days later, while cruising up the lake toward Pointe Martel, I met up with Jake and Harley. They were in an old homemade boat that they had purchased at a yard sale in town the day before. The boat was made of plywood and had an ancient, eighteen-horsepower Evinrude motor. There was a steering wheel up front, but no throttle or gearshift controls. Luckily for the Helms, there were two of them. Jake sat up front on a lawn chair and steered the craft, while Harley kneeled in back in about three inches of water and worked the throttle by hand. As they approached, I could hear Jake shouting orders at Harley, "Slow

135

down, Eaglebeak, or you'll kill us all." Harley replied on cue, "You talkin' to me, Stickman?" as he held the throttle wide open and motored on past the spot where I sat idling.

I watched as they made a wide, arcing turn, then came racing back in my direction. Jake was standing up now, holding the steering wheel in one hand and waving a half-empty bottle of whiskey in the other. The boat swerved wildly as if it also felt the effects of inebriation. Harley was still in the rear, hunched over the motor looking like an angry, green-eyed bilge rat.

When they got within fifty feet of my boat, Harley killed the motor and let the boat glide. "It's stuck in gear," he yelled as they coasted up alongside. Apparently the fellow who sold them the boat guaranteed it would run in both forward and reverse, but said nothing about neutral, because there was none. When the motor was running the boat moved either backward or forward and never stopped until Harley pushed the kill button. Even though Jake shouted out orders and purported to be the captain, it was first mate Harley "Eaglebeak" Helm who controlled the vessel . . . and Harley took orders from no one.

As our two boats drifted alongside each other in the bright afternoon sun, Jake recounted how they had traveled out to North Bay and "practically stole" the boat at a yard sale. "The guy wanted $800 for the boat, motor, and trailer, so me 'n Harley told him to keep the trailer and offered him $650 for the boat. That poor sucker took the bait like a starved catfish. Course the boat wouldn't fit on top of the GTO so we had to pay him $75 to haul it up here, but we still made off like bandits."

While Jake continued talking, Harley was in the back bailing out water with a two-gallon bucket. "It leaks cause it's been sittin' in a garage for three years," Jake explained. "But the feller in North Bay says it'll swell up tight as a drum once it's been in the water for a day or two. Can you believe that fool lettin' this little hummer go for $650?"

"It's hard to imagine, but the world is full of fools," I agreed. I was afraid they would ask to borrow my shotgun again, but the subject of bears never came up. I gave them a couple of pike and a half-dozen walleye I had caught in the river early that morning. "Anything you need from town?" I asked.

"Whiskey," Jake said, tossing the now empty bottle overboard. "We're fresh out."

A week later, on the fateful morning of June twelfth, as the boat with four policemen and the bodies of the five victims from the St. John's School approached Pointe Martel, Jake and Harley Helm had just concluded a toast to their new foundation. By then it was just one or two bottles shy of completion. Of course one good toast deserved another, and they proceeded to toast the trees and the birds, the rocks and the flowers, and life in general, until everything they could think of was pretty well toasted, including Jake and Harley.

They were sitting contentedly under the whiskey tree watching the waves roll in and break along the shore, when around the Pointe came a red, tri-hulled boat full of people. Initially, everything seemed all right, but then the craft turned directly into the wind and disappeared into the gully of a wave. When it regained the crest of the following wave and dropped again into the trough, it was hit very hard by a wave which broke over its bow smashing the windshield and swamping the boat with water. The vessel turned sideways and, just as another wave threatened, it lurched forward and raced toward shore at a speed that seemed reckless if not suicidal.

What happened next became a source of contention and debate between the Helm brothers in the months that followed. Jake claimed Harley had been drinking too much and Harley said the same about Jake. They watched the red boat come crashing up onto the rocks below their campsite, then as four of its crew jumped out and scrambled to safety, the borrowed boat with five of its passengers still onboard slid backwards into the water and sank. The Helms raced down the hill and attempted to rescue the five people who were now floating in the lake wearing life jackets yet unable to make it to shore. Jake and Harley could hear the policemen yelling directions in a language they could not understand, but when they pulled the five people from the icy water they found them not only dead, but already cold and stiff. At first they blamed themselves for being so slow to the rescue, but eventually they learned that in spite of their valiant efforts to save the victims, they had already died the day before. The Helm brothers spent a very sober afternoon helping transport the four hapless policemen and the bodies of the five young victims to Ville Marie by road.

I did not speak with Jake and Harley until nearly two weeks after the accident. The St. John's disaster had a sobering effect on the brothers. They worked hard to finish the foundation on their cabin, then went to town and paid to have a truckload of lumber and plywood delivered to their building site. When we stopped to say good-bye on our final trip up the lake in early November Jake and Harley had four walls up and a plywood roof over their heads. They were hoping to install a wood stove before the first snowfall, but more importantly they had stockpiled several cases of whiskey to ward off the cold of winter.

"Me an' Jake ain't takin' no chances with frostbite," Harley laughed as he tipped a bottle to his lips and guzzled down the remains. After wiping his mouth on his shirt sleeve, he uncorked another bottle and held it up as if making a toast. "You and the missus have a good trip back to Utah and we'll see ya next spring."

I wished them well, then hiked down the hill through a stand of poplars that had carpeted the ground with a soft golden layer of heart-shaped leaves. Passing in between the large silvery tree trunks I caught glimpses of Pat holding onto April in the bow of the boat. Our eighteen-month-old daughter squirmed and reached over the edge toward the glassy water where she could see the reflection of a little girl waving back at her in the bright autumn sunlight. It was a brilliant November afternoon and the end of my fourth season on Lake Temiskaming. Each year had become more significant than the one before, but after the events of 1978, I hoped our future would not involve us in anything that warranted headlines in a newspaper. That kind of news is usually bad.

As for the Helms, we never saw them again. The following spring I stopped at Pointe Martel to see how they had fared through the winter and found the place abandoned. The door to their cabin was wide open and partially eaten by porcupines. Inside there was nothing but a few empty bottles of whiskey and porcupine pellets scattered here and there on the floor. The prickly little pests had also chewed right through the plywood walls, leaving jagged, knee-high openings in the south side of the building. It was obvious by the cobwebs and layers of dust that Jake and Harley had been gone for months. Even their overturned boat, which lay rotting on the beach like the carcass of a whale, had large gaping holes in its belly where porcupines had dined all winter.

Three days later I learned from the locals in Fabre that the brothers had suddenly left the area in a rush the previous fall, apparently with the Mounties in hot pursuit. Jacques, the local mechanic, told me that one afternoon Jake and Harley towed their GTO into town behind a tractor and offered to pay him double to replace the alternator and install a new battery before closing time. "The one with the big nose kept pacing back and forth watching the road out in front of the garage, while the tall, skinny one shuffled boxes from the back seat to the trunk when he thought I wasn't looking. I couldn't see what was in the boxes, but as soon as I was done they paid me and left in a hurry. Later that evening three policemen came by asking questions about them, but they were long gone."

That was the last we ever heard of our wild neighbors, Jake and Harley Helm.

⚜ Dam Update

Thursday, July 9, 1998
Ville Marie, Quebec, 7:30 P.M.

A meeting was held with Hydro Quebec officials and consultants as well as representatives of ARK and other committee members. Tom Brown, a trained fisheries biologist, was also in attendance to speak for and ask questions on behalf of "Les Amis de la Rivière Kipawa." Tom voiced concerns about habitat throughout the river's ecosystem and the possibility of lake trout spawning near the mouth of the river.

Doug Skeggs made another plea that Hydro Quebec move slowly and precisely on their research and impact study of the river's delicate ecosystems. "The river seems to be getting lost in the shuffle with so much attention going into water levels and fish habitat on Kipawa Lake. Other than kayakers, nobody seems to have much concern about what happens to the river."

Henri LaForest took issue with that statement. He recounted the hours, days, and weeks he has spent protecting and improving the river. In 1983 he applied for and received a government grant to employ local youths to build picnic tables, outhouses, hiking trails, footbridges, and a lookout platform at Grande Chute. He was also successful in obtaining a "green zone" status for both sides of the river, which protects forests and trees from logging within three hundred yards of the shoreline. Apparently, the "green zone" status does not apply to protecting the water that HQ intends to divert for their Tabaret project. Nonetheless, Henri is right. No one has done more toward protecting and improving the Kipawa River. Henri LaForest truly is "un ami de la Rivière Kipawa."

Charles Cobbold Farr

Chapter 17

DANCING WITH THE PICOJEESIES

Come to the edge, he said;
he pushed them, they flew.
—Guillaume Apollinaire

Late in the year of 1873, on a chill but dazzling November morning, three men were paddling a canoe along the eastern shore of Lake Temiskaming. Kneeling in the bow and stern were two government surveyors, O'Dwyer and O'Hanley, who had been commissioned to "map out" the Temiskaming region. Perched on top of some gear in the middle of the canoe was an adventurous young Englishman named Charles Cobbold Farr, who had joined the survey crew four weeks earlier in Pembroke, Ontario. Farr was a newcomer to the north. A cheechako. He had signed on as a "dollar-a-day" axeman, which seemed fair enough pay to an unemployed immigrant who was anxious to see new country.

About a mile south of the mouth of the Kipawa River, Farr noticed some "tiny glimmerings" of light on the cliffs high above the surface of the lake. For several minutes he paddled along, quietly watching as the rocks overhead sparkled and glowed in the changing light. By nature Charles Farr was a curious, inquisitive young man, but on this occasion he remained silent. Recent experience had taught him to be cautious when asking questions and voicing opinions in the presence of the two surveyors. O'Dwyer and O'Hanley were veterans of the bush and took special delight in "stringing along" greenhorns and cheechakos whenever the opportunity presented itself.

A few nights before while stopped at an Ojibwa encampment near Old Woman Rock, Farr suspiciously asked his companions what was in the stew offered them by their native hosts.

"Just a bit o' moose meat and wild onions," declared O'Hanley as he ladled a hearty portion onto Farr's plate before passing it on without taking any himself. Farr found the meat to be "tough and stringy," but nonetheless savory, after a month-long diet of "fried pork and dreadful dodger."

As they prepared to embark the following morning O'Hanley took special care to point out the remains of a large haunch of meat hanging from a tree not far from their canoe. Suddenly Farr felt his throat tighten and his stomach lurch. Dangling from the bottom of the mutilated haunch was a hoof with a horseshoe on it.

"Don't pay no mind to that, Mister Farr," chortled O'Hanley. "The Ojibwa are famous for domesticatin' wild creatures. Last time we stopped here for a visit they were in the process of skinnin' a moose that still had a saddle strapped to its back."

Now, as their canoe drew near the base of the cliff not far from the Kipawa River, O'Dwyer noticed the young Englishman staring up at the bewildering flashes of light.

"Kin ye see the Picojeesies up thar, Mister Farr? 'Tis sunlight reflectin' on their wings that makes 'em shimmer so."

"Picojeesies?" queried Farr, expecting to be taken in once again.

"That's right," smiled O'Dwyer as he winked at O'Hanley in the bow of the canoe. "Picojeesies are li'l, wee faeries that dwell high in the cliffs. Ev'ry day when the sun shines down on the rock the Picojeesies venture out to frolic and dance on the ledges."

Farr turned to O'Hanley for reassurance.

"It's true," cried O'Hanley gesturing up at the towering precipice. "The Picojeesies possess the secret to love and good fortune. But only those with the courage to climb up there and capture one can learn the secret."

"I believe you, O'Hanley," said Farr, hoping to bring the conversation to an end. "I have often wondered about the secret to love and good fortune, but for now I'm content to just sit here and wonder some more."

"Whatever suits you," exclaimed O'Hanley as he reached into the folds of his knapsack and retrieved one of the dodgers, a stale, hardened mixture of flour, salt, and water. "However, it'll do no harm to leave a small token o' good will for the Picojeesies," he said crumbling the dodger in his powerful right hand, then leaning out and sprinkling the dust at the foot of the cliff.

In his journals Charles Farr never indicated whether or not he returned to the cliff in search of the Picojeesies. Nonetheless, love and good fortune were his destiny. A few months later he acquired gainful employment with the Hudson's Bay Company where he rose quickly in rank and station. Eventually he married the woman he loved, Georgina Probyn of Pembroke. They settled on some gently sloping ground near the north end of Lake Temiskaming where Farr became the founding father and leading citizen of the town of Haileybury.

On a balmy day in July one hundred and ten years after Charles Farr and his companions paddled their canoe along the base of the cliffs, my sixteen-year-old brother Vic and I went in search of the Picojeesies. We traveled by boat one mile south of the lodge to the place where Farr had seen the "tiny glimmerings" of light. I had noticed the glimmerings on several occasions traveling up and down the lake, but had assumed it to be the sun reflecting on bits of pyrite or "fool's gold."

The sheer cliffs that line much of Lake Temiskaming's shore are largely composed of tonalite, a hard, metamorphic rock in which veins and pockets of silver are commonly found. Near the top of the lake one of North America's largest silver strikes occurred in 1903. The ensuing stampede of miners and fortune seekers, many of whom were returning penniless from the great rush to the Yukon, resulted in the town of Cobalt.

My brother and I arrived at the cliff about nine o'clock in the morning just as the sun cleared the treetops and flooded the area with light. Sure enough, the Picojeesies were already out dancing on the ledges. We could see their silvery wings glistening in the sunlight as they flitted from one point of rock to another. The cliffs rose vertically to a height of 350 feet above the surface of the lake. We had come prepared to scale the precipice with a 150-foot rope, a half-dozen carabineers, and some nylon webbing to make safety harnesses. I also had my camera in tow. Should the legend of the Picojeesies prove to be true, I wanted to have some evidence on film. As we sorted through our climbing gear, Vic noticed a small outcropping of rock about 80 feet above the boat that literally sparkled with light.

"If the Picojeesies are real, we're going to find a whole nest of 'em right up there," he said pointing up at the rock.

Before attempting an ascent, we scouted down the lake a couple of hundred yards and located a break in the cliff where a narrow defile led up to a series of shelves. After studying the area, I determined that with a little luck, we might climb to a level above the Picojeesies, then use the rope to rappel down and take them by surprise. I told Vic that the Picojeesies would be expecting us to ascend straight up from the boat and would likely disappear before we were halfway there. He was quick to agree.

"So we'll leave the boat below them as a decoy, then sneak around the corner and capture 'em from above."

"Precisely," I said, slapping him on the shoulder. "It'll be like shooting ducks on the Seedskeedee."

Seedskeedee is the Crow Indian word for a river which winds through western Wyoming and eastern Utah. Mountain Men later renamed it the Green. Hunting waterfowl along its banks had always been one of our favorite pasttimes, but the success of our hunts was often limited because the river flowed through a deep, narrow gorge which caused the ducks to fly high overhead out of shotgun range. We would shoot anyway, but unless one died of a heart attack, about all we ever got were quacks of laughter as the ducks sped away.

One windy afternoon Vic and I decided to scale the canyon walls and try to ambush the elusive fowl from above. We left our dog down on the riverbank next to our jackets and hip waders. Then, with shotguns cinched inside our belts, we scaled the cliffs to a height of about seventy feet. After loading our guns, we lay down flat on a ledge and waited.

Only a few minutes had passed when I heard Vic chuckling soft and low as a flock of pintails came flying around the bend. There were about twenty birds beating their wings into a stiff headwind, which made them easy targets. Those ducks never knew what hit them. Life had not prepared them for the calamity that occurred as they came winging upriver that day. So accustomed were those fowl to having debris hurled up at them from below, it was as though gravity had betrayed them when suddenly it rained down on them from above. As the smoke cleared, it was obvious that the day belonged to us. By taking the higher ground we had finally succeeded. Perhaps the same strategy would work with the Picojeesies.

The sun was directly overhead when Vic and I began our ascent of the backside of the cliff. We cautiously worked our way up over shelves and through crevices, at times grasping the gnarled roots and branches of stunted trees and brush that virtually grew out of the rock. At one juncture we started up a narrow chimney which became impassable, and we were forced to retreat and attempt a different route.

It was a slow, meticulous climb. Eventually we arrived at a level platform of lichen-covered rock about a hundred feet above the lake.

To determine the exact location of the Picojeesies, Vic and I lay prone on our stomachs and carefully wormed our way out to the edge of the precipice. The view from the rim was breathtaking. Far below, at the base of the cliff, the boat was tethered to a small withered birch tree. It resembled a child's toy bobbing up and down in a swimming pool. Scanning the far side of the lake, we could see Ontario's wild, uninhabited shoreline stretching northward for several miles. To the southwest I pointed out the rugged, inhospitable cove where the survivors of the St. John's disaster had spent the first night of their ill-fated expedition.

As we lay there enjoying the view, the screech of an osprey drew our attention overhead to where a pair of the magnificent birds circled high aloft in the thermal rising up from the water. We rolled onto our backs and watched them for several minutes. The two osprey drifted effortlessly, making wide, arcing turns in the sky while the sun glistened on their wingtips. It brought back to mind the Picojeesies.

"Where do you suppose those little faeries are now?" I questioned Vic.

"I'm thinking this whole thing is a hoax started by a couple of superstitious Irishmen," he replied skeptically.

I pulled myself closer to the edge and looked straight down the face of the cliff. Thirty-feet below, on the narrow shelf that Vic had seen from the boat, there remained a tiny flicker of light. With renewed enthusiasm I whispered, "Something is still down there, Vic. Let's get moving before it disappears altogether."

A short distance from where we lay was a small but sturdy red pine, to which we anchored our rope. Once it was secured, Vic and I each took hold of the line and leaned back toward the edge to test both the knot and the tree's root system. We strained backwards throwing our combined weight against the rope. Everything held firm.

Next we each made a harness by looping a strand of nylon webbing around our waist and thighs, then cinched it tight through the belt loops on our pants. I threaded the rope through the eyes of a figure eight descender and clipped it to the gate of my carabineer, insuring a safe, controlled descent to the Picojeesies.

Vic was eager to go first, but I insisted on being the guinea pig. I felt responsible for his safety, he being my junior by fifteen years and the youngest of my ten brothers and sisters.

"What would Mom and Dad say if I allowed something bad to happen to their golden boy?" I chided him.

"Mom and Dad wouldn't care," he shot back. "They both adhere to the salmon theory."

"The salmon theory?" I reluctantly asked.

"It's simple. If a man and woman produce enough offspring, a few will always survive. If something bad should happen to either of us, I doubt we'd be missed."

On that cheery note, I pulled on a pair of cowhide gloves and sat back in my harness to check the rigging one final time. All was secure and ready to go. The rope began to slide through the figure eight as I fed it slack with my right hand. After taking four or five steps backward I was teetering on the edge staring down at the lake.

The hardest part of rappelling for most people is taking the first step over the edge and leaving the world of the horizontal for the world of the vertical. Some beginners just freeze up or suffer vertigo. All at once, everything starts spinning or the ground comes rushing up at them, and they clutch the rope so tight their knuckles seem ready to burst right through the seams of their gloves. Beads of sweat roll down their faces and breathing becomes an irregular, staccato-like gasping for air. Their knees shake up and down uncontrollably, like the needle on a sewing machine, and if left unchecked, the trembling rapidly spreads to all extremities.

Vertigo can result from looking down too soon or too often and not focusing on the task at hand. Climbing and rappelling are as much a mental exercise as they are a physical challenge. If a climber does not maintain concentration on what his feet and hands are trying to accomplish at that very moment, and begins to worry about what is above or below him, he sets himself up for defeat.

Perhaps there is no other activity that forces a person to exist so much in the present as does mountaineering. When stepping backward off a hundred-foot ledge, it is almost impossible to start worrying about how one will pay the utility bills next month or what to fix for dinner that night. The national debt or the rising price of gasoline are irrelevant when clinging precariously to an overhang with five fingers and ten toes, while your free hand reaches and probes for a grip somewhere up and beyond your field of vision.

As I lowered myself toward the Picojeesies, I continued to see the occasional glimmer of light near the small outcropping of rock below me. The more I descended, however, the fewer in number there appeared to be. When I arrived at the outcropping, the Picojeesies had disappeared altogether. After gaining a foothold on the narrow shelf, I looked up from where I had just come and beheld several glimmerings about halfway between me and the top of the cliff. Somehow I had passed right by them. I stood there perplexed, shaking my head.

Momentarily, I saw Vic peering over the edge. "The Picojeesies are even more elusive than pintails on the Seedskeedee," I called to him.

"This is no duck hunt," he hollered back. "We're on a wild goose chase."

I continued my descent for another thirty feet to a wider shelf that offered better footing, then disengaged my carabineer from the figure eight. The boat was only twenty feet below me now and I wanted to get some pictures of Vic rappelling down the cliff. With the sun directly behind me and an excellent view of the far side of the lake, I had an irresistible backdrop for a photograph. There was just enough space on the shelf to lean back against the rock and hold my camera above my head.

While Vic hauled up the rope, I tried to reposition myself to get a better angle for shooting pictures. The shelf was too narrow to turn completely around on, but by making a quarter turn, I could view perfectly my brother's line of descent. As I turned, I caught a glimpse of something that seemed strangely out of place. Raspberries. Either my eyes were playing tricks on me or I had actually seen raspberries hanging from a branch about ten feet from my right hand. I looked again. It was no hallucination. From a tiny crack where the wind and rain had deposited just enough soil for a seed to germinate, there grew a raspberry bush. The entire plant consisted of three haggard-looking vines with a half-dozen bright, red berries that had somehow survived the ravages of wind, sleet and hailstorms. There it was, a raspberry bush stubbornly clinging to a cliff above Lake Temiskaming; a testament to the tenacity of life. In its own way, no less a miracle than the possibility of finding Picojeesies somewhere in the crevices above.

I raised my camera and focused when Vic appeared at the top of the cliff. He began his descent with a series of small, cautious steps. I assumed he was nervous, trying to overcome the "jitters" while getting a feel for the rock. Suddenly he leaned back and threw one hand in the air like a rodeo rider, then recklessly kicked out from the rock and spun a 360-degree circle around the rope. It caught me by surprise, but I managed to get a couple of pictures before he landed feet-first to the wall.

"Whoop-ee-ki-yi-yo!" he hollered at the top of his lungs, then pushed off again and spun back in the opposite direction. My camera continued to click as he descended in leaps and bounds, looking like a frenzied spider hanging by its web in a windstorm.

"There won't be any Picojeesies within ten miles of here after that ruckus," I called to him as he sailed past me headed for the boat. Either he was not listening or was just too caught up in the moment to reply. I could hear the rope "zinging" through the figure eight when he gave one final push off the wall, yelled "yahoo buckaroo," then launched himself out over the water. He was only fifteen feet above the boat, but when his steel-plated, size eleven loggers hit the aluminum deck, the entire vessel shuddered and rocked as a deafening "crash" reverberated off the cliffs.

"That'll show those little faeries how to get down a cliff without flittin' around and wastin' time," Vic roared as he unclipped his carabineer and beat on his chest.

I smiled but remained silent. Vic's wild demonstration up on the rock needed no endorsement from me.

"I hope you got some good shots of my 360s," he jubilantly cried, while attempting a clumsy pirouette on the bow of the boat.

"We'll never know unless you pass me the rope," I called back from my perch high above. He took the end of the rope and snapped it violently like a bullwhip, which sent a loop snaking up and over to where I could reach it. While lowering myself to the boat Vic continued

to brag and boast about his "marvelous descent." I cautioned him to show a bit of humility. "Between the weight of those logging boots and your overblown ego the boat might sink before we reach the camp." My warning fell on deaf ears. Something had unleashed an enthusiasm that stayed with my brother for days.

In the years since Vic and I first explored the cliffs, I have returned many times to show family and friends the "tiny glimmerings" that Charles Farr made note of in 1873.

"What's up there?" they invariably ask.

"Picojeesies," say I. "'Tis sunlight reflectin' on their wings that makes 'em shimmer so." And thus the lore is passed on from one generation to the next.

There are often a few whose curiosity compels them to climb to the top. They are always rewarded by a spectacular view of the lake but then they must decide whether to walk back down or venture out on the cliff. Rappelling, in many respects, is a leap of faith. Some choose not to take it. The fear of falling is natural. Logic tells a person they have no business hanging from a narrow strand of rope a hundred feet above the ground.

"What if it breaks?" they argue. But that never happens. The only thing that breaks is a person's confidence. Once fear and self-doubt are overcome, many find themselves drawn to the edge like a fledgling hawk yearning to leave the nest.

I have watched my children tremble and shake when they first approach the edge of the precipice. Like young birds, gulping for air and grasping for courage, they tentatively step out into space and disappear from view. For a time all is quiet. They have been swallowed up by the abyss—that great unknown. They have left the security of the nest, yet still wonder if they can actually fly. I know they are struggling, fighting to control the quivering in their arms and the fear in their throats. A silent eternity passes. I offer words of advice and encouragement.

"Sit back in your harness, Michelle. Take a deep breath, little Kate. Feet flat to the wall, Becky babe."

For a long moment there is no response, I feel no movement or change of tension in the rope. Eventually though, the line goes taut and hums like a tightly stretched bowstring, as they push out from the rock and begin their descent to the shimmering ledge.

Suddenly, the air is filled with shrieks of joy as they discover the thrill and freedom of flight, and I know they will never again be the same. They have sprouted wings. By the time they reach the bottom they are somehow changed. There is a lightness in their step and a glimmer in their eyes. They have danced with the Picojeesies.

149

"Whoop-ee-ki-yi-yo"

LIFE ON THE EDGE

A sitter and a doer
Were high upon a ledge.
The doer talked of soaring
As he swung out o'er the edge.

The sitter watched with terror
As the doer disappeared.
He was afraid to follow;
It was himself he feared.

"Look before you leap," he cried.
"Before it is too late!"
But the doer had already gone
Upon the wings of fate.

The sitter watched and wondered
If the doer would survive,
While the doer learned just what it meant
To really be alive.

Death never stopped the doer,
Nor even slowed him down.
The step he took was freedom,
And his soul could not be bound.

The sitter crawled back on the ledge,
Afraid to make the dive.
But his fear of death was foolish,
For he never was alive.

—Scott Sorensen

151

Hauling wood at forty below

Ice bound on Lake Temiskaming.

Chapter 18

THE WINTER OF '83

Ayii, Ayii
There is one thing
And only one thing,
To rise
And greet the new day,
To turn your face
From the dark of night,
To gaze at the white dawn.
Arise. Arise.
Ayii, Ayii.

—An Eskimo Song

The winter of 1983 holds memories of long, dark nights and frosty cold mornings on the banks of the Kipawa River. I spent the winter at the lodge cutting timber and gathering logs for a new cabin. Pat and I had actually closed the camp in late September, then traveled south and west three thousand miles to California, where she would stay the winter at her parent's home while waiting for the arrival of our third daughter. It was a difficult time for us to be apart, but our longtime friend and partner, Don Bair from Indiana, had offered to sell us the entire camp, plus the adjoining 250 acres of land, for a price that was hard to resist. Pat was due to give birth in early December, but the situation required that I return to Canada immediately, and leave her and our daughters in the care of her parents.

In October I departed for Quebec via Utah, where I stopped to see my parents and take on a passenger, Dave Christensen, a young man who was bored and looking for adventure.

"Would cutting timber in the frozen north cure the boredom?" I asked.

"Sounds better than hanging out at the mall," he replied. I assured him that although Canada might be cold, it was not so barren and desolate a wasteland as a shopping mall.

Before leaving California, I told Pat that every night at ten o'clock I would walk out onto the docks and watch the North Star for a moment and think of her and our children. She promised to do likewise. In California, however, the time would be seven o'clock and the temperature would be seventy degrees Fahrenheit. When I took my nightly stroll out on the docks to say good night on December twenty-first, the North Star shone like a ten-carat diamond and the thermometer read minus thirty-four degrees. By morning the surface of the lake had frozen solid enough to walk on.

In spite of the intense cold, Lake Temiskaming is often one of the last bodies of water to freeze over in the region. Its great depth and strong current slow down the inversion process that causes most lakes to ice up earlier. My eighteen-year-old lumberjack apprentice Dave and I took baths daily in the lake up until December fifteenth, when a thin veneer of ice formed around the docks and along the shore. The ice did not put an end to our daily bathing ritual. It merely inconvenienced us by requiring that a hole be cut in the frozen surface before retiring to the sauna to warm up.

Our sauna is a small plywood shed heated by a forty-dollar tin stove. It can reach temperatures of around two hundred degrees Fahrenheit, which seemed "awfully hot" to Dave when we arrived at the camp in early November. Then the daytime temperatures were still in the mid-to-upper forties. But in December, when a three-day-long blizzard sent the mercury crashing to minus twenty-one, having an eight-by-ten foot shack that could heat quickly to two hundred degrees seemed reasonable, if not necessary. Especially in light of the fact that our living quarters seldom got above freezing, no matter how much wood we packed into the stove.

Dave and I had confined our living space to just a fifteen-by-twenty-foot bedroom which we sealed off from the rest of the lodge and heated with a wood-burning stove. It was the same room in which Madame Fleury had tied the frozen wolf to the bedpost back in 1918. Over the years the logs had weathered and cracked and lost most of their capacity to insulate. Daylight could be seen shining through the cracks in a dozen different places where chinking had fallen out from in between the logs. The building's windows were single panes of glass held loosely in place by nails, the putty having dried up and blown away years before. Our attempts to winterize the old cabin required days of work. Even after re-chinking the cracks and putting plastic on the windows, frost would form overnight near the doorways and on the windowsills inside the room.

The roof was a single layer of boards, covered with tar paper but devoid of insulation. Our living quarters actually became easier to heat once a foot of snow formed on the roof and acted as a barrier from the cold above. For drinking water, we went to the river each day and filled a plastic bucket which we kept on the floor in a corner of the room. But as December turned into January, we moved it to a shelf above the stove to keep it from freezing at night.

The nights were without end. It was dark by five o'clock in the afternoon, and stayed dark until almost eight in the morning. We spent the time stoking the fire, reading books, writing letters, and listening to the CBC radio channel out of Sudbury, Ontario. Being isolated, I learned to appreciate the diversity of programming offered by the Canadian Broadcasting Corporation. There was news, weather, and sports (hockey for the most part—anything else is considered child's play up north). I often felt better about the cold around Lake Temiskaming when the weatherman announced the forecasts for Winisk, Fort Albany, and Attawapiskat, a thousand miles to the north. Their temperatures often ranged ten to fifteen degrees colder than ours.

Albeit, I wondered how many times the people in those communities broke ice off their drinking water or woke up in the morning and found their hair frozen to their pillow.

The music on CBC radio varied from classical, folk, opera, and rock 'n' roll. There was not enough of the latter to suit my young companion though. Dave had a Walkman and a few cassettes of heavy metal music that rivalled a chain saw both in volume and quality of sound. Each night when the symphonic melodies of Bach and Beethoven came drifting through the airwaves across the Canadian Shield from Sudbury, Dave would slink off to the far corner of the room looking sick as a gut-shot wolf. He would then jam on the headphones, crank up the Walkman, and lapse into a glassy-eyed coma of contentment. I know the feeling. I was a teenager in the sixties when chain saw music got its start.

During the long hours of darkness there was ample time for reading. My favorite books were about northern people and adventurers such as Farley Mowat's *People of the Deer* and his compilation of accounts of Arctic exploration in *Ordeal by Ice*. Some of the stalwart men of the Franklin Expedition, in search of the Northwest Passage, roamed the Arctic for twelve years trying to escape the ice and snow that had imprisoned their ship. Of the 130 men who left England in 1845, none survived. The stories of their struggles were told by Eskimos, whose advice and assistance they often ignored. I enjoyed reading James Houston's wonderful yet tragic tale of the first whalers to come in contact with the Eskimos in his book *White Dawn*. I read for a second time *Black Sand and Gold*, Edward Lung's fascinating journal of the rush to the Yukon and how close he came to striking it rich on the Eldorado. Perhaps the greatest survival story of all is Alfred Lansing's *Endurance*, a book about Ernest Shackleton's expedition to the South Pole and how he and his entire crew escaped death on the ice after being frozen in for nearly two years. When the mood required something light, I would pull Robert Service from the shelf and recite "The Cremation of Sam McGee" or "The Shooting of Dan McGraw".

As the winter dragged on and outside the snow piled higher, I escaped to the British Isles and read about the "terrible beauty" of Ireland in Leon Uris' tragic novel *Trinity* . Then south to Wales where I descended into the coal mines in Richard Llewellyn's *How Green Was My Valley*. I traveled to Africa with Beryl Markham in her book *West With The Night*, and marveled at what a female bush pilot did for adventure in Kenya in the early 1900s. I also flew with Antoine de St. Exupery in *Wind, Sand, And Stars* in the skies over Europe and North

Africa, delivering mail to remote outposts everywhere. Neville Shute took me on a trip to Southeast Asia and Australia in his classic story of *A Town Like Alice*. Then I sailed the blue Pacific in an enormous dugout canoe with outriggers in James Michener's *Hawaii*. After the islands I returned to my native land and roamed the red rock canyons of southern Utah in Edward Abbey's *Desert Solitaire*.

On days when foul weather confined us to our cabin and the gloom of isolation became extreme, I would read of men exiled from home and country in *The Count of Monte Cristo*, *Les Miserables*, and *Papillon*. Their battles with loneliness and despair, and their determination to rise above grave circumstances, gave my own spirits a boost. At Christmastime, when I longed to see my wife and children, I read *The Education of Little Tree* and *The Yearling*, which brought back memories of my youth and how differently a child views the world.

When the batteries in Dave's Walkman ran out and we had no replacements, he complained about being bored and how each night seemed longer than the one before. I loaned him a book that my dad gave me when I was eighteen and our television was on the blink. I had told my father that there was nothing exciting to do around the house and asked him for the car keys and a little spending money. He handed me a copy of Robert Ruark's *Something of Value*, and advised me to hang on tight and fasten my seat belt. For the next three days and nights, I became lost in the magnificence and terror that was Africa during the Mau Mau uprising. I was caught up in a world that rendered "The Brady Bunch" and "Gilligan's Island" trite and meaningless. The book seemed to have a similar effect on Dave. He read it without saying a word for five straight nights. Late on the fifth night he closed the back cover and said, "Okay, what else ya got?"

Our winter workdays in Quebec began at 8:30 A.M. After a quick breakfast, we would carry our chain saws up the hill behind the lodge and trudge through snow to the stand of timber we had been working the previous day. Our task was to selectively cut about twenty-five hundred mature spruce, poplar, and pine (both red and white) to sell to the various mills and telephone pole buyers in the region. The telephone company would pay by far the most money for any tree that met their requirements. They were only interested in red pines, however, and just one in ten of those were straight and tall enough to meet their specifications. I sold about two hundred red pines to the telephone pole buyer after setting aside fifty of the straightest trees to build a new cabin.

The lumber mill in Bearn, Quebec, bought the remaining red and white pines plus all of the spruce, to be cut into boards. A few of the finest poplar trees were sold to a mill in Ville Marie that produces veneer for paneling. The rest, about 90 percent of the poplar, went to the chip and pulp mill in Temiscamingue, Quebec, to be made into paper or waferboard.

Dave and I would fell and de-limb about three hundred trees Monday through Friday, then Saturday morning two French-Canadian lumberjacks, Luc and Pierre, would arrive with their skidders. Skidders are large, powerful, four-wheel drive, tractor-like machines used for dragging the trees out through the bush to a road. The previous summer the sawmill had cut a road from the highway that runs between Fabre and Laniel down to the edge of our property. I use the word road in a relative sense. Specifically, it was a steep, rough, snowpacked trail that wound its way over frozen bogs and beaver dams. Nonetheless, there were sixteen-wheel tractor-trailer rigs driving in and out all winter long, hauling trees to the mill for processing.

Skidder hauling a hundred-foot white pine.

I had brought Dave to Canada as an assistant, someone to cook, clean, and stack firewood at the camp, but after a few weeks he said he was bored and wanted to work a chain saw. At first I refused. I had no intention of letting an eighteen-year-old, city-raised kid start wrestling ninety-foot-high trees with a chain saw. I had promised his mother I would bring him back to Utah alive and well, and missing no parts. After eight seasons of living in the Canadian bush, I had met too many lumberjacks who were maimed, crippled, or missing some of their parts. And they were the lucky ones—the others were dead.

Dave was persistent though. One night after I disassembled my saw to clean the carburetor and change the bar, he put it back together then sharpened the chain while I was out in the sauna. A week later, when watching me fell several trees, he begged to be allowed to de-limb the ones that were already down. Finally I gave in and told him he could have a go at de-limbing a big spruce that was laying on the perimeter of an area I had cut. Spruce have about ten times as many branches as red and white pines, and each branch is full of gummy sap that flies off the chain and sticks all over the person cutting it. I thought de-limbing a spruce or two might quell his enthusiasm to be a lumberjack.

On the contrary, he took to cutting timber like a duck to water. The spruce trees he had already figured out. After making a quick, clean job of removing the branches, he walked up to me all covered with sap and smiled, "We don't really have to de-limb the spruce you know. Luc just runs the wheels of his skidder along the trunks and the branches snap off like twigs. How about letting me do some red pines now?"

He was right. I had underestimated the kid. After just a few days in the bush, Dave could identify the various trees and most of the tricks to cutting them. He had noticed how Luc and Pierre saved us hours of work by de-limbing spruce trees with their tractor wheels, and also how they de-limbed white pines by dragging them through rough terrain that simply broke the frozen branches off at the trunks. Poplars had just a few limbs very high up, most of which were removed with a single cut when the tree was topped. Red pine boughs were stubborn though, and had to be removed one at a time with a chain saw. That became Dave's job. I told him to work along behind me at a safe distance, then cut tops off all the trees that I felled, and de-limb the red pines. Under no conditions was he to fell any trees—it was too dangerous.

Each morning as we climbed the hill behind the camp, I reemphasized the conditions under which he was to work. Pretty soon, though, I began to suspect my lectures were not sinking in. On a couple of occasions when I retraced my trail at lunchtime to where Dave was de-limbing, it appeared there were more trees down than I could recall having felled. One time, after dropping a big white pine, I shut off my chain saw and heard the crash of falling timber from the direction Dave was working. Later, when I questioned him about the noise, he flashed an awkward grin and told me that some of the red pine limbs were so big that when he cut them they sounded like an entire tree coming down.

Whatever doubts I still harbored about Dave felling trees were put to rest one afternoon as I returned to the lodge on a trail we seldom used. I had been working with Pierre, pulling choker cables from his skidder to the bottom of a steep ravine, where I attached them to fallen trees to be hauled up. While winching the trees out of the ravine, one of the chokers broke loose and sent a piece of steel cable flying into the cage of the skidder where Pierre was sitting at the controls. Fortunately, it missed him, but lodged itself underneath a shifting mechanism which jammed the transmission. The skidder was stuck in reverse.

I told Pierre that I would go to the camp and return with a hack saw and a torch to remove the broken cable. We were running low on daylight, but I knew of a shortcut that led from the bottom of the ravine, then up on a ridge overlooking the rapids near the lodge. Shadows were deepening by the minute so I left in a hurry. While crossing the top of the ridge, I caught a glimpse of something moving in a distant stand of trees. It was too large to be a lynx or even a wolf, but much smaller than a moose. Bears were all in hibernation and deer were very scarce in our area, but it could have been a deer. Quietly, I backtracked a few steps and crouched down low for another look. From behind the trunk of a huge red pine, in an area we had cut several days before, Dave suddenly appeared. He was walking slowly, circling the base of the tree, but he kept looking up into the branches as though counting or measuring something. Then he stepped back from the trunk four or five paces and reached down for an object in the snow. It was his chain saw.

By then, of course, I knew that Dave was going to fell the tree, but I was curious to see how he would do it. His chain saw had a short, fourteen-inch bar for trimming branches off trees, and here he was taking on a red pine forty inches in diameter and a hundred feet tall. It reminded me of another David—the one who fought Goliath with a slingshot.

He approached the tree confidently and began to cut wedges near the base, in the area where the trunk flares out to form the tree's root system. I was encouraged to see he understood the importance of cutting low; the tree was less likely to become a hazard by jumping off its stump, and also, when stacked in a pile to be measured by the buyer from the mill, it would bring more money. The only measurement that counted for much was the diameter of the butt.

From where I stood, about a hundred and fifty yards away, it was difficult to see how Dave managed to cut a big enough wedge with his short blade. But when he stepped back from the trunk, it was obvious he had removed about the right amount of wood. Several questions remained, however; had he correctly determined the tree's natural lean, and how the branch structure might affect its fall? Also, was he aware of the sloping ground on which he was cutting, and what effect other trees in close proximity might have? Nothing is more dangerous than a "hanger." Hangers occur when a tree is cut and falls into the branches of another, then remains there, leaning like an enormous deadfall trap. Pity the unwary soul who then wanders beneath it and becomes its victim. Every lumberjack has stories to tell about close calls with hangers.

Well, Dave was either real smart or very lucky. I suspect a little of each. He had made the right decision on where to notch the tree, then he walked around behind it and began cutting towards the notch from the opposite side. When he got within a few inches of the notch, which again required extra effort with the short blade, he hesitated momentarily and waited for the tree to bend slightly forward and rest on its hinge. The hinge is a narrow band of wood that remains intact in the center of the cut. Now he could be certain that the tree would fall in the direction he intended. As he proceeded to make his final cut, I heard the first loud crack as the few remaining fibers in the hinged area began to pop and tear from the weight of the tree as it fell. I was glad to see that he never turned his back or ran as the tree came crashing down. Neither did he stand too close or endanger himself by continuing to cut through the hinge. He switched off his saw, then cautiously backed away while keeping his eyes on the tree as it thundered to the ground. For several moments thereafter, pine cones, needles, and small branches continued raining down from neighboring trees whose slumber had been disturbed by the thrashing limbs of the magnificent red pine. When the woods were again quiet, Dave looked all around him like a child with his hand in the cookie jar. I suppressed the urge to call out and make my presence known; I wasn't sure whether to scold him for disobedience or congratulate him for a job well done. One thing was certain, the kid was a natural-born lumberjack.

Back at the lodge that night, I said nothing about what I had seen from the ridge top earlier in the day. The subject never came up. After Dave went to bed, I picked up his chain saw, cleaned the filters, and replaced the fourteen-inch bar with a new twenty-four-inch one.

I figured if he was intent on felling trees, he should at least have equipment that was up to the task.

We awoke the next morning to air that was bitterly cold. I had been up twice during the night to stoke the fire in the stove. On the second occasion I stepped outside to a spectacular display of northern lights, probably the best I had seen since the night that Whistler had paddled into our bay five years earlier. The sky was filled with towering columns of pink and blue light, shimmering like crystal above the frozen lake. The mirrored reflection of the aurora on the ice created a scene that was at once eerie and beautiful. I did not linger outdoors very long. Each breath was a lung-searing reminder of the extreme cold. When I exhaled, small clouds of frozen vapor hung around my head, turning my whiskers hoary with frost and nipping my ears and nose. It was the kind of cold that Luc said could freeze the sap inside a spruce tree "til it burst wide open."

As we climbed into our work clothes that morning, Dave asked me if I thought Luc and Pierre would show up for work. It was Saturday morning and there were plenty of logs to skid, but Luc had told us if the temperature ever hit forty below he would not come to work. Not that the cold bothered him personally, but at minus forty it could damage the machinery. At eight o'clock that morning the thermometer was holding at minus thirty-nine degrees.

"We won't know about Luc and Pierre unless we climb the hill and look for them," I said, handing Dave his chain saw. He noticed the long bar and new chain immediately, and he knew what it meant. Suppressing a smile, he reached out and grasped the handle of the saw with his left hand, then extended me his right. We shook hands, then walked from the cabin out into the woods without saying a word, but for the first time in weeks I knew we understood each other perfectly.

For several hours that morning we cut timber, waiting for Luc and Pierre to arrive and hoping the temperature would rise enough to allow them to skid some trees. We had almost 250 pines and poplars on the ground, but a forecast of snow threatened to bury them, making the job of getting them out much more difficult. At noon we lit a small fire by dousing a pile of branches and bark with diesel fuel, then we toasted our frozen ham and cheese sandwiches over the flames. The first day on the job with Luc and Pierre, we learned that all sandwiches eaten by true lumberjacks must first be toasted over a fire of spruce bark and pine boughs doused in diesel. It mattered not what lay between the slices of bread—bologna, cow tongue, or peanut butter—it must be toasted. Anything less was a breach of the lumberjack behavior code.

By the time we finished toasting our sandwiches, we could hear the growl of the skidders coming down the winter road. We ate in a hurry, as Luc and Pierre turned into the clearing and drove past our fire to start hauling timber.

Later that afternoon the temperature had warmed considerably as a south wind accompanied by heavy snow blew into our area. Luc and Pierre were working like mad to skid all the timber out to the road before it was buried. I was cutting trees in a big stand of poplar just over a small rise from where Dave was de-limbing several red pines. I had already laid down about a dozen trees and was cutting into the last one, when I noticed dark-colored chips of dry-rot flying off the blade of my saw.

Luc and Pierre had warned us about poplar trees and dry-rot. They said that poplars were the most dangerous to cut because of the difficulty in determining which way they would fall. Unlike pines, firs, and spruce, whose even-sized branches are distributed symmetrically up and down the length of the trunk, poplars have just a few heavy, odd-sized limbs clustered near the top of the tree. Miscalculating the size and weight of any single branch increased the likelihood of having the tree come down in a direction opposite that intended. Or even worse, the tree could tear completely off its stump and twist or spin as it fell, making it impossible to know which way to move to avoid being crushed. In a tree that has dry-rot, where the center is soft and punky from disease or age, the danger is further compounded. Not only will the tree fall in almost any direction, but the weakened limbs and branches might snap and come hurling down like hundred-pound boomerangs.

Luc had shown me how to identify poplar trees with dry-rot by looking for large toadstool like growths on their trunks. Once recognized, we would bypass the infected trees and move on to healthier ones. The method was not foolproof, however. The tree I had barely cut into showed no outward signs of dry-rot when I first inspected it. As I cut into its center, though, dark punky chips suddenly began to fly, and by then it was too late. Immediately I released the trigger on my saw and jumped backwards as the big tree shuddered and cracked, then began to fall. My first thought was to drop the saw and run, but the sound of breaking branches caused me to look up just in time to glimpse one of those hundred-pound boomerangs whirling at me through the air. I threw myself in the opposite direction of the tree's fall line, then felt a heavy, crushing blow as everything went black.

When I regained consciousness, I was lying in the snow on my side, dazed and weak with shock. My head was still reeling from the blow, and my hard hat, which I believe saved me, was lying an arm's length away near the heavy limb that had struck me. The poplar tree itself never hit the ground. After falling a short distance it had twisted and jumped off its stump, then caught in the branches of a nearby white pine, which no doubt hurled the broken limb in my direction. The tree was still leaning precariously on its neighbor, held up by a couple of rotting limbs that were intertwined with the branches of the healthy tree. Looking up from my hole in the snow, I could see the old poplar teetering on its bad leg, creaking and groaning like a wounded giant reminding me I was lucky to be alive. But perhaps not for long should the wind shift in its favor.

Slowly I raised myself to a sitting position to look for my chain saw and was jolted by a sharp biting pain high up on my left leg. I rolled over onto my right side then glanced backwards into the pocket of snow that had formed where my hip had been. It was soaked with blood. At the bottom of the pocket, sticking up through the crimson-colored snow, was the bloodied tip of my chain saw. Apparently it had still been running when the limb knocked me senseless and I had fallen on top of the blade, which tore through three layers of clothing and into the flesh on the outside of my left thigh. Using my teeth, I pulled the glove from my left hand and reached for the wound. As my fingers probed through the ragged hole in my clothes, I felt the warm stickiness of blood trickling down my thigh.

There is nothing neat or pretty about a chain saw wound. It is neither a cut nor a slice. When it meets with flesh, a chain saw rips, tears, and mutilates. The gash in my thigh was about four inches long and half an inch deep, but the manner in which the flesh had been parted and torn was ghastly. The saw's teeth had removed so much meat from the area between the undamaged skin, I had doubts about stitching it up even if we had sutures available.

The blood continued to flow from the wound so I packed it with snow through the tear in my clothing, then removed my wool shirt and wrapped it tightly around my leg just above the cut and tied a stout knot with the sleeves. It made a crude sort of tourniquet, but nonetheless it slowed the bleeding. I rose to my feet feeling dizzy and nauseous, but the pain in my thigh had been numbed completely by the snow packed over the wound. Once again I looked upward at the huge, leaning poplar as a gust of wind made it rattle and moan, reminding me I was still in harm's way. Hoisting the chain saw in my right hand and clutching a dead branch in my left to use as a walking stick, I hobbled over the rise towards the sound of my partner's saw.

Dave was still busy de-limbing the last of the red pines he had down when I limped out of the trees into his small clearing. As usual, he was wearing his earphones, listening to "music to chain saw by," and never saw my approach. I sat down on the stump of the tree he was trimming, and waited for him to finish. It's bad business to startle a person who is operating a chain saw alone in the bush.

After cutting the last branch Dave turned off his saw, but continued to mimic and hum along with the sound of the steel guitar on his Walkman. He held up his chain saw then spun around wildly, picking and strumming it like Jimi Hendrix in a snowmobile suit. When he saw me he stopped abruptly.

"What's up, boss?" he asked casually, as though strumming a chain saw was an everyday occurrence.

"I've had an accident," I said pointing to the rip in my pant leg. When Dave got a close look at the ragged wound and blood-soaked clothing his eyes got big and he dropped his saw to the ground as though it were on fire.

"That's the ugliest gash I've ever seen," he exclaimed.

I nodded my head in agreement, then told him to go and find Luc and bring back the first aid kit he kept under the seat of his skidder. As Dave disappeared into the trees, I felt pretty stupid to be sending the kid who wasn't old enough to de-limb red pines out for help.

Fifteen minutes later Luc, Pierre, and Dave all came racing back through the trees as if being chased by a bear. Luc, a very strong, tall, long-legged man was the first to reach me. When he bent down to inspect my wound, small clouds of vapor exploded from his lungs as his chest heaved for air. Suddenly he threw his head back and started to laugh. He turned to Pierre who was standing behind him holding the first aid kit and said, "It's only a scratch. The way young Dave talked, I thought he'd cut off his leg."

As they closed up the wound with butterfly bandages, gauze, and tape, I was actually relieved to hear them joke about what an insignificant injury I had sustained.

Pierre set to building a fire for warmth, then sat down on a log and began to roll up the leg of his coveralls. When it reached above his knee he pulled up his long johns revealing a jagged red scar that ran from his shin to the top of his kneecap.

165

"Now that's a wound," Pierre grinned with obvious pride. "But not so bad as Luc," he said, deferring to the older lumberjack. "Show 'em a real wound, Luc."

Once Luc had finished bandaging me, he repacked the first aid kit and handed it to Pierre. Then he unzipped the top of his coveralls and stretched the neck of his undershirt, to unveil a mean-looking scar which ran parallel to his collar-bone for several inches, then out over his right shoulder. Where it ended was not obvious; he left that to our imaginations.

After joking for a few minutes about old wounds and close calls, Luc became serious and told us how his younger brother had died, pinned to the ground by a big white pine. "It was a hanger that killed him, three days before Christmas near Val d'Or. I could see by the marks in the snow that he did not die quickly. Andre was a tough but good-natured kid," he said looking at Dave as if making a comparison. "He struggled to free himself for a time—perhaps calling out to me for help—but I could not hear for the noise of my chain saw. By the time I found him, he was dead."

For a long moment a suffocating silence hung over our fire like a shroud as the four of us stared at each other through the smoke and ashes. Then Luc pulled a smoldering branch from the flames and stirred some snow into the embers making them sputter and hiss. "It happened a long time ago on a job up north, but that doesn't make it any easier. I took Andre home for Christmas, but there was no celebration at our house that year. His death nearly killed my parents. Andre was their baby, the youngest of seven."

In conclusion, Luc pointed the smoking branch at my bandaged leg and said, "Be careful my friend: this is dangerous work we do." Then he stood and marched off through the snow toward his skidder.

Never again did I feel a need to caution or lecture Dave about the perils of cutting timber. From that day on he took the work very seriously and even left his Walkman at the camp. Both of us gained a new respect for Luc and Pierre and the men who spend their lives toiling as lumberjacks. It is a profession whose reputation has become somewhat tarnished in the past decade or two. Perhaps technology is to blame. With the invention of chain saws and heavy machinery many forests have been altered or annihilated with little thought for the future. In our case, however, the lumber mill that cut and harvested trees along the winter road spent nearly a year transplanting and reforesting over a million young trees that will someday supply another generation with homes, furniture, and other products. By building a small but serviceable road, the mill opened up an area that was formerly inaccessible to anything but a few snowmobiles. Now people can drive to a trail head that is only a fifteen-minute hike to Grande Chutes. Before the road existed, not more than a handful of people were even aware of the spectacular waterfall.

The lumber mill is the lifeblood of several small communities in the region. It provides jobs for people like Luc and Pierre who wish to remain in the bush and raise their families in a rural setting. Too many people whose ties to the north go back over a hundred years have been forced to move south to work in the urban sprawl of Toronto, Montreal, or Ottawa.

Luc often recalled the old days when lumberjack festivals were held in his hometown. Loggers would gather from all over the area to celebrate, compete, and demonstrate the skills of their trade. The winners of those competitions were often the most highly esteemed individuals in the community, but now those days are gone and the timber industry is under attack. Some of its most vocal opponents are people who benefit, at least indirectly, from the goods it produces. I love and appreciate forests and wilderness, and I raise my voice in protest to greed and mismanagement of resources wherever it occurs, but for Luc and Pierre and the people whose livelihoods depend on the harvesting of trees I have no contempt. On the contrary, the opportunity I had to spend a winter alongside them gave me a lasting appreciation for people

Pierre, Luc, Dave, and Scott eating diesel-grilled sandwiches.

167

who labor long and hard, seven days a week, with no complaint. They live simply and find pleasure in even the smallest of things. Pierre would spend the entire lunch break watching the antics of a squirrel wrestling with a marshmallow he had suspended from a pine bough with a piece of string. When lunch was over the squirrel was always rewarded for entertaining us with a piece of bread or a cracker from Pierre's lunch box.

Like their Courier de Bois ancestors, Luc and Pierre were born to the out-of-doors. They worked tirelessly under conditions of extreme heat, severe cold, or with clouds of black flies and mosquitos buzzing their heads. Both were quick to laugh but slow to anger, and I seldom heard them criticize or find fault with anyone. They were independent men who took full responsibility for themselves and their families. To whine and complain, or to blame others for circumstances either within or beyond their control, was not a part of their nature. They descended from generations of men and women, both native and French Canadian, who were as much a part of the land as the fox, the bear, and the caribou. They played an important role in the opening up and the development of Canada as a nation. In the Canada of today, however, the lumberjack has an increasingly smaller role and his future is uncertain.

In mid-February Dave and I finished our work in Quebec, then closed up the camp and headed for warmer climes. Dave was yearning to attend a rock concert and eat a Big Mac after surviving for several months on beans, oatmeal, and diesel-grilled sandwiches. I was looking forward to seeing my family and meeting my two-and-a-half-month old daughter, Katie, who had been born on December first, half a continent away. When Luc and Pierre learned that I was the proud father of three daughters they laughed good-naturedly and called me "Many Filles." It was a sobriquet that stuck throughout the winter; "Many Filles has a broken chain saw; Many Filles has cut himself; Many Filles looks tired and hungry."

We said good-bye to Luc and Pierre, who had given us a ride in their skidders out the winter road to Chester LaForest's farm where my station wagon was parked. As Dave and I packed gear into the vehicle, Luc asked me about California and how long it would take to drive there and if I thought he should make a visit sometime. I smiled at the thought of the big lumberjack standing on the beach at Malibu, wearing sunglasses and bright-colored shorts with logger boots on his feet. Somehow, I could picture him in a swimsuit showing his battle scars to the surfers and their scantily clad girlfriends, but I could not imagine him without his logger boots—they were too much a part of his repertoire.

"Of course you should visit California, Luc," I said with a laugh. "Weaving in and out through the bush in your skidder has prepared you well for driving on a Los Angeles freeway."

After a final handshake, we jump-started the frozen Volare, which sputtered and coughed as oily smoke spewed from its tailpipe. I took a seat behind the controls, then looked across the cockpit at my co-pilot Dave, who was happily adjusting his headset after plugging it into the cigarette lighter. I could hear the heavy metallic beat of steel guitar and bass drum arcing back and forth between his earphones as we taxied out toward the highway. Less than a mile down the road his eyes glazed over and his jaw went slack; he had reached nirvana. I turned the radio dial to 96.1 FM and cranked the CBC up as loud as it would go. I knew we were in for a long, turbulent ride.

Six-year-old Jenny with a 9 lb. pike.

❧ Dam Update

Friday, July 10, 1998
Kipawa River Lodge (Topping's Camp), 2:30 P.M.

Two Hydro Quebec consultants (Gilles, a hydrologist, and Jean, a fisheries's biologist) visit the lodge to ask permission to launch a boat this afternoon. They want to set out nets for the summer segment of their fisheries study. I give permission, but question the value and timing of studying fish and habitat when only 5 or 6 cubic meters per second is coming down the river. If they want to get a true reading on fish, they should set their nets when the river is running near its average level of 76 cms. That is when the walleye, pike, whitefish, and lake trout come to the mouth of the river in schools. On several occasions when the river is flowing between 50–75 cmc I have descended with scuba gear (accompanied by Ron Huywan, a divemaster and scuba instructor from North Bay), and seen dozens of pike, walleye, bass, and whitefish feeding in the current. But today, with the gates at Laniel shut off entirely and only 5 cms seeping underneath the dam, I expect the fisheries consultants will catch mostly suckers and ling.

At 5:30 P.M. two men from Laniel arrive at the lodge with a boat and several nets. One of them is Serge Plante, a native of Fabre who helped us recover the victims of the St. John's disaster twenty years ago. Serge informed me that he was here in April setting nets on behalf of the HQ study but they only caught a few whitefish, some cisco, and one lake trout. "Not much walleye here," he said. I told Serge he was at least a month too early. The walleye in this part of Lake Temiskaming spawn in late May and early June because of its depth and cold water.

The next morning Serge and his partner return to the camp to retrieve their nets. The hundred-footer, which was placed directly in the mouth of the river, has a three-pound pike and a four-pound walleye. Each of the two-hundred-foot nets placed along opposite banks about three hundred yards out from the river mouth contains several suckers, ling, and a few small walleye and one seven-pound pike.

I do not believe the study to be a very precise or serious attempt to assess the impact that diverting the Kipawa River will have on fisheries at its mouth. To the contrary, I offer the results of my own twenty-four-year study of fisheries at the mouth of the Kipawa River—when the current is average to high.

Scott with a 15 lb. lake trout.

Becky and Kate displaying their 10 lb. walleye.

Michelle holding an 11 lb. lake trout.

"When the current's high the fishing's great.
Doug Sorensen and a 7 lb. lake trout.

Vic using a come-along and a cant hook.

Chapter 19

BUILDING WITH LOGS

If you have built castles in the air,
your work need not be lost:
That is where they should be.
Now put the foundations under them.
—Henry David Thoreau

When I was a boy most of my friends talked of becoming astronauts, presidents, or professional baseball players. I dreamed of becoming a cowboy, pirate, or Indian chief. Now that I am a responsible, middle-aged adult, I lean more toward Indian chief; however, certain aspects of cowboy and pirate still hold a definite, if not irresistible, appeal.

At the impressionable age of ten I read a book about a frontiersman who trekked off into the wilderness, cleared some land, then built a cabin out of logs for his family. He struggled, worked, and overcame numerous hardships, but in the end he lived happily ever after. To me it seemed so simple and right.

Throughout the ensuing years as I attended high school and university and watched my peers becoming doctors, dentists, lawyers, and soldiers in Vietnam, I never forgot that man who built a cabin in the woods and, at least in my mind, lived happily ever after. In a world fraught with turmoil, upheaval, and unrest, he seemed to have all of the answers.

The spring of 1984 found Pat, our three daughters, and me back on the shores of Lake Temiskaming preparing to build our cabin in the woods. My younger brother Vic, a refugee of civilization, joined us once again. Having graduated from high school, Vic packed a duffel bag, a fifty-dollar guitar, and then fled life in the city like a rat from rising water.

When we arrived at the lodge in May, I showed my family the pile of fifty-foot logs that Luc had neatly laid out on a skidway near the tennis court the previous winter. "Here's our new cabin," I said gesturing toward the small mountain of wood. The logs appeared to be much larger in May than they had back in January when we had the skidder to drag them around like pieces of kindling. "All we have to do is stack them up in a big square then cut out the windows and doors."

Victor and Pat were very quiet as they circled the imposing pile of wood, marveling at the size and length of each massive red pine log. Vic, a stout and husky lad, approached the pile and put his shoulder underneath the butt end of a particularly large log which was resting on top of the pile. He stooped slightly like a power lifter doing a squat and attempted to raise it up. The log never moved. Seven-year-old April scrambled to the top of the heap and exclaimed, "These logs are huge Daddy! How are you going to move them?" By their continued silence I could tell that my wife and younger brother were wondering the same thing. I walked across the lawn and disappeared briefly into the old icehouse, then returned holding a couple of odd-looking tools that resembled a pair of ice tongs attached to the end of a pick handle. "We'll move the logs with these. They're called cant hooks and Luc showed me how to use them last winter."

"Are you joking?" Victor laughed as he took one of the tools and examined it skeptically. "Maybe that old lumberjack was teasing you and told you these are called cant hooks because you can't move anything at all with them, let alone a two-thousand-pound pine tree."

Vic had worked the previous summer for a landscaper and was accustomed to moving large objects with a tractor or backhoe. His experience had left him woefully unprepared for the life of a frontiersman. At least I had April on my side. She looked at me with youthful adoration and proclaimed, "Don't worry, Uncle Vic. My daddy's the strongest man in the world. He can move those logs with one hand tied behind his back."

Her remark drew muffled laughter from Uncle Vic. He walked past me with a derisive grin on his face. "I hope you don't disappoint April by using both hands when you move those logs, Daddy," he laughed, as he shuffled off toward the lodge to get his fishing pole.

I had read several books on log cabin building the previous winter, and what I lacked in actual experience, I made up for in confidence and enthusiasm. I had also taken a course from Barry Story, one of northern Ontario's master log home builders. Barry advised me not to build too big on my first attempt. "It's easy to get discouraged if you bite off more than you can chew," he cautioned. I ignored his advice because I thought it might be my only attempt, and I wanted to build as big as my imagination and the length of my logs would allow. He also strongly recommended the use of a tractor with a front-end loader for moving and lifting the logs. Especially if they were red pines. "Red pines," he explained, "are strong and straight, but heavier than lead." Barry preferred white pines for various reasons; white pines don't shrink as much when they dry, the bark is easier to remove, and they generally have less taper between the butt and the top, making them easier to fit when notching the corners. Nonetheless, I had a pile of the largest and finest red pines in northern Quebec. They were handpicked from a selected group of twenty-five hundred trees cut the previous winter. I was raring to go.

Concerning the use of a tractor, I neglected once again to follow Barry's admonition. It seemed to me that using a large mechanical device (such as a tractor with a front-end loader), would violate the frontiersmen's code of ethics for log cabin building. No doubt I had already violated the code by using a chain saw to harvest the logs, and a skidder to drag them down to my building site. However, I did not intend to further disgrace myself by using a tractor. Every man has a limit to what he will do—a line he will not cross. My particular limit was insufficient funds with which to purchase a tractor. That was precisely the reason I had invited my brother Vic to spend the summer with us; he was a source of cheap sibling labor. I had seen it work with the Helm brothers, Jake and Harley. As long as Jake supplied Harley with plenty of whiskey, the work got done. Unlike Harley though, Vic was a sober and temperate young man to whom whiskey held no allure. Nonetheless, he had a weakness, an Achilles' heel that I intended to exploit. He loved to fish. It mattered not what type of fishing—trolling, angling, or casting a fly. As long as he could spend his evenings out in a boat with a fishing rod in his hands, he would work all day like a slave.

We spent the latter part of May and the first two weeks of June peeling bark from the logs that were stacked on the skidway. Certain logs could be peeled with relative ease. It they were wet with sap we would use a spud, a long chisel-shaped tool that digs beneath the bark and pries it off in big, wide slabs. Working with the spuds we could girdle an entire log and have it debarked in fifteen to twenty minutes. On the other hand, if the bark was dry and flaky we would use a drawknife or a short-handled spade with the tip of the blade squared off and filed down to a sharp edge. Pushing the spade or pulling the drawknife up and down the length of the log would chip the bark off in small feathery pieces. Debarking a red pine in this manner was a tedious hour-long project that left our backs aching and our hands blistered.

One afternoon while Vic and I were hacking away on a particularly stubborn log, a group of teenaged canoeists from a youth camp near Temagami stopped to get a drink from our spring. As the young men sat and sipped the cool, refreshing water in the shade of a large balsam fir, they questioned us about our project. Simultaneously, it occurred to Vic and me that with a few well-chosen words we might succeed at the old Tom Sawyer whitewashing game. I told the kids we were peeling logs for a new cabin and that it was an ancient, nearly forgotten craft perfected by Canadian pioneers, men of such strength, stamina, and stature it would be hard to find their equal in today's society. "Nowadays, it's mostly done by machine, but the old way is better. Doing it by hand not only makes a finer cabin, it builds strong character."

At that juncture Vic piped in. "Not just any old Joe off the street can peel a log the way it ought to be done. It takes a well-trained eye and a supple wrist to make the bark fly in the right manner." Then, with a powerful thrust of his shovel he sent chips whirling from the log like a hatch of hungry locusts.

"I betcha I can do it," chirped a slender, knobby-kneed lad who looked about fourteen years old.

"I doubt it," Vic replied after sizing him up. "You don't look strong enough to me. You'd probably quit halfway through the job." Then he turned back to his task, knowing the gauntlet had been thrown.

"I can do it, Mister! Hand over that shovel and stand aside," screeched the boy, anxious to prove himself.

Vic reluctantly offered him the shovel as though it truly grieved him to quit debarking logs even for a moment. In his eagerness to make a good showing, the skinny kid had bark flying in all directions. "If you get too tired just give the shovel back," said Vic. "I was hoping to get three or four logs done before dinner."

"If he gets too tired, I'll take a turn," cried a red-haired, freckle-faced youth wearing a cap adorned with dozens of pins and badges.

At that point I relinquished my spade to him, then hustled to the shed to get more tools. When I returned carrying three shovels, four spuds, and a drawknife, the boys were all in a pioneering spirit, clamoring for a chance to peel logs and build character.

For over an hour Vic and I relaxed in the shade of the balsam fir, sipping a cup of cool, refreshing spring water. We were impressed at the stamina, strength, and enthusiasm displayed by those young men.

"You're lucky you caught them on the third week of our expedition," commented their twenty-year-old leader, who walked over and sat down beside us in the shade. "You wouldn't have had any takers in this bunch two weeks ago when we started our trip." He explained that the group was fairly typical of most the boys that sign up for the thirty-day wilderness experience. They come from places like Toronto, Detroit, and Philadelphia, and most of them don't even know which end of the sleeping bag to climb into on the first night. Their parents pay a lot of money to give them the chance to cook over fires, sleep in tents, and paddle canoes around northern Canada. Many of these kids have been pampered and indulged all their lives, but this experience gives them a different outlook and a change of attitude. There's something about stepping out of a Mercedes and into a cedar-strip canoe and paddling around in the wilds for a month that gives them a whole new perspective. I know. I came here from Atlanta six years ago when I was fourteen and I've been back every year since."

He told us how the first week is the most difficult for the young men. They complain about blisters, sore muscles, grueling portages, and not having television or video games to entertain them at night. On week number two most of them are reticent, having resigned themselves to thirty days of hell. By the third week they become hardened to the discomforts around them and begin to feel the satisfaction and self-confidence of knowing they are tough enough to handle what seemed incredibly difficult just two weeks before. When week number four rolls around they are sad to see their adventure coming to an end and talk about how it was the best four weeks of their life. "When their parents return to pick them up they are often surprised at how much their son has changed. The boy shakes his father's hand and gives his mother a hug, then opens the door of the Mercedes for her. Some of the parents are so impressed they sign their kid up for next summer right on the spot. 'You've worked miracles with my boy' is a common response as they hand me a hefty tip."

The young men got so involved peeling bark we invited them to stay for dinner and spend the night at the lodge. Even their leader seemed to be enjoying the brief respite from paddling, so instead of pushing on to the camp at the Indian Portage three miles south on Lake Temiskaming, he accepted our invitation.

April and Jenny hung around for about an hour, happy to have some big brother types to talk to and banter with. But when two of the young men began teasing them about being 'a couple of scrawny munchkins,' they took offense and wandered off toward the river. The trip leader overheard the innocuous remark and told the two offenders to lay down their spuds and go pitch all six of their tents and unload the canoes. Vic and I felt that, compared to peeling bark, pitching tents was a reward. The leader assured us however, that setting up tents was considered punishment for bad behavior or slacking off, and that those two culprits had done more than their share of it. I invited them to pitch their tents on the grass inside the old tennis court, which is the most level and least bumpy ground on the property.

During dinner April and Jenny were unusually quiet. They gulped down their food in five minutes, then asked to be excused to go out and play.

"Don't you want a slice of rhubarb pie?" Pat asked them.

"No thanks, Mom. We're working on a secret project down by the river and scrawny boys aren't allowed," they taunted the two "evil-eyed" tent pitchers sitting across the table. Then they scuttled out the back door.

I assumed April and Jenny were just making some improvements on their fort, which was actually a lean-to made out of old boards and plywood scraps set up against the trunk of an immense, hundred-year-old white pine. I was wrong in my assumption. The two little hooligans had spent the afternoon in the marsh catching frogs until they had gathered about four dozen of the bug-eyed amphibians inside an old bait bucket.

After dinner they retrieved the bucket from where it lay hidden behind their fort, and proceeded directly to the tennis court, unzipped one of the tents and released all forty-eight frogs inside. Then they zipped the door shut and ran like the dickens back to their fort by the river. April and Jenny assumed they had placed the frogs in the tent that belonged to the "evil" boys that had teased them earlier that day. After all, they had watched their two tormenters setting up a bright red, two-man tent in the tennis court just before dinner when they were plotting their revenge. Now it was payback time.

As the ten young men and their leader walked from the Main Lodge back to the tennis court, April and Jenny hid themselves in the trees behind the River Cabin fifty feet away from the tents. The sun had set half an hour earlier but the evening sky was still aglow from lingering rays of sunlight reflecting off the clouds far to the west. Smug and confident in their hideout, the girls watched with eager anticipation as the two young men entered the tennis court and proceeded to a dark blue tent just opposite the one that was full of frogs.

180

"What are they doing?" April whispered to her five-year-old sister who was crouching ever lower behind a dense honeysuckle bush.

"I don't know, but that's the wrong tent," Jenny observed with growing apprehension.

As soon as the two "evil" boys had entered the blue tent and the other eight youths had settled into their respective tents, the twenty-year-old leader appeared at the tennis court with a lantern. He checked each of the tents by calling out the boy's names, then marched directly to the bright red, frog-infested tent.

"Now what is he doing? That is not his tent!" April contended with rapt indignation as they watched him unzip the flap and crawl inside.

"I'm getting out of here; it's past my bedtime," Jenny intoned as she turned and began slinking through the trees like a fox leaving a henhouse.

Suddenly the stillness of the evening was shattered by a bloodcurdling scream that resonated out over Lake Temiskaming. It was a scream that could only be described as two parts anger and three parts surprise.

Several years later, when April determined that the "statute of limitations" had long since expired, she confessed to the crime and gave a detailed account of the remarkable scene that unfolded before her eyes that night. Moments after the scream emanated from the red tent, there appeared ten wild-eyed faces from the openings of the other five tents. Like prairie dogs rousted from their burrows by the hiss of a rattlesnake, the boys watched in wonderment as small low-flying objects came whirling out through the doorway of their leader's brightly lit tent. At first the tiny objects came flying out in a rapid succession of pairs and even sets of threes, but eventually the rate decreased to just one at a time every few moments. Even more amazing was the manner in which the objects leaped and caterwauled like grasshoppers on a hot griddle as soon as they hit the ground. The scene played itself out after three or four minutes when the leader ran out of projectiles and profanities to hurl through the opening of his tent. But the excitement was far from over. Wearing a dark, hooded sweatshirt, with eyes glowing like crimson embers, the distraught man emerged from the tent looking like the grim reaper. His chest was heaving like a bellows as deep, raspy breaths exploded from his lungs. When his gaze finally focused on the terror-stricken boys in the blue tent, he lunged in their direction. Instantaneously, their heads disappeared inside their tent and the camp fell silent as death.

"Get out here!" roared the leader as the boys quietly cowered inside, feigning sleep. "I'm going to count to three and if you're not out of that tent, I'm coming in after you. One, Two . . . ."

"But we're in our underwear," squealed one of the boys in a frightened, high-pitched voice.

"So much the better. Now get out here. Three!"

There was a sudden flurry of movement inside the tent, then the door unzipped and out jumped the "evil" ones in a state of near undress. Standing at attention, quivering in their boxer shorts, the two beguiled youths were sharply berated for putting frogs in their leader's tent.

"How could you be so stupid as to do it on the very night I assigned you tent duty? You two are on latrine detail for the rest of the trip."

While the two innocent offenders meekly crawled back inside their tent, April beat a silent but swift retreat down the trail toward the Main Lodge. She overtook Jenny about halfway there. "Serves them right for calling us scrawny munchkins," she said, reveling in victory.

"Yeah, serves them right!" Jenny parroted her older sister, as they clasped hands and vowed to carry their secret with them to the grave.

Quietly they tiptoed through the back door of the Main Lodge and climbed into their beds, fully clothed and ready for reprisal. As least they would not be caught in their underwear like the "evil" ones. Out on the lake a solitary loon chorused its lonesome wail across deep water, "T-e-m-i-s-k-a-m-i-n-g," it cried. Within minutes both girls were soundly sleeping, content and reassured that justice still prevailed on the banks of the Kipawa River.

The two "scrawny munchkins."

By June 15 the logs were completely debarked and ready to be cut and fit. Vic and I began the first round by rolling a pair of enormous base logs down from the skidway and onto a set of four corner posts which would act as temporary footings for the construction of the log walls. This was not the actual building site. It was my intention to assemble the four walls on a level, grassy area right beside the skidway, rather than attempt to move the logs by hand to the permanent location on top of a rocky knoll overlooking the rapids. The knoll was nearly a hundred yards away and much of that distance was uphill over rough, uneven ground. Once the log walls were built, I planned to bring a large farm tractor with a front-end loader down the logging road and transport the entire structure one log at a time, over to the river.

"You must be crazy," Victor objected. "You want to build the cabin right here by the tennis court, then move the whole thing over to the river. This is foolishness; I'm going fishing."

I figured that once Vic thoroughly understood the logistics and difficulty of moving the logs, he would come around to the idea of constructing the walls next to the skidway. Especially in a few weeks when the walls were eight or nine rounds high and each log had to be raised ten feet above the ground. Furthermore, Vic would not likely be present for the task of relocating and reassembling the building anyway. As the summer progressed and the enormity of the project became more apparent, I concluded we would not have the structure ready to move onto its permanent foundation until sometime the following year.

Starting the fourth round.

After the base logs were in place, we rolled two additional red pines from the skidway and positioned them perpendicular to the base logs, forming a thirty-four-foot-by-thirty-four-foot square. It was beginning to look like a building. I cut saddle notches with my chain saw near each end of this second pair of logs so they would fit tight and secure at the corners where they overlapped the base logs.

Having completed the first round, I proudly walked on top of the logs from corner to corner, imagining what the cabin would someday look like sitting on top of the knoll with the rapids thundering past just twenty feet below. It was a great moment. I could envision the finished product right down to the log railings running the length of the covered decks facing the Kipawa River on the south and Lake Temiskaming on the west. Perhaps my exuberance would have been dampened a bit had I known the project was going to require three more summers to complete.

With the first four logs in place, I set out to determine the location of the windows and doors. By planning the main entry door near the center of the west-facing wall, I was able to use several twenty-foot half logs and save my straightest forty-footers to span walls and decks where there were no windows or doors. The same held true when we reached window level on the third and fourth rounds. Each wall was broken up by the placement of two or more windows which required much shorter logs in between the various apertures.

Before starting the second round of logs, I trained Vic in the use of a scribe. The scribe is a tool that resembles a large drafting compass. It has an indelible pencil attached to its upper arm and a pair of levels positioned on top, and is used to mark or "scribe" a narrow section of wood to be removed from the underside of each log. Once the log has been scribed, the wood is removed with a chain saw. This process is what gives the structure a nearly airtight fit between each round of logs. The invention of the scribe and the chain saw has revolutionized the craft of building with logs.

By the middle of August we were working on the eighth round of logs and the walls were about nine feet high. Only two rounds remained, but they proved to be the most difficult. Up until that point we had been able to roll the full-length logs up a skidway using cant hooks for leverage and small wooden wedges for blocks. The short, sectional logs that fit in between windows and doors we were able to lift by hand or with the use of a block and tackle. Now we were faced with the daunting task of lifting eight full-length logs, each weighing about a ton, ten feet off the ground to bridge the window and door openings on each wall.

"I'm going fishing," shrugged Victor as he eyed the remaining logs. "Just give me a holler when you get this all figured out. Sure would be nice to have a tractor right now."

Watching him trudge off toward the lake, I sensed my younger brother was still struggling with my rigid adherence to the frontiersmen's code of ethics. The building process had been doggedly slow and labor intensive. On a good day we were able to lift, scribe, cut, and fit a single log. On an average day we did less, and on a bad day none at all. There were always interruptions, which included trips to town for supplies, broken equipment, bad weather, and so forth. Nonetheless, Vic had been a tireless, congenial, even-tempered worker from day one. He was as steady and stalwart as a plow horse and mature beyond his eighteen years. Our daughters adored him. Every night he would strum his guitar and sing them to sleep with his impersonation of Willie Nelson performing The Redheaded Stranger, or his eloquent version of Elton John's Texas Love Song. Perhaps their favorite though was Vic's rendition of Don Quixote, by Gordon Lightfoot. No children have fonder memories of being serenaded at night with a sweet refrain than do our daughters. In a day and age where knights in shining armor are few and far between, the fair damsels who reside on the banks of the Kipawa River have come to expect nothing less.

Eventually we raised the final eight logs by using a pair of come-alongs suspended from fifteen-foot upright poplar poles set on each corner of the building. It was another tedious, time consuming job, but as I said to Vic, " What is time to a person living on the shores of Lake Temiskaming?"

In September when the final log was scribed, cut, and rolled into place, the four walls had the look of a cabin. When we closed the camp down for the winter, I found myself stopping in between chores and admiring the massive log structure that had slowly materialized out on our back lawn over the past three months. It had been another good summer. While loading the boat in preparation for our final trip of the season down the lake, an early flock of geese appeared high above the bay. Like an arrow on a compass, they formed a perfect V as they honked their way south toward the Everglades. I wondered if the geese were like me, hesitant to leave and already looking forward to the return of spring.

⚜   ⚜   ⚜

The summer of 1985 began with digging. After opening up the lodge, I attacked the rocky knoll overlooking the rapids with a pick and shovel. My goal was to dig a dozen holes down to bedrock into which I would pour cement footings for my foundation. The vast majority of the weight in a log building is in the outside walls. Barry Story, my building instructor, had suggested I put a well-grounded cement pier every eight feet along the base of each wall. Fortunately, I hit bedrock at about three feet in the area I was digging.

Next I built a dozen two-foot square forms out of plywood, then filled each form with cement up to ground level. The cement I brought in by boat from Ville Marie in ninety-pound bags, then mixed it in a wheelbarrow with water, sand, and gravel from the beach in front of the Main Lodge. I kept the mixture dry enough to pack like a good, slushy snowball. The twelve foundation holes required about forty wheelbarrow loads of cement, to which I added rock and Rebar for strength.

Because the rocky knoll had such rough, uneven terrain, ground level for the holes varied as much as five to six feet in elevation. This discrepancy I corrected by building piers of cement blocks on top of each footing to an equal height above the ground. Each pier was also reinforced with cement and Rebar. Hence, the lowest corner of the building had a six-foot-high pier underneath the foundation log, while the highest corner sat on a one-foot-high pier. The other two corners were perched on three-and four-foot-high piers respectively. I determined the height of the other eight piers by using a line level suspended from a taut string running from corner to corner. Getting the holes dug and filled with cement, then building the piers consumed the month of June. At least I could say it was all done by hand, in strict adherence to the frontiersmen's code of ethics. Daniel Boone and Davy Crockett would certainly have given me their nod of approval. But my next move would have them rolling over in their graves.

On July fourth, my friend and closest neighbor, Claude Langevin, came barreling down the logging road in his big four-wheel-drive tractor. We would spend the next two days moving the log walls from their temporary footing near the old tennis court to the permanent foundation overlooking the river. Before disassembling the walls, I carefully numbered every log using different colors of crayon on each corner. It would not bode well to mix up any of the logs because each one was custom cut to fit the contours of the log below it.

Using the bucket on his front-end loader like a small crane, Claude was able to disassemble the four log walls in a couple of hours. As soon as he laid a log on the ground, Pat filled the lateral groove that had been scribed and cut on the underside with narrow strips of fiberglass insulation. The strips were held in place with staples and would insure an airtight seam in between each round of logs when we reassembled the building on its permanent foundation.

By nightfall Claude had transported the first three rounds of logs over to the rocky knoll and set them in place atop the cement piers. I was impressed at the skill with which he maneuvered the big tractor up the rocky knoll, over and in between huge boulders, balancing the two-thousand-pound logs all the while on the bucket of his front-end loader. When the tractor drew alongside the foundation piers, Claude would lower the bucket and set the log in place, as precisely and gently as laying a baby in a cradle. Working with him over the span of ten years, I was constantly amazed at the innate genius he demonstrated in matters mechanical and physical. He was a jack-of-all-trades—welder, mechanic, lumberjack, farmer, veterinarian, electrician, refrigeration specialist, chain saw repairman, to name a few. I presented him with numerous challenges, many of which had me completely baffled, but I never saw him thwarted. I can hardly count the number of times we were in the middle of some difficult task or project when he would stop and show me a faster, safer, more logical way of accomplishing it. Most of our communication was done in sign language. Claude is not deaf, but he speaks very little English. I speak even less French. We used a combination of hand gestures, pantomime, and laughter, useful tools in overcoming a language barrier.

Claude moving the walls one log at a time.

The following day Claude transported the remaining seven rounds (twenty-eight logs) to the rocky knoll and finished reassembling the structure. Then, before returning to his farm, he hoisted three more fifty-foot red pines on top of the building to be used as purlins and ridgepole to support the rafters and roof. The twenty-four foot-long rafter beams I collected here and there along the shores of the lake and brought in by boat. Then, just when I needed some extra hands, my dad and two brothers, Dan and Doug, flew in from Utah in Dad's light plane. For ten days we peeled bark, hoisted rafters, and very cautiously raised the purlins and ridgepole into place. The two-thousand-pound ridgepole had to be set atop two thirteen-foot vertical beams rising up from the second story. Getting it up and into position was a precarious, nerve-wracking, high-wire act. At one point, when a pulley slipped and the ridgepole suddenly dropped two feet, the four of us dove for cover beneath the two-by-tens and empty gas drums we were using for scaffolding. Three hours later, after hoisting with levers, come-alongs, and block and tackle, we breathed a collective sigh of relief when the ridgepole slid into place twenty-five feet above ground level.

Ten days later, after my dad and brother Dan flew back to Utah, Doug and I brought in a boatload of one inch milled lumber to use for the roof. It was a job that would have taken us the better part of a week, but a boatload of good friends from Cobalt, Haileybury, and New Liskeard showed up and the roof was raised in a day. Doug and I spent the final four days of the season tacking down rolls of graveled tar paper to protect the new roof from the weather. And right on cue, as we laid the last roll of roofing along the peak of the building, a skiff of early snow had begun to fall.

Raising the roof.

The following summer, 1986, was spent enclosing the gable ends, adding dormers to the roof, building interior walls and installing windows, doors, and floors. Most of the doors and windows were salvaged and brought down from Bob Topping's old Turtle Camp on top of the hill. Sadly, the beautiful old building had fallen into disrepair after years of abandonment. We salvaged the hardwood maple floors by carefully prying up the two-inch-wide, tongue and groove boards. Pat and the girls patiently stripped off the old varnish, hand-sanded each piece, and then we relaid everything in the new building. The turtle camp also had ceilings of eight-inch-wide, tongue and groove pine which was painstakingly removed, hauled down the hill, and used for interior walls.

After digging a waterline which tied into the spring on top of the hill, I installed plumbing, furniture, and propane lights and appliances, then proclaimed the cabin finished!

"Not so fast," said Pat. "What about a fireplace?"

"Fireplace? We don't need a fireplace. That would require another year's work. What we need is rest and relaxation, and lots of fishing. I'll purchase the best wood stove that money can buy. That would be much better than a fireplace."

My words hung in the room like air pollution. After a moment of cold, heavy silence, Pat put her hands on her hips and began tapping her foot on the floor. I knew what was coming next.

"After three years of backbreaking labor building this castle, you would be satisfied with a wood stove? Why not paste comic strips all over the ceiling of the Sistine Chapel? Shame on you!"

The summer of 1987 was spent constructing a seven-foot-wide, twenty-eight-foot-tall stone fireplace. It began at bedrock, five feet below the cabin floor and extended up through the center of the building for two stories, then came to a head three feet above the peak of the roof, "Whew!" The task might never have come to fruition had we not been joined again by Vic. After a two-year hiatus in Puerto Rico, Victor returned to the Kipawa with his fifty-dollar guitar and a Spanish accent.

We began the process by hauling fifteen tons of stone in the wheelbarrow from a pile of rock on the riverbank seventy yards downstream from the cabin. The rock pile was the remains of an old log anchor which Zeph Fleury had constructed back in the early 1900s. It formerly held one end of a massive chain connected to a line of square-hewn timbers that stretched across the mouth of the river. The log chain was there to catch the wood floating down the Kipawa from the logging operation upstream. For the most part, the stones in the pile that anchored the log chain were the size and shape needed for constructing the fireplace. They were uniquely beautiful stone as well. Some were dark gray granite marbled with white veins of quartz; some had shades of amber and rose flecked with tiny grains of glittering mica.

Vic and I would mix just enough cement and mortar to build about two vertical feet per day. We had been advised not to go too fast so the mortar could sufficiently set and bond before adding more weight. When it came time to line the inside of the structure, I turned once again to the old Topping cabins. On this occasion, however, I climbed the smaller hill to Dan Topping's notorious Club 21. The fireplace in Dan's building was a marvelously crafted work of art. Unfortunately, it had been built on unstable ground back in the 1930s. Ten years later, near the end of World War II, the ground below the cabin shifted and the whole fireplace and chimney tilted backwards about three feet. To this day, while the rest of the building has slowly caved in around it, the immense stone fireplace leans at an awkward angle downhill toward Lake Temiskaming.

The interior of the old Topping fireplace was lined with well-preserved, heat-resistant firebricks, firebricks that I desperately needed. I spent a rainy afternoon huddled inside the old tilting structure chiseling away at the crumbling mortar, removing enough brick to line our new fireplace.

In early August, Victor and I carried the final stones up the twenty-foot-high scaffolding and cemented them in place. We added a fourth coat of varnish to the heavy, white pine mantel, then waited until dark to christen it with a fire. That evening at nine o'clock, with Pat and the girls gathered around, Vic struck a match to a pile of birch and maple in the fireplace and celebrated as the flames kindled and the smoke drafted straight up the chimney. While my daughters roasted marshmallows over the coals, I stood back and watched the golden firelight reflecting on the log beams overhead. It felt good. Four years of hard labor were at an end.

"Our castle is finished," said Pat giving me a hug and a kiss.

"I'm going fishing," Vic whooped. "Anyone care to join me?" I was fast on my younger brother's heels with fishing pole in hand.

Time to relax.

❧   ❧   ❧

In the summer of 1990, three years after vowing never again to undertake such an immense project, I began another log cabin. The old boathouse had begun to collapse, so I took my chain saw and cut its log walls into cordwood and made a magnificent bonfire with what was left. Then, where the boathouse once stood, I constructed a very close facsimile of the cabin on the rocky knoll. Only now I was an expert, and I didn't have my brother Vic around to hinder my progress. Thus, instead of four, long, grueling years of labor, the new building required six. However, as I often said to Vic, "What is time to a person living on the shores of Lake Temiskaming?"

One day in June 1995, I was hauling chimney stone from the docks to the new cabin when a shiny white sedan came bumping down the logging road right past the sign I had posted on the hill above the lodge. The sign read, "CAUTION: STEEP HILL—NO VEHICLES BEYOND THIS POINT." When the car passed my second sign, "PRIVATE PROPERTY—NO TRESPASSING," I began waving my arms and yelling, "Stop. Turn around. Go back!"

Oblivious to my warnings, the sedan approached the steepest part of the hill and careened sideways, then fishtailed all the way to the bottom and out onto the grass until it came to a halt alongside the Main Lodge.

"Can't you read? Didn't you see the signs?" I hollered as I stalked toward the vehicle wondering what sort of mule-headed person would ignore the signs and drive a sedan down a hill meant only for tractors and four-wheel-drives. Suddenly, the car door swung open, and I saw a familiar face. It was the same mule-headed person that had rammed an ice floe with a rubber dinghy on Lake Temiskaming twenty years earlier. Jim Karpowitz had returned to the Kipawa River.

I grabbed him in a bear hug, as his wife, Nancy, and their three kids piled out of the car. "This place hasn't changed a bit," Jim observed as he looked around the property. Then glancing back at the steep, rutted hill, he added, "But who would have thought I could drive here in a Ford Taurus?"

I laughed. "Well actually, Hos, you're the first person to drive down that hill in anything less than a four-wheel-drive. And I'm not sure how you'll ever get it out of here."

"Don't worry!" Jim bellowed. "It's a rental. It can go anywhere."

Jim had spent the previous eighteen years as a wildlife biologist chasing moose, bear, and bighorn sheep around the mountains and deserts of central Utah in four-wheel-drive trucks provided by the Fish and Game Department. It was a line of work that naturally lent itself to the rough and bruising treatment of state-owned vehicles.

Jim and I spent several days fishing, canoeing, and reminiscing about old times. We hiked to Grande Chute with our families, went down the lake to the rappel rock, and even made a little progress on the new chimney.

"Whatever happened to the old dugout?" Jim asked one morning as we set out in a boat to explore the Matabitchewan River.

"It sat on the beach for about five years, then just turned up missing one spring. I guess it was carried away by rising water," I told him.

"Let's hope so," Jim said. "Or pity the thief who stole it. He's probably long since dead."

On the evening prior to their departure, Jim and I were fishing in the mouth of the river for walleye when he posed a question: "Twenty years ago did you ever imagine you'd still be living here on the Kipawa River?"

"Of course not," I grinned. "But someone's got to do it."

"Do you expect to be here for another twenty?" he continued.

I shrugged my shoulders. "I don't know. But if I am, you can bring your grandchildren up fishing."

"Fair enough," he replied as he reached back with his fishing rod and let fly with a cast that sent his lure sailing downstream two hundred feet into the current.

The next morning, Jim and Nancy piled their three kids back into the Taurus and prepared to make a run at the hill. It had rained during the night, leaving the rutted tracks in even worse condition. I had my doubts. Jim gunned the engine, then leaned out the window and said, "Keep your nose to the wind, and your eyes on the skyline." With a roar, the white Taurus lurched forward and bounced and fishtailed up the hill while rocks and gravel spewed from the rear wheels.

"Can you believe they made it?" Pat said as we listened to the sound of the car grow faint in the distance.

"Sure I can. It's a rental. It can go anywhere."

Jose Mediavilla

Chapter 20

DON QUIXOTE DE LA KIPAWA

A veritable account of the never-before-imagined adventure of the brave knight, Jose, who sallied forth to do battle with the dreaded rapids of the enchanted River Kipawa, armed only with a double-bladed paddle and mounted on a hopelessly narrow craft whose sharp, pointed ends resembled that of a javelin, and what perils befell the errant knight for his ill-advised curiosity that led him to challenge the turbulent waters of that mystical river, and other incidents whose impossibility and immensity have caused some to esteem this account as apocryphal, yet nonetheless it remains as wild as it is real and worthy of mention in this most rare but truthful history.
—Scott Sorensen

In the year of nineteen hundred seventy-five when I had lived on the shores of Lake Temiskaming but one month, there descended on the rapids of the Kipawa River a tall, gaunt, black-bearded Spaniard whose brief sojourn remained shrouded in mystery for many years thereafter.

One rainy day in June I was working on the deck of the River Cabin, which stands just thirty feet from the river's most formidable rapid, when out of the bush there appeared what can only be described as a modern-day Don Quixote. He was tall and thin of stature, and his countenance was hawk-nosed, tight-lipped, with dark, deep-set eyes that bore a look of determination, a desire to attempt the impossible.

The strange knight greeted me in an odd mixture of French and Spanish. "My name is Don Jose Mediavilla," he said with a bow. Then brandishing his double-bladed paddle he proclaimed, "I am a soldier of truth, champion of right, and conqueror of mighty rivers" I answered him in Spanish, which for me was more familiar than French, having lived in the Andes Mountains of Bolivia for a time.

He told me he was originally from an area near Valencia, Spain, but for the past several years he had lived a self-imposed exile in northern Quebec, where he taught school in the town of Rouyn. On weekends and throughout the months of summer this native son of Spain would venture forth with his kayak to explore the rapids of various rivers in the region.

Like Quixote of old, Don Jose had a helmet on his head, but unlike the tin washbasin that adorned the crown of his noble predecessor, Jose wore a headgear of white plastic similar to those worn by modern-day hockey players. Instead of an ancient suit of armor, his body was clad in a skintight wet suit, and around his chest, rather than the traditional coat of mail, was a bright yellow life jacket. With his long sleek kayak balanced on his shoulder and his double-bladed paddle held high above his head, he exclaimed, "These are the weapons with which I battle the rapids of the Kipawa River."

At that point he turned to examine the tremendous rapid that boiled and churned behind him. He told me he had successfully run every rapid on the river between Kipawa Lake and the lodge with the exception of the hundred-foot drop at Grande Chute and the rapid that lay before him.

I commended him for his courage and skill, then asked him if any of the rapids he had run upstream compared in size and velocity with the one at our feet. He looked again, then shrugged, "What is it that makes you so apprehensive about this rapid?" In no uncertain terms I told him that a quarter-mile-long rapid with a continuous drop of seventy feet over huge boulders and massive rock shelves was sufficient to make even the most experienced paddler apprehensive. "Perhaps that is true," cried Don Jose, "but when I look at this rapid I see no boulders, drops, or dangerous shelves. I see only a shiny ribbon of water that beckons and calls to men of action and adventure."

I proceeded to tell the intrepid knight that I, too, had heard the call of the river just two weeks before, when I took, Jim Neel, a friend from Indiana on a wild ride through the lower half of the rapid in a two-man, inflatable dinghy. We barely made it fifty feet into the river when misfortune struck. A tremendous wave turned the boat upside down and we were forced to swim with the current, which violently swept us over rocks and dragged us through deep holes of whitewater before spitting us out into the lake like a couple of rag dolls. We were thoroughly beaten and battered, but humbly grateful to be alive.

I rolled up my shirt-sleeves and pantleg to show Don Jose some of the bruises and scrapes that the rocks and boulders had inflicted on my person. He remained unimpressed. "Perhaps your choice of vessel was to blame for your ill fortune." I agreed that a kayak in the hands of a skillful paddler was much better suited for the rapid than a rubber dinghy, but nonetheless, I had grave reservations about an attempt in any sort of vessel.

The gallant knight studied the rapid for another moment, then with a flourish of his paddle he proclaimed, "The day is now late, but soon I shall return to conquer the beast that rumbles and roars in the depths of this rapid." With that he silently bowed, then vanished into the forest. Eleven years were to pass before Don Jose returned to the Kipawa River. When he did, however, it was with unforgettable style.

On a warm July day in 1986, I was skin diving in strong current at the mouth of the river which was running at a high level due to recent rains and a late spring thaw. I had been searching the river bottom for lost fishing tackle when I surfaced for air and noticed my wife's younger brother James waving frantically from the bow of our boat and pointing upstream at the rapids.

I turned just in time to see a large, colorful object flying over an enormous wave, then disappear into a deep hole about halfway through the rapid. As I focused on the hole, there suddenly appeared from out of the turbulence a tennis shoe which was attached to a long, spindly leg that kicked and flailed in desperation before vanishing back into the torrent. Next there emerged a long, sinewy arm clutching a wooden paddle, whose blade slashed and beat against the waves momentarily before being drawn back into the fray. Finally I detected a yellow life jacket and white plastic helmet which I recognized as the property of the long-lost but most valiant knight, Don Jose.

All at once, as though it had grown weary or perhaps bored with its adversary, the river released its hold on the stouthearted knight and he continued his wild descent toward the lake. He was swept by crosscurrents over hidden shoals and in between boulders and rocks whose craggy tops protruded through the foam and spray like dragon's teeth. At the crest of one particularly massive wave the errant knight uttered a deep-throated roar that reverberated out over the lake. Whether it was a roar of victory or a cry of defeat, however, I could not truthfully say. When he yelled a second time, I concluded it was a plea for help, so I swam toward the struggling knight as the river carried him into the lake.

When I reached Don Jose and grasped the collar of his life jacket he was choking and gasping for air. "I thought I was drowned; I thought I was dead," he shrieked several times, as I towed him toward shore. When we arrived at the dock, I hauled him from the lake until only his feet were left dangling in the water. After hacking and coughing for several minutes, Don Jose looked up at me and inquired, "Am I truly alive, my friend?"

"Yes," I replied. "Not only are you alive, but you have survived a savage battle with that raging beast of a rapid."

"So be it!" cried Don Jose, presenting me his paddle. "Now, my friend, it is for you who live on the shores of this river to challenge the beast within."

Thus it was I learned to paddle and roll the long, narrow craft whose sharp, pointed ends resemble that of a javelin. In time I achieved a certain level of success in kayaking most of the turbulent drops in the river, but the formidable rapid next to the lodge I steadfastly avoided because of its immense size and unforgiving nature. Indeed, the rapid had been named Hollywood by two skillful paddlers, Doug Skeggs and Peter Karwacki, who successfully ran it in 1986. They agreed that Hollywood was an appropriate name for two reasons: there had been numerous movies filmed along its shores, and anyone who succeeded in running it in a kayak was a star in his own right.

In the summer of 1988 I decided to make a solo descent of the Kipawa River. Pat transported me upstream ten miles to the small fishing outpost at Laniel, Quebec. I eased the kayak into the river, then carefully slid my legs and hips into its narrow hull. Leaning forward, I stretched the spray skirt out in each direction until the entire opening had been sealed off. I tightened the chin strap on my helmet and pushed out into the current as Pat bade me good luck and farewell.

I paddled through the rapids at Buttonhook and Log Jam without incident. At Broken Bridge, I surfed on the crest of a large wave for several minutes, then advanced downstream with ever-increasing confidence. After executing nearly flawless runs at White Pine and Elbow rapids, I determined that the day had arrived to challenge the drop at Hollywood, to silence the beast that bellows and roars at the mouth of the river.

As I approached the final bend above Hollywood, my heart was pounding and the sound of water crashing over rocks thundered in my ears. There was no time to second guess the river, I dropped over the edge into a deep hole that completely submerged the kayak. Fortunately

I managed to stay right side up, but found myself floating backwards when I emerged from the hole.

Paddling frantically to get the boat turned around, I was carried sideways over a large wave and into a powerful eddy whose current grabbed the edge of the kayak and flipped me upside down. I held my breath for what seemed like eternity while positioning my paddle to attempt an Eskimo roll. With a powerful thrust of my right arm and a quick pivot of my hips I felt myself rising out of the water, but staring straight into the most treacherous part of the rapid.

The entire river funneled into a narrow chute which greatly increased the velocity and power of the current, then the channel made an abrupt right turn before dropping over a seven-foot waterfall. I drew a quick breath and paddled for the middle of the chute. The current dragged and pulled at the kayak from several directions, but as quickly as I had entered the top of the chute, I was flying out the bottom, headed toward the waterfall. The kayak plunged over the fall, which buried me in a deep, tumultuous whirlpool. When I regained the surface I was happily surprised to find myself still inside the boat in a vertical position. "I have battled and won, a star is born!" I yelled triumphantly, tossing my paddle high in the air. My moment of self-adulation was short lived, however, when I decided to try the rapid again and see if my initial success was merely a consequence of luck.

Challenging the beast in Hollywood Rapid.

With the kayak balanced on my shoulder, I returned to the top of Hollywood and paddled out into the river. My plan was to attack the center of the rapid as I had done before, but the current pushed me far to the left into some turbulent water which tipped the kayak upside down. Rather than bail out and swim, I attempted a roll. When I extended my left arm a sudden jolt tore the paddle from my grasp, and something popped inside my shoulder. All at once my helmet began slamming into rocks on the river bottom, and I knew it was time to abandon ship.

The procedure for extricating oneself from an overturned kayak is simple, at least in principle. Once you run out of air, your brain tells the rest of your body it will soon die if it doesn't receive some oxygen soon, so you place your hands on the side of the boat and push really hard until you come out.

Some paddlers maintain that getting out of a kayak while upside down in the water is as close to the birthing experience (from the baby's point of view) as a grown person is likely to get. And in fact, if a kayaker is not successful in extricating himself from an overturned boat with relative expedience, both his complexion and facial expression will resemble that of a newborn babe. Such was the case with me that day. I struggled, pushed, and violently thrashed, but could not get free of the kayak. My left arm had been rendered useless. Eventually I felt myself tumbling over the waterfall and the force of the current literally wrenched me from the boat.

Swimming to shore was as difficult a proposition as was getting out of the boat. Like a duck with a broken wing, my left arm refused to function, and every movement sent waves of pain shooting from my shoulder down to my fingertips.

Temporarily I gained footing on a rock and stood up in mid-current to inspect the damage. My investigation revealed that my shoulder was not where it should have been, but rather it had worked its way forward and down into a dubious position that protruded out from my chest at a strange angle.

Stepping gingerly off of the rock, I continued swimming toward shore with my good arm, while the other trailed loosely behind in the current. As I crawled from the river, I glanced downstream just in time to see my half-submerged kayak disappear around the bend on its way toward Lake Temiskaming.

I hobbled down the trail feeling dizzy and weak as the pain in my dislocated shoulder increased with every step. When I arrived at the camp, the first people I encountered were the McCauleys, some friends visiting from Ohio. Larry, the chief of the McCauley tribe, along with his six grown sons, had been vacationing at the lodge every summer for fifteen years. In spite of the fact that they were mostly bankers, accountants, and grocers, I asked them if they had any experience resetting a dislocated shoulder. "You bet," cried Larry, "me and the boys can fix you up good."

While the two oldest boys held me by the waist, the two youngest bent me forward over the porch railing then Larry told the twins to take hold of my arm and pull until it popped back into place.

After a considerable time of them pulling and me yelling, the situation was much the same. My shoulder was still out of its socket. I thanked the McCauleys for their help and concern then staggered off toward the Main Lodge in a daze.

In the final outcome, I reset my shoulder by grasping the bedpost in our room then leaning back slowly until it popped back into its socket. For several days thereafter I found it impossible to raise my left arm higher than waist level, which had a very negative effect on my volleyball game, but a very positive result on my ability to cut firewood. Even Pat could see I was in no condition to swing an axe or carry a chain saw. The type of injury I had sustained would require several weeks of rest and rehabilitation. Anything more strenuous than sitting in a boat with a fishing pole propped up in my good arm was out of the question.

Thus I suffered for nearly a week, fishing from dawn until dusk with nothing to break the monotony. Then early one morning as I was preparing my boat and tackle for another long, tedious day of fishing, a group of kayakers appeared from across the mouth of the river. Paddling in the lead, wearing his plastic helmet and his irrepressible grin, was my old friend and mentor, Don Jose. "It's a fine day to run the rapids, my friend; come and join us on the river," he cried, throwing me his paddle. Without thinking I reached out and caught the paddle with my left hand and spun it twice above my head before tossing it back to him. Only upon hearing Pat's footsteps on the dock behind me did I realize my mistake. "Still too painful to lift a chain saw?" she queried. "You seem to do just fine flinging kayak paddles around."

I stood speechless, totally lost for words, until Don Jose came to the rescue. With a warm, ingratiating smile he turned to Pat and said, "You must understand, fair lady, the magic and power in a kayak paddle. I have seen sick men raised from their beds at the mere sight of one; I have witnessed invalids and cripples made suddenly strong and well by the healing touch of a kayak paddle.

We have observed such a miracle just now with your husband. You should rejoice and admonish him to join us on the river and before the sun sets this day you shall see an ailing man made whole again."

After a moment's deliberation, Pat turned to me and said, "I'm not going to argue with a wild-eyed Spaniard who claims to have seen miracles performed with a kayak paddle. You go run the river, my dear, and when you return you'll find your axe and chain saw out by the woodpile. I hope by then your recovery is complete. As for me, I'll be out in the boat fishing with a good book propped up in my lap."

Pat lands a lake trout.

⚜ Dam Update

Wednesday, July 8, 1998
Kipawa River Lodge (Topping's Camp), 7:30 P.M.

I spoke at length with the men who have been conducting the surveys on water flow, cubic meters per second, at different levels in various parts of the river. I was surprised to learn from the head of the survey crew that only 5–6 cms flow down the river when the gates at Laniel are closed. Paddlers have always been told (or at least assumed) something like 15–20 cms seeps through and underneath the dam even when it is entirely shut. Now I appreciate what precious little water there is keeping the river ecosystem alive and healthy when the gates are closed. Fortunately, during a year of normal precipitation they are seldom shut down for more that a week or two at a time. More than ever, it would seem environmentally irresponsible to divert water from the Kipawa.

Hollywood Rapid when the dam is closed.

What the river takes shall be mine . . .

Chapter 21

PIRATES OF THE KIPAWA RIVER

Fifteen men on the dead man's chest -
Yo - ho - ho, and a bottle of rum!
—Long John Silver

After several years of losing anchors, fishing tackle, and other sundry items to the rocks at the bottom of the Kipawa River, I decided to invest in a snorkel, mask, and fins and attempt to recover some of my property. I discovered a whole new world beneath the surface of the water. What first caught my attention were the schools of walleye, pike, trout, and whitefish. When a diver goes underwater and encounters fish in their own environment, they seem almost tame. I have found myself swimming in water just six feet deep with a dozen large pike surrounding me at arm's length. The walleye or pickerel stay near the bottom, but will also allow a diver to approach within a few feet. Lake trout, averaging ten to fifteen pounds at the mouth of the river are much more skittish. I have seen them only from a distance.

One day, while observing a school of pike, I noticed in the background the outline of a fish well over three feet. I was hesitant to approach what looked like a monstrous pike, but soon I recognized the striped pattern on its side. It was a tiger muskie, or muskellunge, which can weigh up to thirty or forty pounds.

When I approached the huge fish it maintained its distance, but as I turned to swim the other direction it followed me. On its back was an old battle scar about four inches long, and from its lower jaw there protruded a jagged, wayward tooth which was broken in half, possibly the result of a fight at the end of some fisherman's line. The muskie had grown to such a size, that it seemed quite unlikely it would ever end up in someone's landing net. This was the kind of fish that results in campfire stories about "the one that got away." For several minutes it lurked in the shadows, mimicking my every move as I changed directions and depth in the current. Eventually the big fish disappeared behind a rock and was gone. It left me with a greater respect for the size of fish that inhabit a large freshwater lake like Temiskaming.

The water at the mouth of the Kipawa River is pure and clear and provides excellent visibility for diving in the bay before it mixes with the dark, auburn water of Lake Temiskaming. As I began to search the rocky bottom of the bay, I realized I would never have to spend another dollar on fishing gear. Hooks, sinkers, lures, and anchors were snagged between rocks and jammed in crevices throughout the area. I came across the back end of an aluminum canoe that had fallen victim to one of the rapids upstream from the lodge. One evening, after several boats had been fishing in the mouth of the river, I found an expensive rod and reel in about twelve feet of water. As I hauled it to the surface something began tugging on the other end of the line. I swam to shore, then reeled in a scrappy, four-pound smallmouth bass with a black and silver Rapala stuck in its mouth. Obviously, the fish had taken the bait and pulled the rod and reel overboard when some unsuspecting fisherman was not paying attention. I concluded that the bass had certainly made my day profitable, so I removed the hook from its mouth and released the fish into the river.

On another occasion while diving in about fifteen feet of water, I discovered a moss-covered pair of gold-rimmed prescription glasses which I cleaned up and put on our bookcase inside the cabin. A year later, David Wiwchar, a young friend who lives near Cobalt, Ontario, told us how he had lost his glasses the previous year while windsurfing near the mouth of the river. I showed him the pair on top of the bookcase, which he promptly tried on and found to be his.

I began to search into deeper water for three snowmobiles that disappeared through the ice of Lake Temiskaming in 1967. The ice at the mouth of the river is often thin and treacherous, as two of the snowmobile drivers who went down with their machines found out.

In 1984, Cal Bosveld, a neighbor from up the lake told us how his friend lost a five-thousand-dollar ski-doo at the mouth of the river. It seems this particular machine, which could travel at speeds in excess of seventy miles per hour, had developed a stuck throttle. In order to stop the machine's forward motion the driver had to kill the engine. Then to restart the snowmobile another person had to lift the back of the machine so its track could spin freely while the driver pushed the starter then prepared to jump aboard as the vehicle sped away. Apparently either the driver or the holder missed his cue and they both stood watching in awe as the machine bolted across the ice at incredible speed with nobody at the controls.

When the riderless ski-doo reached the open water where the rapids flow into the lake, it had enough momentum to travel over the surface of the river for quite a distance. For a moment the two astonished onlookers thought the machine might hit the other shore, but their hopes quickly faded as it began to hiss and sputter, then sank from view. We attempted to recover the snowmobile the following year by using scuba tanks and dragging the bottom with a grappling hook, but the water was over a hundred feet deep in the area where it went down.

During the summer months it is not uncommon to see and hear angry fishermen cursing and tugging at snagged lures and stuck anchors which often get lodged in the rocks at the mouth of the river. I have been accused by some of watching smugly from shore while people struggle helplessly in their boats trying to free their lines, knowing full well that only a person with a mask, fins, and snorkel can recover those items.

I am the founder and, so far, the sole member of the Kipawa River Reclamation Society, whose motto is, "what's yours is yours, but what the river takes shall be mine." I bear no ill will or wish no misfortune on those who travel great distances over dangerous waters to catch fish from the mouth of the river. In fact, I have often rendered assistance to those in need.

On one particular occasion a man in a large motorboat stubbornly refused to relinquish his shiny new anchor to the river. After making several runs into the current to try and break the anchor free, he inadvertently severed the tip of his index finger between the anchor line and the chrome running light on the bow of his boat. At that point he gave up his attempt to retrieve the anchor and ordered his wife, who was driving the boat, to "cut the damn thing off!" Looking down at his fingertip, she calmly said, "The damn thing is already cut off, dear," to which he impatiently replied, "Not my damn finger; cut the damn anchor line!" After cutting the rope, she ferried him over to the lodge, where we taped the severed digit back into place. They proceeded to the hospital in Ville Marie, while I descended into the river and, after considerable effort, recovered the stray anchor.

The following spring the same couple returned once again to try their luck at fishing. Within half an hour they lost another new anchor. When they motored up to the camp and asked if I had any spare anchors, I told them I had several for sale. As we walked up the dock toward the lodge to look at my anchor collection I noticed the man's index finger had never fully recovered. It was an inch shorter than the one next to it.

When we arrived at the porch and opened the lid of my reclamation box, which was marked ANCHORS $20 EACH, the man spied his former anchor inside and suddenly became irate and irrational. "That anchor's mine! I had it on my boat here last spring," he cried indignantly.

"Perhaps that is true, but you lost it to the river, which in turn lost it to me, and now for twenty dollars it can be yours again," I explained. Unable to grasp the logic of my explanation, the man pointed his shortened finger at me and scowled, "You're nothing but a bloody pirate, and I'll be damned if I'm going to pay twenty bucks for what's rightfully mine!" I listened patiently as he ranted and raved and shook his stubby appendage under my chin. Then I told him his point was not well taken, and if he snubbed me again I would be forced to cut off further negotiations.

Immediately he quit wagging his stumpy index under my chin. I offered to lend him my snorkel, mask, and fins so he could dive for his anchor. I also told him that he could have a large rock from our beach to use as an anchor at no charge whatsoever.

"You should wear a black eye patch and a gold earing and fly a skull and crossbones from your flagpole!" he shouted.

"Shiver me timbers," I replied. "I'll give that suggestion some serious thought." At that point he threw a twenty-dollar bill at my feet, grabbed his anchor, and stormed off to his boat in a huff.

I thought to myself, people travel to this beautiful river to reap its bounties of fish and expect to give nothing in return. Even when the fishing is slow, is a man not happier to sit in the presence of the Kipawa River and not at his office staring at a computer? Has modern man forgotten the wisdom of the old angler's proverb? "Yea and behold, the worst day of fishing is better than the best day of working!"

Only fools utter harsh words and idle threats when the river lays claim to an anchor or fishing lure. Every pleasure has its price. Even the river will exact a minor toll from those who receive so much in return. It is a wise man who can be content with the knowledge that whatever goes down must sometime come up, for that which is lost shall someday be found. And remember that along the banks of the Kipawa River lives a man with a wife and five daughters who might in some small way benefit from this cycle.

⚜ Dam Update

Thursday, July 15, 1998
Kipawa River Lodge (Topping's Camp), 4:00 P.M.

Peter Leonard (an HQ official) and two assistants: Isabel, a hydrologist and Karen, a university student, paid us a visit. As we stood on the deck of the River Cabin looking at Hollywood Rapid, I mentioned that the men from the water survey had said there was only 5–6 cms coming down the river. Isabel seemed very surprised. "Looking at the rapid I would estimate the level to be at 15 to 20 cms, or at the very least 10 cms," she replied.

I told her that the other hydrologist (Gilles) was also surprised by those numbers. Gilles assured me, however, that the men surveying the water levels are the "best in the business" when it comes to assessing cubic meters per second.

I suggested they have a look at some different rapids like Log Jam or Picnic where the entire river is forced between one narrow chute when the dam is closed. The bottom of Hollywood can be deceiving as the water spreads itself out in between rocks and several small channels.

I invited the three of them into the Main Lodge for something to drink. Peter Leonard and I visited for over an hour while Isabel and Karen went for a swim. I told Peter that some of the local population are laboring under the impression that all of the 200 million dollars that HQ proposes to spend on the project will go right into their own pockets, or at least into municipal coffers, and that one man from Laniel was telling people that if the project goes through, local municipalities and residents will receive a 5 to 10 percent reduction on their hydro bills.

Peter just smiled and shook his head. "Where do such ideas get started?" He said that only a fraction of the 200 million dollars would go into the local economy and even that would end in two or three years once the project was completed. People must understand that the turbines and other equipment will not be produced in Temiscamingue or Laniel. The major construction contracts will be awarded to big companies from down south who have experience in large projects like dam building. Certainly it will be a temporary boon to some local hotels, restaurants, building suppliers, and trucking companies, but when the project is finished only a handful of HQ employees will remain to operate the dam. As for a reduction in Hydro rates for locals, there is no such thing. Perhaps there would be some revenue sharing if the local municipalities come on board as partners in the project."

Peter seems to be a nice man and is well suited to the task of trying to balance the interests of everyone involved in HQ's proposal. His job is to smile a lot and keep us all at the table and talking. Yadda, Yadda, Yadda. Meanwhile, the fate of this spectacular river hangs in the balance. It's a catch-22. In view of the fact that the Kipawa River runs through a wilderness with only one part-time resident along its entire course, few people care very much about what happens to it. On the other hand, the Gordon River, a man-made stream which drains the southern arm of Kipawa Lake and runs right through the town of Temiscamingue, is in no danger of being altered or diverted due to the fact that there are dozens of homes and businesses along its banks. And yet nobody travels hundreds of miles to paddle or fish the Gordon. Who wants to float down a man-made stream and see people mowing their grass or hanging their wash out to dry? Not to mention ending up at the base of a smokestack from one of the country's largest pulp mills. The Gordon River has its place and purpose, both past and present. I begrudge it nothing. But I do resent the built-in protection afforded the Gordon, while the Kipawa, its wild and magnificent neighbor to the north, and the sole natural outlet from Kipawa Lake, is in danger of being reduced to a mere skeleton of its former self—a trickle of water in a big rocky ditch.

Vic wading through Hollywood Rapid at low water

Chapter 22

THE MISSING BOAT

Insanity is hereditary.
We get it from our children!
—Anonymous

"Dad! I think you hit a rock and wrecked the motor."

There is nothing more aggravating than a ten-year-old child telling you something you already know but do not care to hear announced out loud. My back was turned to my daughter, but I anticipated her next question even before it had formed on her lips.

"Dad, if the motor is broken, what are you going to do about it?"

Trying to hide my frustration, I replied, "We will have to spend the night paddling toward McMartin's Point, I guess, Jenny."

"But Dad, we don't have any paddles. Katie and Michelle took them out of the boat yesterday to play with on the beach." The sad reality of that statement became all too apparent as I stared at the bottom of our empty boat. "That's just great," I fumed, up the proverbial creek without a paddle.

For the next several minutes, in a remarkable display of patience, wisdom, and grace, Jenny asked no more questions. I tried to compose myself as I thought back on all the rules I had broken that day. So many times over the years I had warned people not to go out on the lake without extra fuel, life jackets, paddles, warm clothes, and a basic knowledge of where they were going. In less than an hour I had managed to break every rule. Now Jenny and I were adrift on the lake several miles south of the lodge in an open boat with a broken motor, and nightfall was fast approaching.

Earlier that day Pat and I had taken our girls to town for supplies. When we returned to the lodge at 6:00 P.M. our twelve-foot aluminum boat with a five-horsepower motor was missing. I questioned the two oldest girls and learned that the boat had been left unsecured on the beach that morning. A strong north wind had blown the entire day. I told Jenny to accompany me in our eighteen-foot cedar-strip boat to go in search of the missing boat.

In my haste to be gone, I failed to check the boat for life jackets, oars, or any other items that would be useful in case of an accident or emergency. Fortunately, Jenny had grabbed her life jacket from the screen porch as I called out for her to hurry. With only two hours of daylight remaining, we proceeded south on the lake, riding two-foot swells with the wind at our backs.

After searching the Quebec shoreline for an hour, I decided to cross the lake and return to the lodge along the Ontario side. It seemed unlikely that the small aluminum boat could have drifted more than five miles in the wind, and besides we were running out of daylight. Jenny was perched high in the bow watching the shoreline while I sat in the stern running the motor and scanning the center of the lake. We were traveling into the waves just thirty yards from shore when suddenly the motor struck a hidden rock that shook the boat from bow to stern.

The incident took me entirely by surprise. I had traveled past that point dozens of times in fourteen years and never encountered shallow water there. Even though the motor continued to run, I knew we had sheared a pin because the boat lost its forward momentum, then turned sideways to the waves. All at once we found ourselves drifting away from the lodge at the mercy of the wind.

Jenny and I began to assess our situation. The date was June 12, and that morning on the radio the weatherman had issued a frost warning for our area. Underneath her life jacket, Jenny was wearing a lightweight but long-sleeved shirt. I had a windbreaker over my short-sleeved shirt, but no life jacket. We were close enough to shore that the wind would carry us in eventually, but it made no sense to land in a remote place that offered no shelter from the cold or mosquitos.

With little else to do I tilted the motor up out of the water to inspect the lower unit. From where I sat there was no visible damage to the prop or skeg. Determined to have a closer look, I stood up and leaned out over the top of the motor. Unbeknown to me the catch which normally held the motor firmly in place when tilted up out of the water was broken. When I reached down and braced my arm on the lower unit for extra support it suddenly dropped back down into the lake, pulling my head and shoulders with it. My legs and feet managed to wrap themselves tightly around the top of the motor, and had my head not been underwater, I might have figured out a way to extricate myself

212

from the situation with some dignity and dry clothing still intact. But it was not meant to be. The best I could do was to point my toes gracefully (no easy feat wearing hiking boots), then continue my forward somersault into the icy lake.

Not more than five seconds passed from the time I hit the water until I was back into the boat. In early June ordinary people can do extraordinary things to avoid prolonged contact with the water in Lake Temiskaming. Jenny said I virtually flung myself back into the boat, while shouting a very colorful phrase that described the temperature of the water in no uncertain terms.

I quickly removed my wet clothing, then proceeded to wring the water from each article while Jenny looked on in amusement. I gave her my most serious "better not laugh at your old man" look, then handed her my wet shirt and told her to hold it up to dry. I did the same with my pants. With about twenty minutes of direct sunlight remaining, the two of us stood like castaways in the old wooden boat, waving wet clothes in the wind.

"Dad, do you think Mom will come looking for us in the big boat?" Jenny asked.

"Not a chance," I replied. "Mom wouldn't leave the baby alone in camp with your sisters, Jen. We're on our own tonight."

Daylight was nearly gone and the wind began to die as I got back into my damp clothing. I pried a couple of planks from the false floor of the boat to use as paddles. I had installed the planks two years before to avoid standing in the ever-present puddle of water that gathers on the bottom of every old cedar-strip boat.

"Use this board to paddle with, Jenny," I said, handing her one of the rough planks. "The exercise will help keep you warm."

"How far is McMartin's Point?" she asked.

"About six or seven miles, I would guess. If this wind keeps up, we should make it before dawn. There's a nice old fellow named Joe Belanger who has a cabin there. If we're lucky he might be at home and give us a ride back to the lodge in the morning."

"But what about the missing boat?" Jenny asked.

"Now we're the missing boat," I replied.

For several hours we paddled south. Our progress was hindered when the tail wind died down just after dusk. Using the boards for paddles was a slow, tiresome proposition, but it kept our minds off the cold and gave our shoulders and arms something to do.

"Dad, are we having an adventure?" Jenny asked, in between strokes.

"Yes, Jenny, I believe this would classify as an adventure. We certainly didn't plan it. We don't know the outcome and there are some definite risks involved. Sometimes it's hard to recognize an adventure until after it's all over. I suspect we'll know for sure by tomorrow morning."

After a time, Jenny's teeth began to chatter so we huddled close on the seat and rocked back and forth singing "Row, row, row, your boat." Looking up at the sky we located Polaris, the North Star, by lining up the two stars at the end of the cup on the big dipper. I explained how the ancient mariners would navigate by using the North Star as a reckoning point because it was the only star in the heavens that stayed in one place all night long. We found Cassiopeia, the lazy W, which sits exactly opposite the big dipper on a straight line through Polaris. I told Jenny to keep track of those two constellations during the night as they chased each other clockwise around the North Star. By morning they would end up trading places in the sky.

"Dad, when you were a kid did you ever do something dumb like leaving a boat untied and it floated away?"

"Yes, as a matter of fact I did, Jenny." I told her about a time when I was seventeen years old and I asked my father if I could borrow his brand new, twenty-two-foot fiberglass boat and go water skiing with my friends. He said, "Sure, but be careful and don't hit any rocks!" Those words proved to be prophetic in ways my father never imagined.

I hitched the boat to our truck and began towing it up the canyon above Salt Lake City to a lake in the Wasatch Mountains. While approaching a sharp turn on the canyon road, high above a place called Suicide Rock, we hit a bump, which resulted in the trailer coming loose from the truck. I tried to remain calm and slow the truck down gradually but when the boat and trailer passed me on the right going 40 MPH, a feeling of panic set in. "Bad luck," muttered one of my friends; "real bad luck."

It was a strange but awesome sight watching my father's new boat racing down the road in front of us, headed straight for the cliffs above Suicide Rock. The trailer managed to execute part of a turn before it ran off the road and came to a sudden halt just ten feet from the edge of the canyon. The trailer tongue had ploughed into a large mound of dirt and stopped, but the boat was not so fortunate. It continued its forward momentum, and launched like a rocket from off of the trailer out over the side of the canyon.

What happened next was beyond my field of vision, but I got a very good description of it from a fellow who was coming down the road from the other direction with a truck full of turkeys. He said he was just starting into the turn when around the bend, right in the middle of the road, came a boat on a trailer with nothing towing it. His first reaction was to close his eyes and ask himself if perhaps twenty years of turkey ranching had affected his brain, but when he looked again the trailer had run off the road and stopped, while the boat went flying out over the precipice toward Suicide Rock. It remained airborne for the first hundred feet, then it crashed and rolled the last two hundred feet to the bottom. What remained of the hull came to a sudden stop in a creek bed that was only half the width of the boat.

When I pulled up to the edge of the canyon in our truck, the turkey rancher was standing there scratching the top of his head, "Seems like an odd place to launch a boat," he mused. "There's hardly enough water in that creek to float a cow chip, let alone a motor boat."

When I looked over the edge of the cliff, my stomach felt like a deep, hollow pit. There were life jackets, water skis, fishing poles, and other sundry items scattered up and down the side of the canyon along the entire path the boat had rolled. One of my friends turned to me and said, "If that were my father's boat, I would climb back into the truck and continue driving east to Denver or St. Louis. After about ten or fifteen years I'd call home to see if Dad had come to grips with the situation, then I'd decide whether or not it was safe to return."

At that point in the story Jenny stopped me and asked, "Weren't you scared to death when Grandpa found out about the boat?"

"I wasn't as scared about losing the boat as I was about disappointing Grandpa. When I phoned his office and told him that his boat was at the bottom of the canyon in a hundred pieces he was pretty upset. His main concern, however, was that no one was hurt. Grandpa always said that a person who loves boats, cars, and houses more than he loves people is a poor man. If given a choice between losing Grandpa's boat or his respect, I would rather lose his boat."

About midnight I noticed that Jenny was no longer paddling. Fatigue had set in and she was asleep, slumped awkwardly over the edge of the seat. I set my paddle board down and moved her shoulders and head to a more comfortable position on top of my lap. Her small hands felt cold and damp as I tucked them inside the folds of her life jacket. She had not uttered a word of complaint or discouragement the entire evening, but that was no surprise. Along with her mother's dark eyes and hair, Jenny inherited an innate sense of composure and tranquility that Pat has always possessed.

I thought of the day we hiked to Grande Chute when she was eight years old and anxious to take on the world. While removing my shoes to climb to the top of the diving rock, Jenny approached me and said, "I'm going to jump off the rock too, Dad." I just smiled and told her to accompany me to the top then make her decision once she had looked down. The climb by itself is enough to deter most people from making the leap.

When we reached the top I held Jenny's arm as she stepped out on the edge of the rock. After analyzing the situation for a moment, she turned to me and spoke, but her words were drowned out by the roar of the waterfall.

I assumed she was frightened, so I tightened my grip on her arm and told her I would help her climb back down. She looked somewhat dismayed, then spoke to me again, but her words were still inaudible. I leaned over close and said, "Don't feel bad about not jumping today, Jenny; there will be other chances." She turned to me and yelled in frustration, "Let go of my arm so I can jump!"

The moment I loosened my grip she lunged forward off the rock and was gone. She landed feet first with a splash, then disappeared beneath the water. When her head resurfaced a huge grin spread across her face as she laughed out loud and raised her arm triumphantly.

I tried to imagine what it would be like to be a kid again, and to see the world through the eyes of an eight-year-old. I remember the first time I swam in the ocean and felt the power of the surf lifting my body up off of the sand. It was like nobody else had ever done it before. I was the first to experience it. It seemed as though I was inventing life as I went along. Every day was a new adventure, every night a chance to dream bigger dreams.

Around 2:00 A.M. Jenny woke up shivering uncontrollably, so I started the motor and let it idle, hoping it might radiate some heat through its cover. I was playing with the shifter, when suddenly the gears caught in reverse and the boat began to move backwards. By a stroke of luck a piece of broken sheer pin had worked itself into a position to spin the prop. I turned the boat around and proceeded, stern-first, toward McMartin's Point.

Up until that night I had always considered a motorboat going in reverse to be a sluggish, unwieldy vessel, but after paddling with a floorboard for six hours, it felt like we were flying on the wings of eagles. Jenny suggested that I try to put it in forward gear. I thought it best not to tempt fate but rather be content with our present good fortune.

For half an hour we chugged along in reverse, then out in the distance I glimpsed a flickering light. "McMartin's Point," I called to Jenny. "We should be there in another twenty minutes, and it looks like Joe Belanger has been waiting up for us. He'll probably have hot chocolate on the stove by the time we make land."

"Let's keep moving," Jenny muttered through clenched teeth.

When we landed on the beach, Joe was standing on his cabin porch holding up a lantern. I jumped from the bow of the boat, but sprawled face-first in the sand like a child still learning to walk. After sitting immobile in the boat for so long, it required several minutes to get my land legs back under me.

"It's a cold, dark night for fishing," Joe called from the porch. "Come on in and warm yourselves. There's cocoa on the stove."

Jenny flashed a big smile at me as we hobbled, stiff-legged, up the beach. "I think I've had about enough adventure for one day," she sighed.

"Me too," I replied. "I'm looking forward to a couple of days of routine boredom. Maybe some kayaking or windsurfing. Anything but searching for lost boats."

As we entered Joe's cabin, the sweet, rich smell of hot chocolate was overpowering. He poured us each a huge, steaming mug and said, "I was just about to turn off the light and go to bed when I heard your motor out on the lake. I wasn't sure because it sounded so far off and didn't seem to get any closer for a long time. It's been a strange day. With that strong norther blowing I haven't seen anyone out on the lake, but just before dark a small aluminum boat with a five-horsepower motor drifted into the bay. When I hauled it up on the shore there was nothing inside but an empty tank of gas and a half-dozen paddles. Why do you suppose someone would have all those paddles in such a tiny boat?"

"That's hard to say, Joe," I replied, as Jenny shot me a nervous glance. "It probably belongs to someone with lots of kids. Strange things happen all the time to people with lots of kids."

Adrenaline rush on the Kipawa River.

Dam Update

Monday, July 21, 1998
Montreal, Quebec

At 9:30 P.M. a meeting was held at Hydro Quebec's headquarters in Montreal. Henri LaForest and I flew in this morning from Rouyn, Quebec, to be in attendance. Also present were Peter Leonard from HQ, Doug Skeggs representing ARK, Dave Pollard representing "D'eau Vives" (a Quebec whitewater association), Pierre Trudel, the Director General of the Quebec Federation of Canoe-camping, and a half-dozen Hydro Quebec consultants as well.

This turned into the first "nuts and bolts" meeting I have attended that really addressed the concerns of whitewater enthusiasts on the Kipawa River. We looked over drafts of various questionnaires that will be circulated among users of the Kipawa River, including kayakers, canoeists, rafters, hikers, climbers, sightseers, and fishermen. among others.

Hydro Quebec seemed open to the suggestion that a study be funded for potential commercial whitewater rafting, kayaking, and canoeing on the Kipawa River. We proposed that HQ request water releases from the Ministry of Natural Resources to open the dam in Laniel for two weekends in September where various levels of cms might be procured. Two river rafting companies, Owl and Esprit, have expressed interest in bringing rafts with professional crews from their operations on the Ottawa River to assess the potential for commercial rafting and kayaking on the Kipawa. This is the first meeting I have attended concerning the proposal that left me feeling cautiously optimistic with the approach that Hydro Quebec is now taking.

220

Chapter 23

BABES IN THE WOODS

*There are people who pray for eternal life and don't
know what to do with themselves on a rainy day.*
—Chesterton

One rainy day in August of 1992 my two eldest daughters
were bored and frustrated. They were acting like teenagers. "This is
the pits, Dad! There's nothing to do but work and watch it rain. It is
so boring around here." My suggestion that, in spite of the rain, they
go water skiing, skin diving, kayaking, canoeing, fishing, or just sit
in the sauna then go for a swim, was received with derision and scorn.
"You always say that, Dad. We want to do something fun. You are so
boring." They were in an awful rut. The monotonous routine of water
skiing, skin diving, kayaking, canoeing, and fishing every day was
getting to them. They needed a challenge and a change of scenery.
They needed an adventure.

I recalled the summer I turned fifteen and told my parents
what a "boring place" our home was in Salt Lake City. The next day
my father loaded our seventeen-foot canoe on top of his truck and
hauled my cousin and me to southern Utah where he turned us loose
on Lake Powell for ten days. Dad gave us a map and told us to
explore every tributary, canyon, and passage of the hundred-fifty-
mile-long lake. For a couple of teenage boys it was the adventure of
a lifetime. We felt like Tom Sawyer and Huck Finn rafting down the
Mississippi to New Orleans. We ate catfish and rattlesnake, and slept
one night on the floor of an ancient Anasazi cliff dwelling with
strange and mysterious petroglyphs chiseled into its sandstone
ceiling. For ten days the world was at our fingertips. We were the
masters of our destiny.

The experience on Lake Powell forged within me a love of wild places and a desire to seek new and distant horizons. It was a gift from my father that I hoped to pass along to my daughters, which is how they ended up in a boat on Kipawa Lake the morning after that "boring, rainy day" in August of 1992. I waved good-bye from the wharf in Laniel as their small aluminum boat disappeared into the great shimmering expanse of the northern Quebec wilderness. Fifteen-year-old April, the idealist, sat up high in the bow with a map spread across her lap and a faraway look in her eyes. She was dreaming of the possibilities. On a lake with over a thousand miles of shoreline, a dozen major channels, and hundreds of bays, islands, and inlets, the possibilities seemed endless. Thirteen-year-old Jenny, the realist, sat behind her in the stern with her feet planted firmly on the floor and her left hand tightly grasping the motor handle. Shielding her eyes from the sun with her forearm, she scanned the water directly in front of the boat. Nothing beyond mattered. Should they hit a rock or a log their excursion would come to a grinding halt. Three years earlier Jenny had become an expert on what not to do in a small boat on a large lake. She understood the consequences of running aground and being adrift on unfamiliar waters. Harsh experience had taught her how quickly an outing could become an ordeal. The day before, when April drew up a list of food and supplies for their four-day adventure, Jenny went through the list and doubled everything. "No point in going out shorthanded," she remarked. The following morning when April surveyed the pile of food, clothing and gear Jenny had assembled for the trip, she smiled and said, "If we die it won't be from cold or starvation." This is their story as told from the pages of April's journal.

Wednesday, August 5, 1992—Laniel, Quebec:

We began our four-day journey on Kipawa Lake on a calm, sunny afternoon in a small aluminum boat with a six-horsepower motor. Jenny and I laughed and licked the orange-powdered remains of Cheetos from our fingertips as we lounged on the boat benches in our swimming suits. The only waves we encountered on the lake all day were those created by the boats of fishermen that sped past us along the main channel.

That evening at seven o'clock we made land on Jawbone Island near the southern end of the lake. It was a warm, pleasant evening. While gathering rocks to build a fire ring we heard a loud commotion from across the channel. Standing on a wharf in front of a small village, a group of people were cheering and yelling as a water skier was being towed behind a float plane through a veritable typhoon of wind and spray created by the plane's propeller as it taxied noisily around the bay. "Now that's an interesting way to pull a water skier," Jenny said as she cleared and leveled an area to pitch our tent on. We ate hot dogs and baked beans for dinner, then lay in our bags on the hard, bumpy ground. For a while I talked to Jenny about the events of the day and what marvelous adventures we would likely have on the rest of the trip. Her only response was a soft, rhythmic snoring through the folds of her sleeping bag. I remember listening to the comforting songs and laughter of Frenchmen in their cottages across the water as I drifted off to sleep.

Thursday, August 6, 1992—Jawbone Island, Lake Kipawa:

The longest day of my life. We awoke at eight o'clock to the crying of loons out on the lake. Small patches of mist hung between the trees like damp sheets on a clothesline. After a leisurely breakfast of apples and oatmeal, we spent two hours repacking the boat and preparing for the day's travel. We were not holding ourselves to any schedules.

We headed north to McKenzie Island, then turned right off the main channel toward Hunter Lake. When we reached Corbeau Island I was relieved to find a camp with someone at home. Our fuel tank was almost empty. The owner of the camp, a burly, black-bearded man with only one arm, was in a hurry to get to town. He seemed a little put out when I asked him to sell us gas and oil. When I handed him our little boat can, he muttered something about "kids wasting his valuable time." He filled it up, though, and seemed happy enough to take our money. "That'll be twenty-three dollars and forty-five cents. The oil's already mixed in." The price seemed pretty steep, but I could see he had a corner on the market. I counted out twenty-five dollars and told him to keep the change. He grinned and then, jamming the money into his pocket, he climbed into a big launch and roared off to town.

"Keep the change?" cried Jenny. "That was nearly a third of the money Dad gave us for the entire trip. Way to go, moneybags."

I told her not to worry. We only needed a couple more tanks of gas and there was nowhere else to spend it anyway.

We slowly approached Hunter Narrows, a tiny channel that connects Kipawa Lake to Hunter Lake. The entrance to the narrows was almost invisible and we got lost in a false inlet for awhile before finding the right passage. The passage turned out to be as shallow as it was narrow, so I sat up on the bow with a paddle directing us through a maze of huge boulders. Just when I thought we might have to turn back the narrows opened up into a large body of water. "Full speed ahead," I shouted back to Jenny; "this must be Hunter Lake."

As we ventured further out onto the water the lake grew in size. Large, gray waves began to lift and jostle our boat as we struggled to keep the bow pointing into the wind. The distant shores were heavily wooded like those on Lake Temiskaming, but the hills were flatter and seemed to go on forever. The woods loomed dark and sinister beneath the overcast sky. The place gave me the creeps. I began to wish we had chosen a different route.

In a bay to our left along a rocky shoreline stood a cluster of small run-down cabins. Jenny and I shared our amazement that anyone would build in such an eerie, inhospitable location. Compared to this, our home on Lake Temiskaming seemed like paradise. As the waves continued to mount, we were momentarily tempted to make a run towards shore, but the prospect of turning sideways to the big whitecaps frightened us both. We were too young to remember the overturned canoes and the drowned boys on Lake Temiskaming, but nonetheless, we had heard the sobering tale a hundred times.

Eventually we came to a second set of narrows and were surprised to see a group of Boy Scouts coming toward us in an odd-looking craft. It turned out to be three large canoes tied side by side with a white sheet rigged in the middle for a sail. Happy to see some fellow travelers on the lonely lake, we waved to them and called out a greeting as they approached. They continued staring straight ahead as if we were invisible. We stood up and yelled but they passed by like a boatful of mannequins. It left us with a strange, uneasy feeling.

It had taken us nearly two hours to cross the first half of Hunter Lake in the rough water. We had hoped to reach a small outpost labeled Mungo on our map, but after passing through the second narrows and finding an even larger body of turbulent water, our plans quickly changed. Mungo was just too remote to hold any attraction for us. Mom always said that the three most important considerations in real estate are "location, location, and location." Mungo lacked all three.

Jenny and I resolved to stop at a small island just beyond the second narrows. The constant beating of wind and waves on our boat was wearing us down both physically and mentally. We pulled into a shallow bay on the lee side of the island, then clambered up on shore to a small height of land. Both of us hoped that getting out of the boat would raise our spirits. It didn't. If the lake was destitute and scary, the land was only ten times worse. When our feet touched the ground, all of our energy and optimism seemed to drain right out through the soles of our shoes. The island felt empty and dead. There were no signs of bird or animal life and even the trees had some sort of ugly grayish blight hanging from their limbs. In the center of the island was an old tumbledown shack surrounded by piles of rusted cans, wine bottles, and the skeletal remains of some long-dead creature.

"Let's just go. I don't like it here at all," Jenny said. I agreed. We returned to the boat immediately and motored back out into the channel toward Turtle Island.

It felt good to be leaving the Hunter Lake area, but as we wound our way along the eastern shore of Turtle Island massive thunderclouds came rolling in from the southeast. Neither of us had eaten since early that morning, so I rummaged through our food box looking for something that could be fixed in a hurry. While I spread peanut butter and jam on slices of bread, large heavy raindrops began beating down all around us. Jenny continued steering the boat but seemed a little distressed. Hoping to put her at ease, I handed her a sandwich and said, "Soggy peanut butter and jam for lunch." Forcing a smile, she replied, "Better than pine gum and ants."

Jenny was referring to a story that Dad used to tell of a trapper named Joe Meek, who was lost and starving in the mountains. For several days he wandered, surviving on roots, pine gum and pieces of buckskin which he cut from the fringe of his leggings. One afternoon when he was nearly played out, Joe stumbled onto a large anthill. The tiny insects went scurrying in all directions. Mad with hunger and fatigue, Joe sat down and began to eat the crunchy little morsels "one bug at a time." Soon it became obvious he was expending more energy catching each one than it was worth. At the rate he was going he would likely perish from starvation anyway. Suddenly Joe had a flash of brilliance. Reaching into his possibles bag he found a piece of pine gum which he proceeded to rub vigorously onto the palms of his hands. Once they were coated with sticky sap, he placed his hands on top of the anthill with the palms facing up. It wasn't long until they were covered with writhing insects. Now he could simply "lick 'em off." Meek was so famished he said they tasted like "nuts 'n' honey." Several months later, having survived the ordeal, Joe was riding across the prairie and his horse kicked the top off another anthill. "Why not try it again?" he mused as he swung down from his saddle holding a chunk of pine gum. Apparently he wasn't as hungry though; on that occasion he spit them out and said they just tasted like ants! Thinking about the lost trapper munching on bugs made the soggy peanut butter sandwich a bit more palatable.

By the time we reached the northeast corner of Turtle Island, the rain had changed from a downpour to a deluge with no end in sight. We were soaked to the bone and miserable. At least there had been no lightning or thunder to add to our woes. As we rounded the final point of the island the channel opened up into another vast body of water filled with churning whitecaps. I turned to speak to Jenny, but the look on her face said everything—we could go no further. It was then I noticed a sandy beach in a small, protected cove directly behind us. We had overlooked the little sanctuary when rounding the point in the pouring rain. "Let's turn back," I said, motioning toward the beach. Jenny responded by pushing the tiller hard to the left and opening up the throttle. The closer we came to the beach, the more inviting it looked. When our bow nosed up onto the sand, however, we noticed a sign painted in bold, black letters nailed to a birch tree. It read: "Buffy's Bare Ass Beach." Jenny stared at the sign and then turned to me and asked, "Does that say "Buffy's Bare Ass Beach", or am I hallucinating?"

"That's right," I answered, stepping out of the boat. Beyond the sign, hidden in a stand of scruffy jackpine was a small cabin. "Hopefully no one's at home," I said to Jenny as we cautiously approached the side of the building. Neither of us was looking forward to meeting someone named Buffy in a state of undress.

The cabin was built from chipboard and painted a putrid shade of green. After knocking on the screen door several times, we walked around the building, stiff-legged from sitting in the boat so long. Once we were sure that no one was there, we unloaded our dripping belongings on to the screened porch, then changed into dry clothing. We arranged everything where we hoped it would begin to dry in the wind. There was a mattress leaning up against one wall and a table with four chairs around it. We lay our wet map out on the table along with several cans of food, then sat down to rest. Jenny was looking a little forlorn.

"Are you okay?" I asked. She started to say "No," but her face crumpled up and she began to cry. "I don't know," she said. "This is stupid. I don't even know why I'm crying." Jenny does not get discouraged often, and she never cries, but it had been a long, trying day.

226

We laid the mattress down and zipped our sleeping bags together for warmth. Fortunately, they were both still dry. After climbing into our bags we leaned against the cabin wall and attempted to warm up our feet. I could still hear Jenny softly crying so I picked up my book and began to read to her out loud. Neither of us expected the woods here to be so vast and desolate.

After a while Jenny and I began to talk about the events of the day. I said that the land seemed empty and godforsaken. She profoundly replied, " Our tiny spirits cannot fill the terrible loneliness of our surroundings." I had to agree. It seemed as though our souls were so small compared to the overwhelming emptiness of the land, that it had left us feeling weak and vulnerable. We had spent the day fighting a sort of battle against the great void of the Hunter Lake woods.

Evening was fast approaching and we needed a warm place to sleep. The night was going to be too cold and damp to stay on the porch. We considered getting back in the boat and trying to reach Corbeau Island, but the thought of being out on the lake again was nerve-wracking. I circled the cabin, searching for a way inside. The door was locked but I found a window on the porch that slid open.

Feeling like a criminal, I climbed through the window and let myself down onto a couch to reach the floor. When Jenny followed I put my hands on my hips and scolded her in a motherly voice, "Now, you know better than to stand on the furniture with your shoes on, Dearie. I guess you can do the dishes by your lonesome tonight."

She laughed and replied, "What dishes, Ma? I thought we were having peanut butter sandwiches again."

After unlocking the front door, we carried our gear inside and lit a fire in the woodburning stove. Jenny chopped up some potatoes and carrots to boil, while I continued to explore the building. At one end of the couch was a revolving panel filled with paperback books and old tabloids. I thumbed through the stack until I found something familiar. It was one of our childhood favorites, "She-Ra, Princess of Power," from the series *Too Long at the Fair*. "Have I got a surprise for you," I called to Jenny, as she added hot dogs and onions to the pot of boiling vegetables. We giggled and laughed as I read excerpts from She-Ra, while our dinner bubbled and steamed on the glowing stove. The smell of hot food was enough to make me faint. We ate until we thought we would burst. Then, just like a pair of Goldilocks, we wandered back to the bedroom and laid down on the twin beds and fell fast asleep.

Later that night I dreamed that a large, naked, wild-haired lady with the name Buffy tattooed on her chest, was chasing us down Bare Ass Beach. Jenny was in the lead, as usual. No one beats Jenny. I was second, with Buffy fast on my heels. It was strange because we kept running past the same boldly painted sign in front of the cabin, as though we were circling the entire island every couple of minutes. The naked woman was tireless. Every time I looked back over my shoulder she would utter a piercing, devilish scream that sent chills down my spine. And yet, she never gained any ground. At one point I stumbled and rolled in the sand, expecting to be crushed by my tormenter, but I found she had stumbled at exactly the same moment. When I slowed down to catch my breath, she also slowed, maintaining the same distance. I quit running altogether and tried walking. Sure enough, she walked at the same pace. We finally escaped by jumping into our boat and pushing out onto the lake, while Buffy taunted and cursed us from shore. After the dream I fell asleep utterly exhausted. Thus ended the longest day of my life.

Friday, August 7, 1992 — Turtle Island, Lake Kipawa:

We awoke at 7:00 A.M. , loaded the boat, and left the cabin in a hurry. "What's the rush?" Jenny asked irritably as I piled half-packed gear and loose cans of food in her arms while prodding her down to the beach. Rather than explain my scary dream, I simply told her we should make haste while the lake was calm and the skies serene.

What a glorious morning! As we pushed off from shore, velvety shafts of sunlight penetrated the treetops and gently touched the glassy water like long, golden fingers in front of our bow. "Those are the fingers of God," I thought to myself as I gazed up through the rays of light at a perfectly cloudless sky. The mirror like surface of the lake was momentarily broken by a small fish, maybe a trout or mooneye, leaping skyward toward a tiny insect that was making lazy circles in one of the beams of light. The fish made a half-dozen acrobatic leaps, each one higher than the last. It seemed determined to better its effort with every jump, like a pole-vaulter raising the bar after each successful attempt. On its final leap the little fish appeared to sprout wings. It soared to an even higher point, then suspending itself in mid-flight, snagged the unwary fly, cartwheeled once, and dropped back right through the center of the ring of ripples it had created when it broke the water.

I wanted to applaud, but instead turned to Jenny who was sitting in the back of the boat with her arms and legs crossed and her eyes half-shut. "Wasn't that fantastic?" I exclaimed. Barely moving

228

her lips she muttered, "I guess if you're a granola-head you'd get off on something like that." Rather than take offense, I smiled and said, "You'll feel better after some breakfast, Jen. How about some raisins and a granola bar?"

She responded by yanking the pull cord on the outboard which popped and sputtered to life, and brought to a close that perfectly tranquil moment.

As we motored up the channel I carefully surveyed the map. We were debating whether to go north to Hunter Point (no relationship to Hunter Lake), or turn east towards Laniel via Corbeau Island. It was mainly a question of fuel. Dad had encouraged us to visit the old mission and Hudson's Bay post at Hunter Point where Charles Farr had spent several years as chief trader. It sounded intriguing, but my calculations told me we would run out of gas about halfway there. Our only safe bet was to travel east toward Laniel.

An hour later we were still headed north looking for the channel, when to our utter amazement, we saw the steeple of a church looming high above the trees. "Could it be?" I turned and asked Jenny, unwilling to trust my vision without my glasses. She nodded her head yes, and continued steering the boat. We rounded the bend and there, in the outer reaches of Kipawa Lake on a deserted peninsula, stood a large white church with a towering steeple. After landing the boat, we approached the front entrance and found it unlocked. Jenny and I went cautiously inside. Judging by the layers of dust on the pews the church had not been in use for years. High up on the front wall were ornately painted statues of Jesus on the cross, the Madonna and Child, and various saints and angels. Obviously we had missed the channel to Corbeau Island and had ended up at the old mission. "The trading post can't be far off," Jenny said. "I hope there is someone there who can sell us gasoline."

We climbed back into the boat and traveled a short distance, about half a mile, when suddenly the motor began to sputter and cough. Jenny quickly pulled the manual choke partway out and tilted the fuel tank while I pumped on the gas line and prayed our boat would not die in mid-channel. Five minutes seemed like an eternity. We continued chugging along even after the pump on the hose went flat. Just as the motor gave a final gasp and quit we glimpsed the shingled roof of the old trading post at the base of a nearby hill. What a welcome sight. I set the oars in their locks and happily rowed the final distance to shore.

As we pulled up to the docks, a little old man with baggy pants and bright red suspenders walked out to greet us. He was hunched over, and something in his demeanor made me lapse into my Utah dialect.

"Howdy, we need some direction as to our whereabouts."

"Your whats?" he hacked.

"Our whereabouts," I responded a bit louder.

"Where ya headed?" he asked, scratching the white bristles on his chin.

"To Laniel by way of Turtle Point and Corbeau Island," I replied.

"Well you're going the wrong direction. You must be lost," he said tugging on his suspenders.

"Not really, Sir, we're just out exploring the lake a little."

"Oh," he coughed. "Thought you were a couple of women biologists or somethin'. Lot's of 'em these days, women biologists. Most of 'em are lost, or hungry, or out of gas. 'Twould appear you are all three."

Jenny and I looked at each other and laughed. He filled our gas tank, gave us a loaf of bread, then told us to stay to the right as we headed down the main channel and to watch for the white rocks in front of a small island.

"Can't miss it," he assured us. We had already missed it once.

"There's a little bit of a dock and a small chute just beyond that. Gets pretty narrow though." He continued mumbling something about women biologists as he turned and shuffled back inside his cabin.

We still had some trouble finding it, but eventually Jenny sighted the narrow chute and we passed through the channel. After stopping at Corbeau and picking blueberries for a couple of hours, we proceeded to the east side of McKenzie Island and made camp in a majestic stand of white pines. The wood we found was too wet to build a fire and cook on, so for dinner we ate peanut butter sandwiches stuffed with fresh blueberries. It was a feast. While we laid out our sleeping bags, a large, yellow-haired porcupine came lumbering through the middle of camp and climbed a tree right next to our tent. When it reached a point about thirty feet high we noticed another porcupine nestled there in the fork of two heavy boughs. Probably its mate. We crawled into our tent and fell asleep to the familiar clucking sound made by the prickly pair in the branches overhead.

230

Saturday, August 8, 1992—McKenzie Island, Lake Kipawa:

We awoke in the morning to the sound of animals raiding our camp. Jenny quietly unzipped the tent flap just enough to observe two fat chattering chipmunks chewing their way into a bag of trail mix. They were stuffing their faces with raisins and nuts. "I'll teach those greedy little camp robbers a lesson," she said, pulling on her boots and stomping out of the tent in her long johns. The chipmunks quickly scattered into a pile of rocks. Jenny picked up the bag of trail mix, then walked to the boat and stowed it safely inside our food box. She returned momentarily, holding a fishing pole in one hand and a bag of unshelled peanuts in the other. "I'm going fishing for chipmunks," she announced with a mischievous grin. After removing a hook and sinker from the end of the line, she tied a peanut securely in its place. Positioning herself partway inside the entrance of the tent she raised the pole and gently cast her line towards the pile of rocks. The peanut landed about ten feet from the place where the chipmunks had hidden themselves. We didn't wait very long. Within a minute two fuzzy little heads popped out of the rocks to survey the situation. From my sleeping bag I could see them testing the air for any sign of danger as their tiny noses wrinkled and sniffed in every direciton. Just then Jenny lightly flicked the fishing rod which made the peanut jump ever so slightly. It was too much for one of the bright-eyed creatures to resist. Scampering from its hole, the chipmunk made a beeline for the peanut, grabbed it in its mouth, and began a hasty retreat towards the safety of the rock pile. Jenny allowed the fishing line to play off the reel until the chipmunk was bounding in full stride. When it got within a couple feet of its hole she cranked the reel and hauled back on the pole. "Gotcha!" she cried, as the tiny ball of fur went catapulting head over heels like a miniature circus clown. Jenny and I rolled with laughter while the surprised chipmunk tumbled to a halt, shook its head, then, with renewed determination, went right back after the peanut.

"I can't believe it's going to try that again," Jenny smiled. She reeled the peanut back in a bit then released the drag to give the plucky little rodent another chance at the prize. She was having a great time. I could see this would be the highlight of her trip. Without hesitation the chipmunk returned to the bait, picked up the nut, and took off like a racehorse. This time Jenny only allowed it to get halfway back to the rock pile before bringing it up short and sending it into another series of somersaults. She laughed until tears came to her eyes. "This beats fishing any day," she crowed while retrieving the line once more. On its third attempt the chipmunk approached the peanut a bit more judiciously while its mate chattered and squealed out warnings from its hole in the rockpile.

"Obviously, that one's a girl," Jenny whispered. "She's trying to tell Mr. Macho to be careful and quit showing off." Her warnings went unheeded. Mr. Macho grabbed the bait a third time and ran "hell bent for leather," as Dad would say, until the line snapped taut and threw him for another loop. This time he was slower to recover. He laid on his stomach panting for breath with his eyes bugged out. As if to save him from further humiliation, the other chipmunk leaped from the rockpile, grabbed the fishing line in its mouth, and chewed through the knot which held the coveted peanut in place. "Yep, that one's the girl," I said to Jenny as we watched her retreat to the rockpile with the treasure in tow.

After breakfast we broke camp and prepared to spend the day slowly winding our way back to Laniel. We were supposed to meet Dad at the public dock at 5:00 P.M. , but after two short hours on the water we found ourselves already there. How embarrassing! It was barely 11:00 in the morning. After tying up our boat we walked to Al's Store and spent our last seven dollars on a bag of Oreo cookies, two candy bars, and some crackers. Anything but peanut butter or oatmeal. We hung out behind Al's for awhile, munching our food and lounging on the picnic tables beneath a sign which read, "For customer use only."

"Customers, that's us," Jenny said taking the last cookie and pulling it apart then licking all the icing out of the center. "You want the rest?" she offered, holding out the two black wafers sans frosting.

"Thanks, but no thanks," I nodded.

At 2:00 we returned to the wharf to check on our boat and get a drink of water. While we sat on the pier with our legs dangling over the water, a noisy flock of tame ducks came paddling our way.

"Let's give 'em the rest of our oatmeal," I suggested to Jenny.

"That sounds like animal cruelty," Jenny replied, as she jumped in the boat and dug into our food box. She returned, swinging a bag of oatmeal in one hand and a jar of peanut butter in the other.

"Ducks won't eat peanut butter, you silly thing."

"Perhaps not willingly, but who knows what they'll do with a little oatmeal to tempt them."

I shook my head and wondered if any creature was safe in the vicinity of my strange little sister. Perhaps some traumatic experience with an animal warped her personality when she was very young.

232

Jenny began by throwing a couple handfuls of oatmeal into the water, which sent the ducks into a cackling frenzy. While they scooped up the crumbs in their bills, Jenny, the evil and cunning temptress, prepared a dozen little globs of peanut butter rolled in oatmeal to disguise them from the unsuspecting fowl. "I call these little delicacies Peanut Butter Surprise," she said with an impish grin. "Here ducky, ducky," she coddled and coaxed as the birds approached, craning their necks in eager anticipation of another handout. "There's no such thing as a free lunch," she cried out with a sweep of her hand, scattering chunks of oatmeal and peanut butter into the lake. With a beating of wings and kicking of feet the fine-feathered friends burst into a wild cacaphonous squabble to see which one could get the most. Even though there was plenty to go around, there was hissing, biting, and pecking as they pounced and dove in all directions. Then suddenly all was quiet. Except for a soft, chewing noise like the sound of children with big wads of gum in their mouths. That was followed by a deep hacking noise not unlike a dog with chicken bones caught in its throat. Then, all at once the entire flock broke into a chorus of coughing, spitting, and gagging as they tried to rid themselves of the gooey globules stuck in their throats and bills. Jenny howled with delight, "Now they know how I've felt for the past four days surviving on peanut butter and oatmeal."

I turned to her and said, "You are a sick child, Jenny. We must see that you get some help right away."

At 4:20 P.M. we decided to get back into the boat and motor down the lake to the nearest point and watch for Dad. We wanted him to think we had just barely pulled in from our rigorous expedition, instead of hanging around Al's place most of the day. At ten minutes to five we saw the Suburban and trailer approaching the wharf. We scrambled back into the boat and came puttering around the point just as Dad climbed out of the vehicle. He waved and called out, "Great timing, eh girls?"

"Right on the money, Dad," we hollered back. He was so excited to see us he nearly fell in the lake helping us dock the boat. Then he grabbed each of us in a bear hug, lifting us right off the ground where everyone could see. How embarrassing!

An hour later when we arrived at the lodge everything seemed different. The screen door to our room still squeaked and the floorboards had the same uneven sag in the middle but somehow the place looked smaller. The entire building appeared to have shrunk. Could this be the lodge we left just four days and a thousand years ago? Could a place change that much in four days? It left me feeling a bit melancholy, as if I'd come home to somewhere I'd never actually been. Jenny crossed the room to her tape recorder and pressed the "play" button. After a long, silent pause the words "Hey Jude," came blaring from the speakers. Jen and I looked at each other, then smiled and heaved a sigh of relief. "The Beatles," I cried. "Finally something is familiar."

"Yeah!" Jenny agreed. "We're home at last."

Home Sweet Home

❦   Dam Update

Friday, August 7, 1998
Kipawa River Lodge (Topping's Camp)

At 1:00 P.M. two paddlers from South Carolina (Jim and Billy) arrived to see if they could get a shuttle back upstream after running the Kipawa. I agreed to give them a ride. I advised them to float down from the park and forget the upper section between Laniel and the park, there is not enough water to make it worthwhile. We are experiencing one of the driest, warmest years on record—the effects of El Nino.

At 7:15 P.M. Jim and Billy come bumping their way down Hollywood. "How did you like the Kipawa?" I asked them.

"Wonderful, awesome, fantastic!" cried Jim. "We had the whole river to ourselves," Billy raved. "In South Carolina when we get water releases from the dams people line up by the hundreds to go kayaking. On certain rivers you must draw a permit just to paddle for a day, otherwise the river would be wall-to-wall boaters. But this is incredible. Ten miles of whitewater all to ourselves! What a perfectly pristine stretch of water."

Jim went on to explain how they had run about a dozen rivers in the past twenty days from South Carolina to Quebec, "but none have the remote beauty or water quality of the Kipawa. We kept doing Eskimo rolls and opening our eyes underwater just to watch the air bubbles recirculating clear to the bottom. What an amazing river! If the Kipawa were in South Carolina and someone was trying to divert the water, the public outcry would be heard all the way to the capitol. Losing this river would be a travesty." They asked me to thank Mike McCubbin for putting the word out on the Internet.

Jumping at Grande Chute.

Chapter 24

THE DROWNING OF JEAN GUY GOULET

Life is either a daring adventure or it is nothing at all.
—Helen Keller

"There's a policeman at the trailhead to Grande Chute and he wouldn't let us pass. He said the trail is closed for the day because a man was swept over the falls."

I recognized the voice. It was Rob Simpson, one of our perennial guests, talking to his friend Bernie. I could hear bits and pieces of their conversation from where I was working on the Boathouse deck. It had been a quiet, peaceful August weekend, but things were about to change. Dropping my hammer, I jumped to the ground and walked toward the two men.

"Is he dead?" Bernie asked.

"Most likely. It's a hundred-foot drop over some real nasty rocks," Rob replied.

As I approached they both turned to greet me. "Did I hear you say there's a policeman at Grande Chute?"

"That's right. There are two of them. They came from Ville Marie in their patrol cars and they're blocking the trail to Grande Chute. A man from Fabre went for a swim above the falls and the current dragged him down. One of his friends and two of his children saw the whole thing. They were sitting in one of the squad cars when we were talking to the police. I think they're in shock. What chance would a person have of surviving those falls?"

"Probably none," I replied, visualizing the violent, churning boil at the base of Grande Chute. "My guess would be that his body is somewhere in the calm stretch of water between Elbow and Hollywood rapids. If not there, then right here in Lake Temiskaming."

"That's kind of a sour note to finish a perfect weekend on," Bernie said as they turned and walked toward the River Cabin to pack their gear. They were headed back home to Toronto. It was Monday afternoon, August 5, 1996, the final hours of the summer Civic holiday observed across Canada every year.

I followed Rob and Bernie toward their cabin, but then walked out in front of the deck to look at the river. Hollywood rapid was running slightly higher than normal for the time of year. My three youngest daughters—Katie, Michelle, and Becky—were playing in the Jacuzzi with a couple of their friends. The Jacuzzi is a smooth, naturally-carved basin of stone situated in the center of Hollywood rapid. When the river is raging in the spring, the Jacuzzi is buried underneath eight feet of white water. In mid-to-late summer, as the river drops, it is right at the surface level, with its own small, swirling channel of water creating a perfect whirlpool bath large enough to accommodate nine or ten people. The kids often play in it for hours then jump on top of their inner tubes and float down through the bottom of Hollywood into Lake Temiskaming. As I stood there watching them play, I thought about the man who had been swept over Grande Chute a mile upstream, and I began to wonder how long it might take him to drift down to the lodge. It was a grim, unpleasant thought.

"I want you girls to get out of the river now and help me mow the lawn," I called to them.

"But Dad, we mowed it four days ago; it's not even tall enough to cut again," Michelle complained.

"That's okay, babe, we can lower the wheels on the mowers and cut it even shorter. Now hurry up and get out of the river."

With heads hanging like a trio of indentured servants, the three girls sullenly climbed onto their tubes and floated down Hollywood toward the lake. As they kicked and paddled their way into the river mouth they passed a pair of boats anchored in the current with fishing poles suspended from each side.

I hustled down to the kayak rack and lifted my bright yellow Corsica from off the top, then carried it thirty feet to the water's edge. Even though I had purposely avoided saying anything to my daughters about the accident, I thought it best to inform the fishermen and prepare them for whatever might come floating downstream. Perhaps they could even be helpful in recovering the victim.

When I paddled my kayak up alongside the first boat and explained the situation to the three men on board, they said they would be willing to assist in any way they could. The second boat contained an elderly couple whose reaction was quite different. They were horrified at the thought of a corpse drifting somewhere upstream and said that they had come to catch walleye not a drowning victim. With that they pulled up anchor and sped away toward their home in Haileybury, thirty miles up the lake.

I paddled back to shore, hoisted the kayak up on my shoulder, then took off for the tennis court where our Suburban was parked.

"What's all the excitement?" Pat called out as I jogged past the kitchen window.

"Someone's gone over Grande Chute," I yelled gulping for air. "Can you get my mask, fins and snorkel, then meet me at the Suburban? They might need some help up there."

Halfway across the back lawn, seventeen-year-old Jenny ran up alongside me dragging a second kayak. "I'll go with you, Dad. I know that part of the river almost as well as you do and I heard you say they might need some help up there."

Apparently Jenny had overheard my brief conversation with Pat through the window. I thanked her for the offer, then asked her to hike upstream from the lodge and search the shoreline alongside Hollywood. "I will meet you at the bay at the bottom of Elbow, Jen."

"But Dad!" she protested, "I want to go with you in the kayak and . . ."

"Not today, Jenny," I said cutting her off in mid-sentence. "Keep a sharp eye on the rapids as you go and take some rope. If you find him floating in the water, secure his body to a tree, then hurry upstream and find me."

For a moment Jenny gaped at me in wide-eyed silence. The thought of finding a corpse in the river had not really sunk in. She swallowed hard and pulled her long, dark hair back from her face. "What makes you so sure he's dead?"

"I hope he's not Jenny, but apparently he went over the falls with nothing more than a swimsuit on for protection. It would be a miracle to find him alive."

"Then I'll hope for a miracle," she cried, as she turned and bolted for the lodge with her kayak in tow. "I'll get some rope and meet you at the bottom of Elbow in an hour. Good luck, Dad!" Jenny added as she raced around the corner of the building and ran headlong into Pat who was carrying a load of diving gear. "Sorry Mom!" she shrieked, as fins, mask, snorkel, and wetsuit went flying in all directions. Then without missing a step she yelled, "Hurry up Mom! Dad's in a rush to get to the Chute!"

After gathering up the scattered gear, Pat arrived at the Suburban still shaking her head. "What's wrong with Jenny? She acts like she's seen a ghost."

I recounted the sobering conversation we had just had about searching for a body in the river. "Jenny's just trying to be helpful. I told her to search Hollywood, then meet me in the bay at the bottom of Elbow. "

Pat seemed distraught as we loaded the kayak and gear into the Suburban. "I just can't believe someone went over the falls. I keep thinking about Zeph Fleury and the accident with that stunt man at the Chute seventy years ago. Deja vu!"

As we drove up the steep hill behind the camp I watched the Main Lodge getting smaller and smaller in my rearview mirror and the great silvery expanse of Lake Temiskaming disappearing in the background. Things had certainly changed since the logging road had been cut to Grande Chute thirteen years ago. Prior to 1983 the majestic waterfall could only be accessed by a long and difficult hike through the bush or by taking a treacherous canoe trip down the river from Laniel. Only a few hardy souls like Zeph Fleury and Jose Mediavilla had ever seen it. Today a bright yellow sign on the highway beckons travelers to come visit Grande Chute via Topping's Road, only five miles by car down a dirt road, then a ten-minute hike on a footpath. The journey has become too easy. Now that anyone can see the falls with minimal effort, it is often taken for granted. Before the road was built we never picked up pop cans, beer bottles, candy wrappers or cigarette butts alongside the falls.

It was four o'clock when Pat and I arrived at the trailhead where the police vehicles were parked. One of the officers told us that a thirty-seven-year-old man from Fabre, Jean Guy Goulet, had attempted to swim across the river fifty yards above the falls. Apparently the man had done it successfully in previous years, but this summer the river was higher and the current stronger than normal. After swimming about three-quarters of the way across, he suddenly disappeared and was carried downstream over the brink. At least that's how the man's friend and two of his children who were standing on shore described it.

"We have temporarily closed the trail to the chutes until the area has been searched by a rescue team," said the policeman.

"How soon might that happen? Is anyone down there searching right now?" I asked.

"Not yet. It is unlikely that a rescue operation will be organized before tomorrow morning. We have already sent the man's friend and children back to their homes in Fabre. It hardly seems possible that he could survive the power of those chutes."

I agreed that his survival seemed doubtful. Two and a half hours had elapsed since the accident had occurred, but nonetheless someone should be searching downstream. Perhaps he had made it to shore seriously injured and was unable to walk. Even if he had not survived, time was of the essence in recovering the body. Should the current carry him downstream to Lake Temiskaming the man might never be found. The lake known as deep water had a history of claiming victims and not releasing them. How much worse for his family and friends to be left wondering what had ever happened to Jean Guy.

I showed the officers my kayak and told them I was familiar with the falls and the rapids below. "My daughter is already hiking upstream from our camp to help us search. Can you give me a description of the man?"

One of the officers seemed amused by my request. "He's tall, athletically built, and wearing white swim trunks. Why do you ask? Do you expect to find more than one person in that river?"

Before I could answer, he turned to his partner and they held a short conference in French. Then he wrote my name on a pad of paper and handed me a card which read: "Sgt. Brisson—Enqueter—Surete Quebec." He told me to proceed downriver and to report anything which might assist him in his investigation.

I returned to the Suburban and pulled on my wetsuit, while Pat stowed the spray skirt and helmet inside the kayak along with the dive gear. "Would you like some help carrying this out to the falls?" she inquired. I readily accepted her offer. The trail to Grande Chute is a narrow path which meanders through stands of poplar and pine for a quarter of a mile. It feels twice that far, however, hauling a kayak loaded down with gear.

Pat took the lead, grasping the bow strap, and I followed, carrying the stern in one hand and my paddle in the other. After a short distance we descended into a gully where a narrow footbridge crosses a small stream. "Step lightly and move fast," I cautioned Pat. "Underneath this thing is a large nest of short-tempered wasps." I had discovered that nest two weeks earlier when my daughters went bouncing over the bridge in front of me on a hike to the falls. By the time I reached the bridge the girls were fifty feet beyond and the bees were in an uproar.

"Look at Dad run!" They hooted and howled as I scrambled backwards out of the gully flailing my arms and beating my head and shoulders with my baseball cap. I was forced to detour upstream and cross at a large beaver dam, which took just enough time for me to calm down and regain some semblance of dignity. As I approached the girls on the other side, I could hear their partially stifled laughter.

"You gotta be faster crossing that bridge, Dad," chirped twelve-year-old Katie. "There's bees underneath it and you might get stung!" Katie has a knack for pointing out the obvious.

"Thanks for warning me, Kate. Next time I'll make sure I'm in the lead."

Pat and I crossed the bridge without incident, then climbed the hill on the far side of the gully. Five minutes later we paused on the ridge above Grande Chute and set the kayak upside down on the ground to serve as a bench. We were both tuckered out. For a moment I just lay back against the kayak catching my breath and listening to the deep, low rumbling of water crashing over rock. Pat sat down and leaned against my shoulder. "Why did you ask the police for a description of the man? It seemed like an odd request."

"You remember that incident with the missing climber on Mt. Timpanogos fifteen years ago? That's why I asked."

In the spring of 1980, while teaching an outdoor education program at a high school in Utah, I was approached by a man from Tacoma, Washington, who wanted to borrow some mountaineering equipment. He claimed to have made a solo ascent of Mt. Rainier the previous winter and said he would be in Utah for a few days and planned to climb Mt. Timpanogos. Timpanogos is a twelve-thousand-foot monolith of granite, limestone, and glacial scree under whose shadow we reside each winter. More than a few people have fallen victim to its rock slides and avalanches over the years. I told the man I could not loan him any equipment and cautioned him about the hazards of climbing solo on Timpanogos in the winter.

Five days later a pair of climbers were crossing a glacier on the east face of the mountain when one of them lost his footing and disappeared into a crevice of melting ice and snow. The man's companion quickly descended the mountain to obtain help but several hours had elapsed before a rescue party arrived on the scene.

Four men with headlamps, harnesses, and rescue equipment descended into the crevice and searched for an hour in icy, knee-deep water before locating a body. They wrapped the body in a blanket, secured it to a litter, and hauled it back to the surface of the glacier. When the victim's companion came forward to make an identification the blanket was parted just enough to expose the man's face. "That's not him!" gasped the surviving climber, staggering back from the corpse with his mouth agape. "You've found someone else. My friend is still down there."

The four incredulous members of the rescue team descended into the abyss once again and resumed their search. Forty minutes later they reappeared with another body. "That's him," acknowledged the surviving partner, having barely recovered from the shock of finding a second victim in the same crevice.

Three days later the other victim was identified. It was the man from Tacoma. Having gone ahead with his attempt to climb Mt. Timpanogos alone, he fell into the crevice and perished. He had not left word with anyone concerning his plans and thus had not been missed.

"We'd better get moving or Jenny will wonder what has happened to us," I said, hoisting the kayak onto my shoulder. Pat stepped close and gave me a hug. "Be careful," she intoned. "I hope Jenny hasn't already found that poor soul floating in the river somewhere. Do you think it was a good idea letting her hike upstream all alone?"

"Probably not," I replied as I thought about how Jenny had been playing volleyball on the beach an hour ago with some friends. Now she was out searching the river for a body. On the other hand, Jenny had done a number of things that most seventeen-year-olds had not. "She'll be just fine," I concluded as I waved good-bye to Pat and started down the steep, winding trail that leads to the base of the waterfall. While weaving my way through the tangle of cedar and birch, I recalled the day of Jenny's birth and the words of my mother-in-law who was present in the delivery room. "Surely you will not raise my precious granddaughter in the wilds of Quebec." At the time, I could not decide if it was a question or a mildly veiled threat. My only thought was that bears and wolves raise their kids in the wilds and they do just fine. Fortunately, I did not verbalize that thought. Three years later, when the opportunity to purchase the lodge afforded itself, Pat's parents were the first in line to support, encourage, and offer financial assistance in the matter, thus aiding and abetting the delinquency and wildness of their own granddaughters.

When I arrived at the riverbank I placed the kayak on a broad, sloping rock, then studied the surface of the water for several minutes. It was difficult to determine where a body might end up. At the base of the falls is a powerful recirculating eddy that pulls branches and pieces of driftwood into its clutches and churns them around and around for hours on end before releasing them downstream. Perhaps Jean Guy was trapped in the eddy somewhere beneath the surface. Alongside the eddy, at the base of the diving rock, is a deep, clear pool, the bottom of which is visible at twenty feet. I could see no sign of him there.

Beyond the pool, sixty yards downstream from the falls is Elbow, the longest rapid on the river. Elbow was named because of an abrupt, left-hand turn in the river channel where water cascades between rocky ledges, then funnels into an enormous pour-over shelf behind which lurks a huge, turbulent hole that eats kayakers for breakfast each spring. Beyond the pour-over, the rapid opens up into a long series of standing waves that empties into a broad, calm bay half a mile below Grande Chute. That was where I expected to meet Jenny. It was also the most likely place to find Jean Guy.

Sitting in my kayak atop the wide, sloping rock five feet above the water, I pushed off into the river. "Whoosh!" The kayak submerged momentarily, then popped back to the surface like a cork. I had my mask and snorkel in place strapped on beneath my helmet which allowed me to search the eddy at the base of the falls without leaving my boat. I simply flipped upside down and let the current pull me around in circles through the eddy while I scanned the bottom through my mask. When I needed to rest or get another bite of air, I set my paddle and rolled back up Eskimo-style.

Visibility in the river was very good. Perhaps too good. I could see the bottom in some places at a depth of twenty five feet. When the current pulled me close to the falls, however, my vision was severely restricted by the turbulent mixing of air and water as the falls crashed over rock then spilled into the pool. There was also an area where the depth exceeded twenty five feet and all I could see were dark shades of green and gray. It gave me the jitters. Every time I passed over the deep hole, goose bumps formed on my skin and my imagination ran wild staring into the shadowy depths. The situation was made even more eerie because of the tunnel vision created by my mask. I could only see what was directly in front of me, while objects suddenly appeared and disappeared to the right and left of the mask as I floated upside down in the current. The effect was chilling. Each time I passed over the dark hole I would see something, either real or imagined, drifting in the shadows below, then the bottom would suddenly reappear as if rushing up to meet me.

I kept thinking about a scene from the movie Jaws, where Richard Dreyfus is scuba diving at night, investigating a mysterious sunken boat. He manages to get down near the bottom of the vessel where he discovers a large, jagged hole torn out of its side. After a moment's hesitation, he shines his light through the hole. Suddenly there appears the distorted, shriveled face of a dead man floating inside the wreck. Of course, everyone in the theater knew exactly what was going to happen, but nonetheless they all screamed as if the devil himself had grabbed them by the ankles.

After making three complete circles through the eddy, my heart was racing and my lungs were aching for air, so I rolled the kayak upright and paddled to the opposite side of the eddy. Even had I found Jean Guy I was not sure I had the fortitude to dive down and haul him back to the surface. Subsequently, my thoughts turned again to Jenny. By now she would be waiting at the bottom of Elbow wondering where I was. Perhaps she had already done the very thing I was dreading and had found Jean Guy. Certainly Jenny would not hesitate to enter the river. Six months earlier, while competing at the Utah State High School Swim Finals, she had exploded off the blocks and won first place championships in two of the most difficult events. If Jenny located Jean Guy in the river, she would likely go in after him.

After making a fourth and final pass through the eddy at the bottom of the falls, I paddled my kayak toward the first big drop in Elbow rapid. Over the previous ten years I had run the rapid at least fifty times, but never alone in search of a body. As I approached the pour-over shelf, I nosed my kayak into a small eddy on the south side of the river. From there I could see the center of the immense hole created by the pour-over. Six weeks earlier, I had watched an inflatable raft with seven frantic paddlers being dragged sideways into the wild, frothing hole. One of the paddlers was my eldest daughter, nineteen-year-old April. Later she gave me a descriptive account of how the raft flipped end for end, dumping all of its passengers into the river. As she fought her way to the surface, April felt a tremendous force pulling her back upstream into the pour-over hole. She had the presence of mind however, to quit struggling and allow herself to be drawn back into it, then curl up tight in a ball and let the strong undercurrent drag her down and push her out downstream. One young man who was thrown from the raft recirculated through the hole four times. He continued fighting for air and struggling to stay near the surface where the dangerous reverse current kept taking him backward into the pour-over. Eventually he grew weary and gave up. Then he was pulled down deep enough for the downstream current to carry him away from the pour-over.

I paddled through Elbow looking behind rocks and in eddies but found no trace of Jean Guy. When I floated into the calm bay at the bottom of the rapid, I was relieved to see Jenny about three hundred yards away, advancing slowly upstream stepping over windfalls and rocks along the north shore. I whistled and signaled with my paddle to get her attention. She waved back and continued to walk in my direction.

"Did you find him, Dad?" Jenny called out as I approached her.

"No luck," I replied shaking my head. "Let's check the bottom of the bay." I pulled the kayak up to shore at Jenny's feet, then squirmed out of the cockpit and reached back into the hull to retrieve my dive gear. While I adjusted my mask, fins, and snorkel, Jenny knelt down and reached forward into the kayak and shortened the foot pegs so she could paddle around on the surface while I searched the bottom. By the time I was in the water and breathing through my snorkel, Jenny had traversed to the far side of the bay and disappeared into a narrow channel behind a small island about two hundred yards away. I hated losing sight of her. If and when I found Jean Guy, I hoped Jenny would be close at hand to assist me, or vice versa for that matter.

With a thrust of my fins I propelled myself toward the channel where Elbow rapid spilled into the bay. My plan was to enter the current at the bottom of the rapid, then work my way to midstream and see where it would carry me. With my mask in place I had good visibility to a depth of about twenty feet. In most places the bay was no more than twenty five feet deep so I could vaguely see the bottom, which was scattered with pieces of waterlogged driftwood and sunken debris all covered with moss from years of being submerged in the river. A corpse in white swim trunks would be easy to see. Subconsciously I began to hope I would not find him. Perhaps through some miraculous occurrence he had survived the falls, floated to shore, then walked out through the bush and hitched a ride back to town. Maybe at this moment he was sitting at his kitchen table telling the incredible tale to his wife and children. Doubtful.

As I approached the channel where Elbow pours into the bay, the current grabbed hold of my legs and began pressing me backwards. It was surprisingly powerful. Immediately I turned sideways to the flow and kicked and stroked to midstream where I put my face down and let myself drift along as I studied the river bottom. At the mouth of the channel the water was perfectly clear and less than ten feet deep. The bottom was a bright mosaic of polished stones laid out in neat, concentric patterns formed over centuries by the strong, undulating current rushing down from Grande Chute. Further downstream the force of the river diminished and the bottom dropped to about twenty-five feet. The water took on a dark green murkiness. I could still make out shadowy outlines of boulders, sunken logs, and gnarled driftwood directly below me. This was the place I expected to find Jean Guy, if in fact he had not made it out of the river alive. Then I saw him. Or at least a glimpse of a contorted, white figure pushed up against some debris on the bottom of the riverbed. With my pulse racing and my heart pounding, I jerked my head above waterline, ripped the snorkel from my mouth and gasped wildly for air. The current continued to carry me downstream so I took a bearing on a large, gray rock along the shoreline to mark my position. Then I looked around for Jenny. She was still out of sight behind the far side of the island, less than a hundred yards away. I started to call out but then thought better. Before sending out an alarm, I wanted to confirm if what I had seen was actually the body of Jean Guy.

For a moment I treaded water and took several deep breaths in an attempt to calm my nerves. Mentally I traded places with the figure at the bottom of the bay. I imagined myself down there and Pat and my five daughters worrying and waiting for me back at camp. It would not be enough to go to Jean Guy's home and tell his family I thought I saw him at the bottom of the bay. Or something that looked sort of like him. There was really no alternative to diving down and making an honest attempt to recover his body.

I replaced my snorkel in my mouth then turned and swam back into the current until I was directly upstream from the area I had seen the white form. Once again, I drifted with the current until the pale, contorted figure came into view. Gulping a huge breath of air, I tipped my head and shoulders down and began kicking with my fins straight towards the bottom. "Try not to look at his face," I thought to myself as I struggled to get deeper. "Just take hold of his arm or his hair and pull him up to the surface." At a depth of fifteen feet the blurry form took on a familiar shape. Suddenly I was overcome with relief. It was nothing more than a dead birch tree with a couple of limbs still intact. It had recently fallen into the Kipawa and drifted downstream before settling on the bottom of the bay. Lying there in twenty-five feet of water with its white bark and twisted limbs, nothing could have looked more like a body in white swim trunks. I was off the hook.

By the time I regained the surface my lungs were exploding and my head was pounding from the pressure. I tore the snorkel from my mouth, rolled onto my back, and lay there gasping for oxygen.

"What's wrong?" called Jenny as she paddled the kayak up alongside me.

"Nothing Jen. I'm just out of breath. Let me rest a minute and we'll continue searching downstream."

Together Jenny and I paddled and swam towards the end of the bay. When we approached Hollywood rapid the channel constricted and the current quickened. I could feel the river pulling on my arms and legs as the shoreline slipped by at an ever-increasing speed. Looking down through my mask, there were large rocks passing beneath me like traffic under a bridge. It was time to get out of the river.

"Grab hold, Dad; I'll tow you to shore," Jenny yelled as she positioned the kayak so I could reach the safety strap on the stern. We pulled into an eddy at the top of Hollywood with only a few yards to spare. Around the turn the rapid was hissing and howling like a pack of hungry wolves. Once on shore, Jenny and I traded places. She set off walking down the trail toward the camp carrying my dive gear, while I reentered the kayak to make a run down Hollywood in a final attempt to locate Jean Guy.

My descent to the lake was slow and thorough. Even though Jenny had searched the rapid from the riverbank, there were a dozen or more pools and eddies where a body might snag and remain hidden from view behind ledges or in between large boulders. There were also a couple more pour-over shelves where he could have been trapped and recirculated. My ten-minute paddle through Hollywood turned up nothing. I returned to the lodge feeling weary and dismayed. After searching every likely place I could imagine between Grande Chute and the mouth of the river, I concluded that Jean Guy's body was out in Lake Temiskaming and might never be recovered. The thought gave me the shivers as I stood on the dock looking out over the gloomy gray surface of the lake. He was out there somewhere and until he was found that knowledge would haunt me every time I went for a swim or a paddle.

That evening after dinner I decided to go fishing in the mouth of the river. Fishing had been slow for several days; nonetheless, I wanted to be outside doing something, even if it were nothing more than practicing my casts and watching the sunset. I couldn't quit thinking about Jean Guy.

Accompanied by my friend Derek Spriggs, who was visiting from Utah, I anchored the aluminum boat in the center of the mouth of the river where I had an unobstructed view of the rapids. Attaching a dark-green, yellow-bellied shad rap on the end of my line, I began casting toward the south shore then slowly retrieving the lure, but all the while my eyes remained fixed on Hollywood.

Fifteen minutes later a fiberglass boat with three passengers on board came racing into the river mouth. Initially I thought it was the same three fishermen I had talked to earlier that day who had so kindly offered to assist in watching for Jean Guy. But then I noticed it was a slightly smaller boat with two men sitting on the front deck, and a woman at the steering wheel. She headed straight for Whistler's Point on the south side of the inlet. When the boat touched land, one of the men jumped out and started hiking upriver toward Grande Chute. Then the boat idled across to the north side where the other man disembarked and began walking upstream on the path that led directly in front of the River Cabin. It was obvious they were searching for Jean Guy. After the second man had disappeared into the bush, the woman maneuvered the boat back into the mouth of the river and dropped anchor about fifty feet away from Derek and me. For several minutes she remained standing, holding the steering wheel and staring intently upstream at the rapids. I did not recognize the woman, but when she looked in our direction, I greeted her with a wave of my hand. She waved back but offered no explanation for their visit. Worry and concern were etched in the lines on her face.

"Do you know Jean Guy?" I called out to her. She turned to me with an expression of utter despair. My question had caught her off guard and I regretted asking it as soon as the words had left my mouth. Tears welled up in her eyes then rolled down her cheeks and a sob wracked her entire frame.

"I'm sorry," I said, but she immediately waved off my apology.

"I am Jean Guy's sister and the two men walking upstream are my brothers. We will search until dark and if we have not found him, we will return tomorrow and search again."

I explained how we had learned of the tragedy from the police and of our efforts to locate Jean Guy. "I am truly sorry about your brother," I said a bit uncomfortably. "My daughter and I looked everywhere we could imagine between the falls to the mouth of the river, but found no sign of him."

She graciously thanked us for the assistance, then turned her gaze back upstream and continued watching the rapids

Jean Guy never turned up that night. Nor the following day. His family members continued the difficult and desperate search to locate him, but with each passing hour hope was fading and a tragic conclusion seemed inevitable. It struck me as unusual that the brothers, sisters, nieces, and nephews were all out looking for him even before a search and rescue team had arrived, like something that might have been common a hundred years ago, but exceptionally rare in 1996. Nowadays when someone is lost or in trouble, I get the impression that it is turned over to the police or the search and rescue unit, while the family sits at home around the kitchen table wringing their hands and drinking coffee. Such was not the case with the family of Jean Guy Goulet that warm August night on the Kipawa River.

The search dragged on for three days until all possibilities had been exhausted with the exception of Lake Temiskaming or the whirlpool at the base of Grande Chute. If it proved to be the lake, there was nothing to do but wait for the body to come to the surface. If he was still in the eddy at the bottom of the falls, the river might have to be shut off so the body could be released from the powerful, recirculating current. Eventually that is what happened. The flumes at the dam in Laniel were closed and scuba divers descended into the pool at the base of Grande Chute where they located and recovered Jean Guy's body. For several weeks after the incident there were questions asked about Jean Guy's behavior and judgement. "Why did he try to swim the river in such a dangerous place? Didn't he realize what would happen if he were swept over the falls? Whatever possessed that man?"

I never met Jean Guy, but I have known people like him— regular, ordinary people who for some reason feel compelled to do unordinary things. A few of the kayakers who paddle the Kipawa River like to "push the envelope" when it comes to running rapids and drops that reasonable people would deem crazy and reckless. But for those who possess unusual skill or perhaps unusual heart and courage, the action is neither crazy nor reckless. It is something they simply feel compelled to do. It is merely a calculated risk. Some people do it by playing the stock market or the blackjack tables. Others, like Jean Guy, do it by swimming rivers, climbing mountains, and jumping out of airplanes. Each offers its own risks and rewards whether physical, financial, or emotional.

I have a friend who visits the lodge from time to time with his wife and ten children. His favorite activity is to swim across Lake Temiskaming and back. I have accompanied him on occasion, but only when conditions are calm, sunny, and warm. Terrel, on the other hand, will undertake the challenge any hour of the day or night, and whenever the urge to "take a little swim" strikes him. On one occasion he and his family arrived at the lodge at dusk. While his wife and children were getting settled in at the River Cabin, I asked them where I could find Terrel. "Oh, I suppose he's out swimming across the lake," said his wife, Janet. "Just leave a lamp burning in the kitchen window of the Main Lodge so he can find his way back." An hour and half after dark, with a big yellow moon reflecting on the surface of the water, Terrel appeared on the beach looking happy and well. "Nothing like a swim across the lake to cleanse the body and renew the spirit," he proclaimed as he sauntered off toward the sauna.

On another visit Terrel showed up all by himself on a weekend that was "just too boring in town." I was busy working on the Boathouse roof when he set out backstroking for the Ontario shore. Every now and then I looked up from my work to check his progress. Twenty minutes later a surprise thunderstorm blew in from Manitoba replete with lightning bolts and sufficient wind to create two-foot whitecaps. I scanned the surface of the lake for Terrel, but he was already lost from view in the waves. Subsequently, I climbed down from the roof and took a boat out to search for him. With lightning striking all around and torrents of rain driving into my face, I proceeded through the storm to the other side of the lake, then returned to the lodge without sighting him. An hour later, when the storm had passed, I was lounging on the screened porch wondering how I would tell Janet and his ten kids that Terrel had drowned in a violent thunderstorm, he came side stroking into the docks looking happy as a loon. His first words to me were, "What in the world were you doing out on the lake in a boat during that squall? You could have been killed! Whatever possessed you, man?"

According to Terrel's line of reasoning, standing up in a metal boat "acting like a lightning rod," was infinitely more dangerous and foolhardy than swimming in the water. "Have you ever heard of a fish getting hit by lightning? Of course not!" Terrel said, wagging an accusatory finger in my direction. "Only people standing up in boats get hit by lightning."

Shortly thereafter I found myself apologizing to Terrel for my irresponsible and reckless behavior. There was no point in trying to explain that I had actually ventured out in the storm to rescue him. Any suggestion of that sort would have been deemed preposterous and irrational by a man who believes that swimming across Lake Temiskaming in a thunderstorm holds no more risk than a walk in the park on a windy afternoon. I allowed him to continue laboring under the illusion that I had merely gone out there to satisfy an unquenchable thirst for adventure. "It was just so boring working up on that roof watching you swim across the lake in those waves," I told him.

Terrel put his hand on my shoulder and said he understood what I was feeling, but I needed to use more restraint and better judgement before setting out in a boat under such perilous conditions. "After all, you have a wife and five children counting on you for support." I suppressed the urge to remind Terrel that he has exactly twice that number of children depending on him for support. It would have been a waste of breath. Terrel has a degree in accounting and a way of playing with numbers that would have resulted in making me seem all the more foolish.

Five days after the drowning of Jean Guy Goulet a funeral was held in town. The Catholic church was filled to capacity with friends, relatives, and neighbors. The unexpected death of a man so young and vital affects everyone in a community as small and tightly knit as Fabre, Quebec. His body was laid to rest in the cemetery on the hill overlooking the village. I was not there, nor should I have been. I never knew Jean Guy Goulet. Nonetheless, I pay tribute to him for his strong and wild heart, and the unbridled spirit that compelled him to swim the Kipawa River. There is a brotherhood of restless souls who were not born to play it safe or content to always walk the beaten path. Certain individuals set their own track through life and step to the beat of a different drummer. Perhaps he is one of them. I hope that wherever he is now, there might also be a river as wild and beautiful as the Kipawa for Jean Guy to swim across.

Chapter 25

HAM THE CAT

Ignorant people think it's the noise
which fighting cats make that is
so aggravating, but it ain't so;
it's the sickening grammar they use.
—Mark Twain

I have never been fond of cats. It is a prejudice I inherited from my father who said that cats are "lacking in character, loyalty, and the ambition to do anything but lay in the shade and kill birds." Generally speaking my father was right, with the exception of Ham.

Ham was a big gray tomcat, a one-eyed street fighter from the alleys of North Bay, Ontario. He was on loan to us from Ron and Audette Huywan, who said he was a good mouser. That was an understatement. Ham the cat tracked down, killed, and tried to devour everything that walked, hopped, or crawled on its belly. He swatted flies and moths on the windows. He caught frogs, minnows, and crayfish at the beach. He chased rabbits and squirrels from our garden and tangled with skunks, snakes, and woodchucks wherever he encountered them. Mice he considered small game, easy prey—mere appetizers.

On his first day at the lodge, Pat offered Ham a bowl of cat food from a bag we had purchased in town. It was a gesture of good will on her part. She wanted the cat to feel at home in its new surroundings. He sniffed the food suspiciously, then with a powerful swipe of his paw, scattered the bowl and its contents all over the kitchen floor.

"What a rude, ungrateful animal," Pat fumed as she reached for the broom. For a moment, it was unclear whether she intended to sweep up the mess or give the cat a sound thrashing. With a contemptuous snarl, Ham stalked out the front door and disappeared into the brush alongside the river. Twenty minutes later I found him on the back porch chewing on a big fat mole. Obviously he preferred to catch and kill his own meals.

Ham the cat was a hunter from head to tail. In the fall whenever I trekked upriver with my shotgun looking for woodcocks, grouse, or ducks, Ham would trail behind me lurking in the shadows like a little gray ghost. He was as silent and stealthy as a wolverine. When I flushed a grouse or jumped a duck, he would spring from his hiding place and attack with deadly precision. And pity the poor fowl that fell to the ground wounded. Like a tiny enraged boxer, Ham would pounce on it and bat its head to and fro until the unfortunate bird succumbed to the pummeling. In battle Ham gave no quarter and showed no mercy.

Like most cats, Ham was aloof and demonstrated little affection for anyone. At times he would look at me as if he were sizing me up for his next meal. Ham and I were not pals, just hunting companions.

On occasion Ham would disappear into the bush on forays of his own that lasted for several days. Once, when we had given him up for dead, he suddenly reappeared all battered and scarred but nonetheless proud to have survived. He was a cat with a swagger and an ego. Perhaps he suffered from delusions of grandeur and perceived himself as a mountain lion or a lynx.

One day a smartly dressed couple in a large leisure craft pulled up to our docks and asked permission to moor their boat while they hiked up along the rapids. They were accompanied by a coiffed but feisty beagle with a pretty blue bow attached to its collar. I noticed it matched the one in the woman's hair. She called the dog Sweeticums. I warned her about Ham the cat and told her she might want to put the dog on a leash. She smiled and said, "Sweeticum's bark is worse than his bite. He won't harm your cat." She misunderstood. It was Sweeticums I was worried about, not Ham.

As they were tying their boat alongside the dock, Ham came strutting around the corner of the Main Lodge with a half-eaten chipmunk hanging from his mouth. The sight of the gray cat was more than the high-strung beagle could stand. With a loud yelp he lunged from the deck of the boat and bolted toward Ham with reckless abandon. The man turned and threw up his arms in frustration, while the woman yelled, "Come back, Sweeticums. Come back!"

Ham held his ground until the charging beagle was four feet away, then he leaped into a small birch tree that grew next to the walkway. The crazed beagle took that as a sign of surrender. He barked and jumped high in the air snapping wildly at the cat's tail, which hung from a branch barely beyond his reach. Meanwhile, Ham sat calmly in the tree while finishing his lunch.

Eventually the beagle grew weary and turned to walk back to his master's boat. That was a grave mistake. Sweeticums had not taken two steps when Ham came flying out of the tree, pounced on his back, and began raking the dog's eyes and ears with his claws. The terrified beagle bolted toward the dock, howling like a hound from hell, which only encouraged the one-eyed monster clinging to his back. Ham scratched, bit, and pummeled the panic-stricken animal all the way back to the boat. Only when the dog's owners resorted to beating Ham with life jackets did the angry cat relinquish his hold on the beagle's head.

"Poor, poor Sweeticums," cried the horrified woman as she lifted the whimpering whelp onto her lap and reached for a towel to staunch the flow of blood from its lacerated ear. The pretty blue bow was now a tangle of crimson shreds hanging limply from one side of the dog's neck.

Ham remained on the dock, pacing back and forth with a smug look on his face. He seemed to be taunting the poor, disillusioned beagle who lay whining on its mistress's lap.

"We must get Sweeticums to the doctor," the woman implored her husband.

The man quickly boarded the boat, then turned to me and said, "Your pet is a menace. It should be put to sleep!"

"You're right," I replied apologetically. "He is a menace, but he's not my pet. He's just my hunting partner."

One night in early September a large bat found its way into the lodge and proceeded to fly in circles from one end of the room to the other. Pat and I were sitting near the fireplace trying to read, but every time the bat swooped overhead, I found it difficult to concentrate on my book. Ham, who had spent the afternoon terrorizing chickens in the backyard, was lounging contentedly on our bed when the bat caught his attention. For several minutes he studied the flight pattern of the strange, flying mouse as it dodged between the cupboards and shelves and dove beneath the rafters. When the bat passed over the bed, Ham was ready and waiting. He leaped skyward with his forepaws fully extended; then, like a baseball player reaching over the centerfield wall, he grabbed the bat in midflight and pulled it down to the bed.

Pat missed the amazing feat but turned just in time to see the grinning cat stuff the squirming, winged rodent into its mouth. My wife's expression turned from one of shock to utter revulsion as the sound of the squealing bat gave way to the soft crunching of bones inside the cat's mouth. With the tip of one wing still protruding from his jaws and a look of sheer gratification on his face, Ham rolled over and went back to sleep.

I have never been fond of cats, but for Ham I made an exception. He was a cat with style, flair, and a passion for life. In a world of feline mediocrity, Ham was a tomcat extraordinaire.

Grouse hunting with Ham the cat.

Dam
Update

Thursday, August 20, 1998
Kipawa River, 10:45 A.M.

My friend John Muise and I put on the river to make a low water run. John and I have made at least thirty runs down the Kipawa together over the past twelve years. We never cease to be amazed at the unique beauty of the river or thrilled by the excitement of descending its rapids.

John and I have also paddled together on the Salmon River in central Idaho, the Green River in western Colorado and the San Juan River in southern Utah. Each is a unique and marvelous stretch of wilderness whitewater, but the Kipawa plays second fiddle to none.

John is a detective in metropolitan Toronto and his job in the city has given him a deep appreciation for wilderness. All morning as we paddled from Buttonhook to Hollywood he fired off questions about HQ's Tabaret project. I informed him of the roller coaster ride we have been on since June 5, the night Charlie Hastings burst through the cabin door with the news that Hydro Quebec had a proposal to divert the Kipawa River.

"It's a shame to even consider a project that could alter and possibly destroy a place this wonderful," was his response. John and I agree that if the

A Toronto cop in Hollywood.

proposal goes through and the river is diverted, we have been part of the lucky few to have experienced the breathtaking beauty and unparalled paddling afforded by the Kipawa River.

Au revoir . . .

Chapter 26

FAREWELL OH KIPAWA

You children of space, you restless in rest,
you shall not be trapped or tamed.
For that which is boundless in you abides
in the mansion in the sky,
whose door is the morning mist,
and whose windows are the
songs and silences of night.
—Kahlil Gibran

"Scott, we have spent nearly half our life together at this cabin in the woods. Maybe it's time to return to the city once and for all and get on with our lives." Even as Pat spoke those words, I detected a note of melancholy and regret in her voice.

"You could be right," I replied. "There might be more to life than watching seagulls play tag in the wind over Lake Temiskaming."

Pat and I were struggling with an acute case of mid-life crisis, wondering where we were headed after so many years in the wilderness. Back in the States, the people we had grown up with were building big houses, driving fancy cars, and establishing themselves in careers that would ultimately take them places. It seemed like they had made their mark on society, while we were still out chasing rainbows over the horizon and trying to cut enough firewood on the side to stay warm. At times we felt like incurable wanderers drifting north and south of the border like migrating geese whose fate is controlled by the seasons.

After leaving his cabin on Walden Pond, Thoreau reminisced, "I left the woods for as good a reason as I went there. Perhaps it seemed to me that I had several more lives to live, and could not spare any more time for that one." The search for another life, or maybe something more to live for, was part of the reason Pat and I decided to put the lodge up for sale and return to civilization once and for all.

Fall had come early that year to the Kipawa River. On September 15, a strong north wind blew down from Hudson Bay leaving a sharp chill in the air. The cold nights and frosty mornings that followed turned the birch and poplar leaves from a deep green to a brilliant gold, and soon thereafter the maples broke out in fiery patches of orange and red. For several days we waited in anticipation, hoping the south wind would battle back and regain some of the frozen ground it had lost to its nemesis in the north.

Five days later, on September 20, the wind and rain from the Arctic subsided and the sun peaked out from behind the clouds, bringing hope for an Indian summer. Although it was cold, I encouraged the kids to take off their coats and put on their shorts in an effort to convince the south wind it was too early to surrender the territory for the winter. For almost an hour we played on the beach in front of the lodge while our legs turned goose-bumped and blue. It was a brave show, but before nightfall the polar express came roaring back with a vengeance. Freezing rain mixed with sleet and snow plastered our roof and windows, while the sunshine and our hopes for an Indian summer retreated southward.

The following day we packed our belongings and prepared for our final departure. I spent most of the morning covering the cabin windows with boards and pieces of plywood, a task I had performed every fall for more than twenty years, knowing that the following spring I would be back to open them up again. This time it seemed as though I was driving nails into the coffin of a close and intimate friend. The sound of the hammer left me feeling empty, for I knew that something familiar and dear was slipping away.

After the last board was in place, I walked into the Main Lodge and found Pat sweeping the floor, a ritual she performs whenever she leaves a building. It makes no difference whether she is leaving for three hours or three months. She sweeps. Pat believes that a swept floor and a clean counter are true signs of a woman's character and virtue. If that be true, in character and virtue my wife has no equal.

Once the floors were swept, the windows secured, and the doors shut tight, we boarded the boat which was piled high with children, gear, and Ham the cat. Altogether we formed a rather demure, solemn-faced group, knowing this might be our final trip up Lake Temiskaming. Nobody spoke as I untied the boat from its mooring and started the motor. The decision to direct our lives on a different course had been difficult, but I felt that once we had gone around the bend and the lodge had disappeared from view, the path would be clear and easy.

As we pulled away from the docks I resisted the urge to turn around and bid a last farewell to our home in the woods. Saying good-bye to a place that held so many memories would be a difficult thing to do. If not for Ham, I don't think any of us would have ever looked back.

We were about a hundred yards from shore when the old gray cat, with a crazed, demented look in his eye appeared from beneath the seat and began to climb the mountain of gear in the middle of the boat. When he reached the top he looked once at me and once at the camp, then contrary to all that is natural in cats, he made a flying leap overboard, splashed into the lake, and then began swimming back to shore.

My first impulse was to let the deranged animal drown, but the kids began to yell and Pat reminded me that Ham was strictly on loan, so I turned the boat around to initiate a rescue. We pulled up alongside the struggling cat, who, in spite of making considerable progress toward shore, had now begun to flounder. Pat reached over the bow and grabbed him by the scruff of the neck and hoisted him out of the water. When she set the dripping animal on the deck, he looked more like a shriveled rat than a once-proud street fighter. Ham shook himself off indignantly, then, looking sullen and mean, he skulked back underneath the boat seat.

When I reached to start the motor, I noticed Pat and the kids had their eyes transfixed on something to the east of us. I turned to look just as the sun broke out from behind the clouds and flooded the view of our lodge with a soft but radiant light. All at once the years and the memories came rushing at me like the waters from the mouth of the river. It was a scene that touched me deeply. For though I had seen it a thousand times, I might never see it again. I wanted to take it all in, to commit each feature to memory, to engrave every detail forever in my mind.

To the north I could see the hill that my partner Jim and I had slept on all night in the rain when lost on our first trek into the lodge. To the south was Whistler's point where the red haired stranger had camped for a week. Beyond that were the great granite cliffs, home of the Picojeesies, where we had taught our children to climb and rappel.

On the beach in front of the lodge, turned upside down and long since retired from service, lay the old wooden boat in which Jenny and I had spent the night adrift on Lake Temiskaming. Adjacent to the lodge stood the icehouse, where the black bear had slept one winter and confronted us the following spring. In front of the icehouse where the boathouse once stood, loomed the new cabin that had consumed six summers of labor. Directly behind the Main Lodge I could see the roof of the two-story cabin we had previously built over the span of four summers, and running alongside it all was the Kipawa River along whose banks we had laughed, and loved, and lived so well.

For many years and throughout every season the river had been our close and constant companion. Its tumbling waters had greeted us with a symphony each morning and lulled us to sleep with a lullaby at night. The sound of the rapids was like the music of life; we had worked, and played, and danced to its rhythm. Its melody, though familiar, was continually changing. There were days when it softly whispered and times when it thundered and roared. On the cool autumn morning when we paused in our boat to rescue the cat from the lake, I could still hear the music, but it was somber and subdued, like a song of farewell.

Adieu . . .

So we said good-bye to the river and lake, then bid adieu to our home in the woods, and charted a course for a new time and place.

⚜ Dam Update

Thursday, August 27, 1998
Kipawa River Lodge (Topping's Camp)

At 3:15 P.M. Doug Skeggs, the vice-president of ARK, came for a visit. He had just met with native councilman Lance Haymond from the Eagle Lake band of the Algonquin Nation in the town of Kipawa. Lance told Doug that over a month ago the native council had requested that Hydro Quebec cease all studies and assessments concerning the Tabaret project. Hydro Quebec responded by sending a letter to the Algonquin First Nations agreeing to discontinue any further work on the proposal until after the native council had an opportunity to meet and form a consensus on the project. When Doug suggested that perhaps some of the members of First Nations would like to participate in the September 12–13 kayaking-rafting weekend, Lance told him perhaps at some future date, after the band council had convened and determined a unified course of action.

Doug agreed that ARK would cancel any plans for a water release or a feasibility study on commercial rafting and kayaking so as to be in compliance with the agreement between Hydro Quebec and the council of First Nations.

I asked Doug to pass on my sincere regards and deep appreciation to Lance and the other native leaders for their decision to move slowly and cautiously with respect to any proposal that would alter the Kipawa River forever. Perhaps the juggernaut has been slowed.

"We throw the small ones back."

Chapter 27

HOME AGAIN

Under the wide and starry sky
Dig the grave and let me die.
Glad did I live and gladly die
And laid me down with a will.

This be the verse that you grave for me
Here he lies where he longed to be.
Home is the sailor, home from the sea
And the hunter home from the hill.
　　　　　　　　　　　　—Robert Louis Stevenson

For two long, drawn-out years we lived in the city "leading lives of quiet desperation," as Thoreau said, "Making ourselves sick trying to lay up something against a sick day." I had found a reasonably good nine-to-five job, but the routine was stifling and the confinement left me gasping for breath. The air we breathed in the city never tasted whole or free. It was secondhand air, diluted by the spawn of tailpipes and smokestacks, then passed on through the lungs of a thousand unsatisfied customers. By the time it reached us it tasted stale and used up. All the good had been sucked out of it. How often we had taken for granted the pure, sweet air of northern Canada. Like ether for the soul, it was invisible yet intoxicating. It never hung over our rooftop in a filmy yellowish cloud, causing our eyes to water and our throats to burn.

In the city we had a comfortable home with all the modern conveniences, but it was crowded in by thousands of other homes just like it, each one a sterile, airtight cubicle where the refugees of city life could escape for a few hour's rest before racing off again the next morning.

I would sit in the confines of our living room (an imaginative name for a place where living is seldom experienced) staring at a picture of the lodge on the Kipawa River. Fortunately, our halfhearted attempts to sell the camp were ineffective. Somehow I managed to dissuade the only buyer who had made us a serious offer. When he told me he had plans to pave the logging road into the lodge and build condos at Grande Chute with a chain link fence surrounding the falls to keep out "uninvited guests and nonpaying sightseers," I declined his offer. It felt too much like selling one of my children into slavery.

I was homesick for our cabin, where we would read by the light of kerosene lamps while shadowed figures from the fireplace danced across the log walls. I longed for the sound of rain spattering down on the thin board roof and the sight of tiny drops forming here and there between the cracks and falling to the cabin floor. I missed seeing the occasional chipmunk, garter snake, or bullfrog hopping across the room in search of a moth or mosquito. We had traded the sight of the sun rising over Lake Temiskaming for the dull, monotonous blur of the television. The sound of the Kipawa River rushing down its course had been replaced by the drone of airplane engines, automobile horns, and ringing telephones.

In December Pat and I felt restless and talked about taking a trip. I had sixteen days of vacation, and even our children were clamoring for a change of climate and scenery. "How about Mexico?" I asked. They stared. "What's in Mexico?"

I told them about San Blas, a tropical paradise where my parents took my ten siblings and me for Christmas when I was fifteen. San Blas is a three-hundred-year-old Spanish seaport nestled in a shallow cove along the Pacific Coast and surrounded by steep, rugged, jungle-covered mountains. One week before Christmas we began the seventeen-hundred-mile journey south through Mexico. Our Suburban and trailer were packed with toys and clothing donated by friends and relatives to share with an orphanage near Mazatlan. Our spirits were high—adventure stirred in our bones.

Two hundred miles south of the border on a lonely, desolate stretch of road between Hermosillo and Los Mochis was an overturned, burned-up hulk of a vehicle with words spray painted on its door panel. Throughout Mexico travelers grow accustomed to seeing the remains of wrecked cars, trucks, and buses left on the roadside like graphic billboards with warnings painted on them: "Don't Drink and Drive," "Speed Kills," etc. But the writing on the wreck we approached on the road south of Hermosillo formed a question rather than a warning: "Que Buscas?" (What seek ye?)

Initially I thought, "How strange that some wandering Mexican guru was roaming the countryside with a can of spray paint and posing deep philosophical questions on the sides of wrecked vehicles. Nevertheless, the question made a lasting impression that impacted the rest of my trip. Delivering the toys and clothes to the orphans near Mazatlan was a gratifying experience, but I kept asking myself, "What in this life is really important? What am I truly seeking?"

We continued south to San Blas, where we built castles in the sand and strolled around the plaza at night to the accompaniment of firecrackers and mariachi music. We ventured by boat up a spring-fed river and watched our children swing from vines and land with a splash in a crystal-clear pond next to a log with big yellow eyes. The log turned out to be a seven-foot alligator named Felipe. Looking up from her book momentarily, Pat casually asked our Mexican navigator, "Will Felipe eat my children, Señor?"

"No Señora," the man calmly replied, tilting his sombrero down low on his face. "Felipe ate yesterday. He will not be hungry again until tomorrow." Reassured, Pat turned back to her reading.

After a week and a half in paradise, it occurred to me how much our vacation in Mexico was like living on the shores of Lake Temiskaming. For ten days we had hardly looked at a watch or a calendar. Instead of getting up each morning and running off in seven different directions, we had shared every experience and savored every moment. Once again our lives were a circle of peace and continuity rather than a frenzied three-ringed circus.

As we drove north to the United States border, I kept thinking about the wedge of land bordered by Lake Temiskaming on the west and the Kipawa River on the south. At night when we made camp on the beaches of Sonora, I would toss and turn in my sleeping bag, distressed at the thought of returning to our life in the city. Two days later on the same desolate stretch of road between Los Mochis and Hermosillo, the Mexican guru struck again. Spray painted on the top of a rusted-out bus which lay on its side surrounded by chaparral and cactus were the words "Has encontrado?" (Did you find it?) I lifted my foot off the accelerator and let the Suburban coast to a stop alongside the road. Pat gave me a worried glance as I opened the door and stepped out of the vehicle. "Have we broken down?" she asked.

"No, I just want to check the tires," I lied, walking back behind the trailer. As I approached the overturned bus, I felt as if someone or something was watching me. Ever since leaving San Blas, it seemed like someone was reading my mind and filling my head with unanswerable questions.

When I was about fifty feet from the front of the bus, I heard a low whimpering noise from inside, like the sound of a child when it's hurt or afraid. I stopped abruptly and listened. With a chill running down my back I shouted, "Quien Es?" (Who's there?) Suddenly a shadow appeared in an opening at the front of the bus where the windshield had once been. I froze momentarily, torn between an urge to back away and a curiosity to get closer. All at once a coyote jumped from the shadows out through the opening into the bright light of day. For an instant the animal looked me straight in the eye. In its mouth was a large dead bird. Then, with the shake of its big, bushy tail the coyote took three bounding leaps and disappeared into the dry chaparral.

As I looked out over the arid landscape I caught one fleeting glimpse of the coyote dodging through the brush. I howled at the top of my lungs, but the sound was instantly absorbed by the vast, expanse of the desert. Then I realized the bird in the coyote's mouth was a roadrunner. In all those cartoons I watched growing up the coyote had never once caught the roadrunner. He had always been the hapless fool who fell over cliffs and ran headlong into the sides of mountains, while the roadrunner sped away smiling. But not that day in the desert south of Hermosillo. The coyote won.

After walking around the battered old bus and reading again the words "Has encontrado?" I heard someone honking the Suburban horn. When I returned to the vehicle I was greeted by five restless daughters and an anxious wife. "Where have you been? Is everything okay?" asked Pat.

"Everything is fine," I said. "Let's head for home."

Three weeks after our trip to San Blas I was still thinking about the Mexican guru and the questions he posed on the wrecked vehicles. What am I seeking? Where will I find it? Oddly enough, it was an insurance salesman who convinced me it was time to return to the Kipawa River. One evening after an exceptionally long day at work, Pat and I were sitting at the kitchen table when the doorbell rang. Neither of us felt like answering, but the ringing persisted, and was followed by a loud and prolonged knock. I got up and walked down the hallway. About halfway to the door I remembered the night Whistler had knocked on our door in Canada. This was the same sort of knock. It had the undeniable sound of destiny and a ringing of fate.

When I opened the door I was greeted by a small man who was dressed in a dark, pin-striped suit and holding a formidable briefcase. He nodded and said, "Good evening, Sir, my name is Theodore. I have come with an important message concerning you and the future of your entire family. May I come in?"

Theodore had dark, vacillating eyes, a thin mustache, and a smile set in concrete which revealed a shiny gold tooth that reflected in the porch light. He was wearing a starchy pink shirt with a white button-down collar and a wide fluorescent tie emblazoned with palm trees and a hula girl whose grass skirt appeared to sway in the breeze as he shifted nervously from one foot to the other. I stood mesmerized. Destiny had knocked, so I invited him in.

As he followed me down the hall toward the kitchen, Theodore stopped in front of a family portrait of my brother with his wife and children all dressed in their Sunday best. Having mistaken my brother for me, he remarked, "What a fine-looking family you've got here, Sir. There's nothing more important in this world than a man's family and planning for their future." I agreed, then told him he was looking at a picture of my brother's family, but right behind him on the other wall was a picture of my family.

Perhaps it would have been kinder to let him believe that the cherub-faced group in my brother's portrait was mine, rather than directing his attention to the grim spectacle that met his gaze on the opposite wall. It was a slightly faded photograph of my family standing in the rain in front of the lodge. Pat and our four older daughters were holding up a huge, slime-dripping stringer of fish. I was standing next to them with a thirty-eight-inch northern pike in my right hand, while my left hand grasped the ankles of our three-month-old baby, who was hanging upside down and naked alongside the fish.

As Theodore focused in detail on the picture his eyes grew large and his jaw went slack. "What's that in your hand?" he gasped incredulously. "That's a seventeen-pound, thirty-eight-inch northern pike," I responded with obvious pride.

"I can see the fish," he stammered, "but what's in your other hand?"

"Oh, that's a twelve-pound, eight-ounce baby girl," I grinned. "Usually we throw them back when they're that small, but she was extra plump and feisty so we kept her and named her Becky."

I ushered him into the kitchen where Pat was sitting at the table with her nose between the covers of a book. There are very few things in this world that can distract my wife while she is reading. When I introduced her to the salesman she took one look at his briefcase and beat a hasty retreat to the bedroom. One time while perched on top of a raft traveling down the Colorado River, Pat became lost in the pages of a Pearl Buck novel and floated right through the most violent rapids without even missing a line. People all around her were screaming and yelling and holding on for dear life, but Pat never batted an eye.

"Wouldn't your wife care to join us?" asked Theodore. "What I have to offer you this evening would be very beneficial to her as well."

"I'm sure it would," I sympathized, "but once my wife gets past the third page of an interesting book she enters a state of nirvana and ceases to exist in the realm of the living."

Theodore sensed the hopelessness of our situation, then sat down opposite me at the table. He began to talk about life being a journey into the unknown, and how every man who embarks on that journey takes on certain risks and responsibilities, and no one knows when or under what circumstances the sojourn might suddenly end.

He continued talking like that for about ten minutes, and still I could not figure out what he was trying to sell. I began to suspect he was a travel agent for one of those high-adventure outfits that backpacks the Himalayas or explores the jungles of New Guinea. I was almost ready to sign up when suddenly his briefcase popped open and out came charts and graphs showing me how long I could expect to live and what would happen to my wife and children when I died. He told me about investments, wills, stocks, bonds, trusts, mortgages, and how all of it related to me dying someday. The more he talked, the less it sounded like a trip to New Guinea.

Theodore showed me a plan that could protect my family from death, illness, and funeral expenses by sending him money once a month. He called the plan life insurance, but strangely enough he kept talking on and on about death, injury, and medical bills. He never said anything about what might happen if by some happy chance I were to go on living. When I asked him about that he said, "In the event that you continue living, and keep up your monthly installments, you will be fully covered. Should you die, however, you would receive a full remuneration plus interest once the death has been legally certified."

"Hold on just a minute!" I protested. "This whole thing sounds like a horse race that's been rigged. In order for me to win, I have to bet that my horse is going to lose. On the other hand, if my horse wins, I have to ride him over the edge of a cliff to collect the winnings."

270

"That's an interesting analogy," smiled Theodore, "but on one point you are confused. To intentionally ride one's horse over the edge of a cliff is an act of suicide. For that you get nothing."

I shook my head in disbelief. Theodore and I were light years apart, barely in the same universe. Perhaps I had missed something or maybe we just needed to find some mutual frame of reference and start from there.

I crossed the room to our bookcase and pulled out a photo album marked "Kipawa." Returning to the table, I moved his briefcase and flip charts to one side and said, "Theodore, we have talked long enough about dying; now let's consider some reasons for living."

I opened the album and turned the pages, hoping to strike some common ground. It was an exercise in futility. As we looked at the photographs and talked, Theodore told me he had never tasted fish caught fresh from a stream, or paddled a canoe on a moonlit bay, or run barefoot along a sandy beach. For thirty-five years he had confined himself to the city. He had never once slept on the ground in the woods by a fire, felt the pull of current on his feet in a river, climbed up a tree on a windy autumn day, heard the cry of coyotes echoing through a canyon at dusk, or the hysterical laughter of loons on a foggy lake at dawn.

Theodore had been born and raised in East Los Angeles, a world of brick walls, paved streets, and heavy traffic. His closest connection to wilderness had been the jungle cruise at Disneyland. His idea of adventure was a cheeseburger, fries, and a drive-in movie. No wonder he spent his waking hours talking to people about death. He had never learned to live.

Theodore was a man so far removed from the earth and the basic elements of life that there was nothing natural left in his existence. When a person completely loses touch with the joy and wonder of nature, something within him dies, like a wolf locked up in a zoo. The fire of life soon disappears from its eyes, until it becomes little more than a dog in wolf's clothing panting for its next meal.

Theodore and I parted company, having failed completely in our attempts to communicate anything to one another. As I sat alone at the kitchen table still looking at the pictures of Canada, my mind began to wander back to a time when life seemed simpler and happiness rose with the sun each morning and lingered long after dark every night. Perhaps Theodore had indeed taught me something of value, or at least helped me crystallize my feelings of discontent. I think I always knew where I would find what I was looking for. It had been right under my feet.

For two years I had lived much the same as Theodore. I had forgotten Henry Thoreau's warning about buying and selling and spending my life like a serf. After all, I had rationalized, a man could not live forever in the wilderness like an eagle or a bear. There comes a time to settle down, shoulder some responsibility, and share in the burden of civilization. Most people seemed happy enough living in cities and towns, elbow to elbow, layer upon layer. For some it is security in numbers; for others it is just shared misery.

I once had a flock of chickens that wandered freely around the lodge, eating grass, catching bugs, and laying eggs in obscure places. They were content and I never gave them much thought until one night a fox attacked and systematically tore each one to pieces. The following morning as I gathered up bones, feathers and feet, I felt sorry for having brought the unfortunate birds to such a wild and remote setting.

One year later I visited a poultry farm and saw twelve thousand chickens crammed into a single barn where they were provided with water, food, and light twenty-four hours a day for ten weeks and then slaughtered for meat. I came to the conclusion that the chickens I had raised on the Kipawa River were the lucky ones. They had lived well and died swiftly. Perhaps to a chicken such things are not important. They are to me.

During her first visit to our home in the north my mother offered me some advice: "Scott, do not become accustomed to this type of living. It's very uncivilized." Even then I think she feared I might never return to live in the city and raise her grandchildren to be proper, civilized human beings. Ironically, that same dear woman gave me a copy of Walden Pond when I was at the impressionable age of nineteen. I devoured the book whole and never looked back.

Several years ago, after spending a long, quiet week at the lodge, a lady from Baltimore remarked, "Living on the Kipawa River is rather quaint and simple. You folks don't demand a whole lot from this world do you?"

"Yes ma'am, you're absolutely right," I answered. "Quaint and simple is good enough for us." But for those who can see a little farther, climb a little higher, and dive a little deeper, the answer is not so simple. Only the question is quaint.

To live on the banks of the Kipawa River is simplicity on the grandest scale. Everything that is trivial, meaningless, or insignificant is swiftly brought to bay. That which is superficial and synthetic disappears like dew in the morning sun. There is only time and space for that which is real, substantial, and of consequence.

In early May we decided to return to the Kipawa River. I quit my job, rented our house, and packed the Suburban and trailer for Canada. Upon arriving in Quebec we found the lodge in an awful state. After two years of neglect and abandonment, I had expected a certain amount of deterioration on the property. After all, most things manmade and left on their own are eventually reclaimed by nature. However, the damage our camp sustained was not an act of nature, but rather the ravaging of men. The doors and windows had been broken and smashed, and the buildings stripped bare of all their furnishings. Things too large to be carried off had simply been destroyed or used as firewood. Looters and thieves are seldom rational. Even the cabinets and plumbing had been torn out and hauled away at greater expense and effort than it would have cost to buy the items in town.

As we walked from room to room, stepping over shattered glass and broken furniture, Pat heard our youngest daughter crying on the back porch. We found her clutching the head of an old rocking horse, a toy she and her sisters had once loved to play with. It had been torn apart and partially burned in the fireplace. Pat wiped away the tears and told her we could make another rocking horse.

To our younger children the whole affair was like a natural disaster. In their minds only an earthquake or a flood could have wreaked such havoc on our home. A child does not easily comprehend that other human beings would intentionally and maliciously cause such damage.

After recovering from the initial shock, we swept out one of the rooms, and laid our sleeping bags on the floor. For supper we ate peanut butter and honey sandwiches by candle-light, and chocolate chip cookies for dessert. When the girls fell asleep, Pat and I walked out to the edge of the lake.

For several minutes we sat in silence on the end of the dock watching a pair of mergansers diving for minnows in their never ending quest for food. "Sometimes life seems like such a chore," I said to Pat. "Do you think we will ever get ahead at this game?"

Pat could sense my discouragement but was not in the mood to indulge in self-pity. She turned to me and said, "Try to imagine what this place was like in 1918 when Zeph Fleury and his wife came here to live in a tent while they built their first cabin." I looked toward our bedroom, which so many years ago was home to the Fleurys. Like a ghost from the past I envisioned Zeph swinging an axe as he notched the final log and raised it onto the building. "I guess old Zeph would have counted himself lucky to have arrived here and found several cabins ready to occupy once he replaced a few windows and doors."

I put my arm around Pat and held her close as the moon began to shine through the branches of a large white pine across the river. It occurred to me then that the vandals and thieves had failed in their attempt to steal the treasure. They had merely run off with a few trappings. The real treasure lay hidden beyond their reach in the roar of the rapids, the cry of the loons, and the sighing of the wind through the pines on top of the hill.

The riches and wealth of the Kipawa River can only be measured in the years of happiness and contentment that come to the people who visit and live on its banks. For us there are few regrets and numerous joys. There is something priceless in the knowledge that each day lived on the shores of this river is time well spent.

I thought about old Mrs. Topping, the Whistler, Don José, the boys from St. John's, the many kayakers and fishermen, the five children we had raised at this camp, and I knew our life was here. Here were the memories that gave value and meaning to the past. Here were the dreams that brought promise and hope for the future.

As Pat and I sat looking across the lake, the northern lights began to dance and shimmer on the far horizon. For a moment I felt infinitely small and insignificant in the presence of so much sky, water, and wilderness. When compared to the immensity of nature, a human being can seem as inconspicuous as dust in the wind. On the other hand, nature has a way of filling the soul and enlarging the spirit to a point that makes a person feel whole and immortal. That is the feeling I get on the Kipawa River. If ever a place had the power to reach out and take hold of a person's heart, that place for me is where the rapids of the Kipawa River tumble into the waters of Lake Temiskaming. That is the place I call home.

Addendum

On the eve of a new millennium the treasure and magic that is the Kipawa River is at risk. If Hydro Quebec is successful in its bid to siphon off as much as 80 percent of the water that flows down the river annually, the treasure will be lost. And it will not be replaced or repaired like shattered windows, broken doors, or stolen furniture. It will be gone forever.

For those who love and appreciate the majesty and wonder of the Kipawa, the loss will be tragic and monumental. For future generations the loss will be incalculable. They will only know it from faded photographs or words in a book, and that is nothing more than an obituary.

The Kipawa River has a natural beauty and a historical significance that warrants our respect and merits protection both provincially and federally from the powers that be. It is unsurpassed, and in many ways unequaled, by other waterways that have already received protection from the onslaught of growth and technology that threatens to destroy lakes, rivers and wilderness all over North America. Let Hydro Quebec look elsewhere to generate a few megawatts of electricity for the huddled masses of New York, Boston, and Atlantic City. Society will pay a very dear price to power a few more washing machines, blow dryers, and streetlights if it is done at the expense of silencing the Kipawa River.

Scott Sorensen
Lake Temiskaming
May 1999

Paddling the Kipawa River
Laniel to Lake Temiskaming
by Doug Skeggs

Distance:	16 km (10 miles)
Difficulty:	Class III-IV river rating
	Class III-IV individual rapids (volume dependent)
Gradient:	30 feet per mile
Volume:	0 cms (740 cfs) to 357 cms (13,209 cfs)

History

The first exploratory river runs on the Kipawa were made in the early 1970s by Jose Mediavilla and a group of paddlers from Rouyn, Quebec. There was no take-out road at that time so running the Kipawa meant a 7 km walk back out to Highway 101. In 1985, Jose introduced the river to a couple of northern Ontario paddlers—Doug Skeggs and Peter Karwacki—who in turn christened most of the rapids with their present names. Doug, Peter, and a handful of other paddlers formed NOLAC (Northern Ontario Liquid Adventure Club), and the Kipawa River Rally began that same summer. Traditionally the rally is held on the third weekend of June. Over the past twelve years, the rally has introduced hundreds of paddlers to the Kipawa River's unparalleled natural beauty, and its magical mood swings.

Scenery

The Kipawa is a beautiful pristine river. There are no roads, buildings, or cottages along its 16 km length with the exception of "the park," where the river winds close to Highway 101 for a short distance. The forested banks are a mixture of spruce, pine, balsam, poplar, maple, birch, and cedar. Particularly beautiful is the lower half of the river, below Broken Bridge Rapid, where stands of majestic red and white pines tower over shoreline cedar.

Wildlife

There are loons, mergansers, and herons on the flat stretches of the upper section and ducks along the entire river. In the lower section where Hollywood flows into Lake Temiskaming osprey, merlin, and peregrine falcons have been sighted. Occasionally moose, bear, deer, beaver, and muskrat have been seen as well.

Description

The Kipawa River is, plain and simple, one of the best, and perhaps even the best, intermediate whitewater run in eastern Canada. The river is runnable at all levels. At lower levels the river does not get above a Class III, with the exception of Pete's Dragon, the middle three drops in Hollywood Rapid (a tight technical Class IV).

Note: The following descriptions of various rapids can change according to water level. Remember to scout each rapid and check for debris or obstructions when paddling unfamiliar water.

The Dam
(Class III all levels)

The flood control dam under the highway bridge in Laniel is runnable at any level above 120 cms. It has been run at levels as low as 100 cms but the drop becomes steep and it is not recommended. Below 100 cms it should be avoided altogether. Above 250 cms a hole starts to form, reacting off the pillar between the two floodgates, but it's fairly easy to work around on either side.

Rock and Roll
(Class III–IV+ level dependent)

Named by a river guide from Wilderness Tours on a low-water run in the mid-'80s, Rock and Roll is routinely walked by boaters who don't like its steep rocky character. The typical run is to enter right of center, just to the left of a couple of very small holes reacting to a rock shelf near the surface. Move right, then straighten out to run a narrow deep-water channel that passes to the right of all the big holes out in the middle. Move left, back out to the center of the drop, as soon as you pass the big holes. Alternative run at levels from very low up to 140 or 150 cms is to start from just left of center and work left down a slide drop so that you work to the far left of the rapid about halfway through it, then run the bottom half hugging the left shoreline through a steep, abrupt hole. This is an easy run at low water when you can actually eddy out halfway through. It gets progressively tougher the more water there is.

Tumbling Dice
(Class III at all levels)

Around the bend past Rock and Roll the river narrows a bit, signaling the start of a long, easy rapid called Tumbling Dice. The second drop in the rapid has a very sweet surfing wave called the Two-Four Wave. Always there above 120 cms but best experienced at levels between 140 and 220 cms. Tumbling Dice continues around the corner in a series of easy waves that end with the beginning of a stretch of flat water that runs past a bend in Highway 101. There is an abandoned highway picnic park here that is no longer maintained. It's a perfect spot for camping, very private, lots of parking, no camp fees, no one bothers you. In low water (15–75 cms), most paddlers choose to begin their run at the park. There is little to be gained by starting at the dam in this level.

Buttonhook
(Class III–IV+ level dependent)
At low water, Buttonhook is where you get your first real look at the Kipawa's rocky riverbed. Put some water in the river, and Buttonhook is where you get your first taste of the Kipawa's strength and dynamic character. At high water, people who aren't comfortable in big pushy stuff call this rapid a Class V. At low water, pick your way down. At levels above 80 cms run the classic line, start left of center, move almost immediately to the center, move right toward the bottom of the upper section to get to the big eddy on the corner. Run the bottom section starting right, then working left at lower water, and staying right at higher water.

Three Blind Mice
(Class III all levels)
Three little drops. Easy run. There is a small play wave on the left in the second drop.

Broken Bridge
(Class III all levels)
If you happen to be on the Kipawa at a level somewhere between 120 and 130 cms, bring your favorite Beach Boys album . . . because this is surf city. There is a glassy 3-boat wave that just won't quit. Enter from either side. A river-left entry requires pulling your boat up alongside the log foundations of the old bridge. The wave is surfable between 80 cms and probably 220. It gets difficult to get on at the higher levels, but there are two waves below it that come into play then. Whatever the level, chances are you will have fun.

Island Rapid
(Class III all levels)
Below Broken Bridge the river splits around an island. River left is easier. River right is runnable at all levels but gets a little rocky at low water and requires a bit of care in running. The river flattens out for a bit after Island Rapid.

Log Jam
(Class III all levels)
This is the start of the steepest part of the Kipawa. Do not off yourself or your boat to the upstream side of Log Jam Island. We've seen the log jam at low water. Take our word for it, it's undercut. Run with the main flow on the left side of Log Jam Island. Pick a line just right of center and stay on it. Easy run.

Zipper
(Class III–IV level dependent)
There is no memory of how Zipper got its name, however, it is the home of the biggest wave on the river. The run is always the same. Run with the main flow around on the left side of the river. Down around the corner, there is a shelf that forms a hole on the right side of the river and a wave on the left. The wave is sometimes rolling back on itself but is always runnable. At levels above 175 cms, this wave gets big. At levels above 220 cms, it gets huge. At levels above 315 cms, it reaches galactic proportions. This wave pushes you to the left, which is no fun. The left-hand shore is rocky. If the wave looks pushy, hit it moving right and you'll be fine.

Upper White Pine
(Class III all levels)
This is a series of corners and waves that is the home of a small, but very popular surfing spot.

Lower White Pine
(Class III all levels)
Also known as Cattle Prod, this is a short, steep drop that is actually a five-foot ledge at low water. Good fun with diagonal waves and lots of quick action. Run left down the chute.

Picnic
(Class III–VI level dependent)
Picnic, named after the picnic table up the rocky shore on the right is a river-wide hole that is an easy run but can be a problem above 100 cms. At 357 cms there was a large tree recirculating in it, which presented an opportunity to a walk the right-hand shore. At low water, pick a line and go. At medium to high water run from center, pushing right to hit the corner where the reactionary wave coming off the shore joins with the edge of the big hole. Or run far left, but be careful of the ledge hole below.

Le Grande Chute
(Don't even think about it)
It's a ninety-foot waterfall with three Class IV-V drops above it that we have run at low water. The two-drop falls have not been run. The walk is on the right.

Elbow
(Class III–IV+)

Put-in below Grande Chute and you are in Elbow Rapid. On a 130 cms run of Elbow in 1985 a Quebec paddler broke a two-foot section off the front of his glass boat in the big hole down around the corner. We never saw the boat again. In 1996 we watched a fifteen foot inflatable raft flip end for end in the same hole. At low water, just pick your way down. At medium to high water, start right and work immediately to the center, and then to the left as you hit the corner. The objective is to miss the big hole on the right side of the river, where all the water is going, and make the big eddy on the left side of the river where all your buddies are. The bottom section of Elbow is a fun, straightforward run through waves and small holes.

Hollywood
(Class IV–VI level dependent)

This rapid was named as a tribute to the moviemakers who made the property here their summer home years ago. This rapid would look good on any river, anywhere. It's a tough run, and an even tougher swim. At low water the rapid is runnable top to bottom. The middle section, Pete's Dragon, is named after Peter Karwacki, the first kayaker to run it. It is essentially three drops with not much breathing space between. Run the first drop through a small chute on the right, through a small but steep hole that can mess with your line a bit (the tail of the Dragon). Most boaters skirt around the edge of this thing rather than punch it. Then you are immediately in the second drop. Run up onto the big rock pillow on the right then let your boat turn a bit and slip sideways to the left. You end up dropping down and bracing onto a curling reactionary which sets you up to run the rocky slide in the last half of the second drop (the belly of the Dragon). Try and make your move so that you end up in the eddy river right. Then you will have a chance to look back over your shoulder to sight your run over the ten-to-twelve-foot fall behind you (the mouth of the Dragon). The fall is not a problem. Less of a plunge the further right you go, but we've run it everywhere. This has been run up to, I think, about 75 cms. You decide. At higher water Pete's Dragon is not runnable. There is a rocky sneak down the right shore that essentially keeps you out of the rapid and is not much wetter than the portage. At all levels you can run from the top to take out above Pete's Dragon, but keep in mind that you will need to get your boat to a small eddy in solid Class III+ water above a very serious drop. If you are not comfortable with that, best to do the carry. It's a short walk around Pete's Dragon, then back in your boat for the bottom half of Hollywood. Ferry out to the center and then to the left side of the river. This is a fairly easy run in big swirling, churning water with lots of "where the heck did that come from" waves in it. The objective is a run down the left side at the bottom, when most of the water is trying to talk you into going right. The consequences of a right-side run is a rude awakening in Davey Jones Locker, a rather large, very dynamic hole. Hollywood surprises a lot of paddlers, and there is usually an audience with cameras ready to capture that special moment.

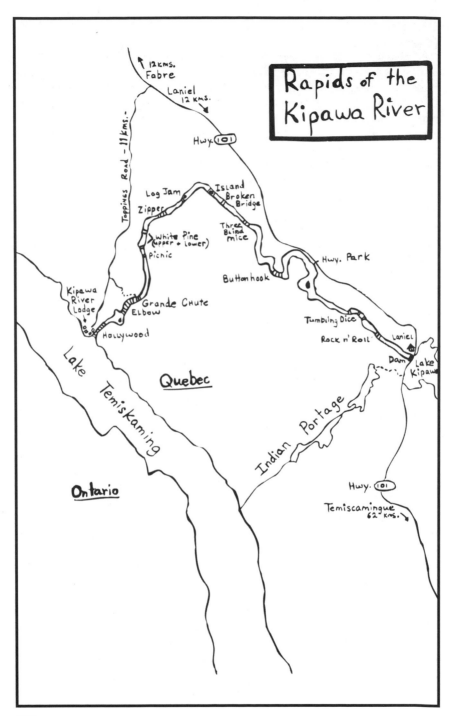

Rapids of the Kipawa River

12 kms. Fabre

Laniel 12 kms.

Hwy. 101

Toppings Road – 11 kms.

Log Jam

Zipper

Island
Broken
Bridge

White Pine
(upper + lower)

Three
Blind
mice

Picnic

Hwy. Park

Buttonhook

Kipawa
River
Lodge

Grande Chute

Elbow

Tumbling Dice

Hollywood

Rock n' Roll

Laniel

Dam

Lake
Kipawa

Quebec

Lake Temiskaming

Indian Portage

Ontario

Hwy. 101

Temiscamingue
62 kms.

BIBLIOGRAPHY

Cassidy, George L., Arrow North, The Story of Temiskaming, Temiskaming Printing, New Liskeard, Ontario, 1976.

Chenier, Augustin, Notes Historiques sur le Temiscamingue, Ville Marie, Quebec, 1937.

Fancy, Peter, Temiskaming Treasure Trails (The Earliest Years), Peter Fancy, 1992.

Farr, C. C. ed. Roach, T. Tales of the Wild North-East, Highway Book Shop,
Cobalt, Ontario, 1980.

Farr, C. C., The Life of Charles Cobbold Farr, private printing, 1967.

McLaren, David, Turn of the Century, Highway Book Shop, Cobalt, Ontario, 1992.

Mitchell, Elaine A., Fort Temiskaming and the Fur Trade, University of Toronto Press, Toronto, Ontario, 1977.

Paradis, Father Charles, From Temiskaming to Hudson's Bay, Buffalo,
New York, 1888.

Smith, Donald B., Long Lance, The True Story of an Imposter, MacMillan of Canada, 1982.

Taylor, Bruce, The Age of Steam on Lake Temiskaming, Bruce Taylor, 1993.

Theriault, Madeline, Moose to Moccasins, Natural Heritage/Natural History, Inc.,
Toronto, Ontario, 1992.

Sorensen Family

Scott, Pat, April, Jenny, Katie, Michelle, Becky

Scott Sorensen and his family spend their summers in Quebec and their winters in Utah. During the school year Scott travels to schools throughout the western United States giving seminars and performing assembly programs on Mountain Men, Indian Lore, and the history of the American West.